Rural America: Aspects, Outlooks and Development

Mental Health and Rural America

Overview and Annotated Bibliography

Rural America: Aspects, Outlooks and Development

Additional books in this series can be found on Nova's website under the Series tab.

Additional e-books in this series can be found on Nova's website under the e-book tab.

RURAL AMERICA: ASPECTS, OUTLOOKS AND DEVELOPMENT

MENTAL HEALTH AND RURAL AMERICA

OVERVIEW AND ANNOTATED BIBLIOGRAPHY

PAMELA RHODES
EDITOR

New York

Copyright © 2014 by Nova Science Publishers, Inc.

All rights reserved. No part of this book may be reproduced, stored in a retrieval system or transmitted in any form or by any means: electronic, electrostatic, magnetic, tape, mechanical photocopying, recording or otherwise without the written permission of the Publisher.

For permission to use material from this book please contact us:
Telephone 631-231-7269; Fax 631-231-8175
Web Site: http://www.novapublishers.com

NOTICE TO THE READER

The Publisher has taken reasonable care in the preparation of this book, but makes no expressed or implied warranty of any kind and assumes no responsibility for any errors or omissions. No liability is assumed for incidental or consequential damages in connection with or arising out of information contained in this book. The Publisher shall not be liable for any special, consequential, or exemplary damages resulting, in whole or in part, from the readers' use of, or reliance upon, this material. Any parts of this book based on government reports are so indicated and copyright is claimed for those parts to the extent applicable to compilations of such works.

Independent verification should be sought for any data, advice or recommendations contained in this book. In addition, no responsibility is assumed by the publisher for any injury and/or damage to persons or property arising from any methods, products, instructions, ideas or otherwise contained in this publication.

This publication is designed to provide accurate and authoritative information with regard to the subject matter covered herein. It is sold with the clear understanding that the Publisher is not engaged in rendering legal or any other professional services. If legal or any other expert assistance is required, the services of a competent person should be sought. FROM A DECLARATION OF PARTICIPANTS JOINTLY ADOPTED BY A COMMITTEE OF THE AMERICAN BAR ASSOCIATION AND A COMMITTEE OF PUBLISHERS.

Additional color graphics may be available in the e-book version of this book.

Library of Congress Cataloging-in-Publication Data

ISBN: 978-1-63321-122-3

Published by Nova Science Publishers, Inc. † New York

CONTENTS

Preface		vii
Chapter 1	Mental Health and Rural America: 1994-2005 An Overview and Annotated Bibliography *Office of Rural Health Policy*	1
Chapter 2	Prevalence of Mental Illness in the United States: Data Sources and Estimates *Erin Bagalman and Angela Napili*	253
Index		267

PREFACE

This book presents a comprehensive summary of the knowledge base around mental health issues in rural and frontier America. Challenges facing rural areas in meeting the needs of its citizens with mental illnesses and substance use disorders are highlighted. The book also reports on opportunities captured and unique solutions available. It briefly describes the methodology and selected findings of three large federally funded surveys that provide national prevalence estimates of diagnosable mental illness: the National Comorbidity Survey Replication (NCS-R), the National Comorbidity Survey Replication Adolescent Supplement (NCS-A), and the National Survey on Drug Use and Health (NSDUH). The book presents prevalence estimates of any mental illness and serious mental illness based on each survey and ends with a brief discussion of how these prevalence estimates might inform policy discussions.

Chapter 1 – Mental Health and Rural America:1994-2005 represents the third edition of a comprehensive overview and annotated bibliography focused on rural mental health. The previous editions (Flax, Wagenfeld, Ivens & Weiss, 1979; and Wagenfeld, Murray, Mohatt & DeBruyn, 1994) have been frequently cited in the rural mental health literature and have served as valuable sources of information relating to rural mental health in the United States.

The previous editions, and the current, have reviewed the environment of rural mental health at points-in-time over the past three decades. Not surprising to those engaged daily in the delivery of mental healthcare in rural America, much has changed and much has remained the same across this span of time. This new edition will examine both what is new and what remains unchanged.

Chapter 2 – Determining how many people have a mental illness can be difficult, and prevalence estimates vary. While numerous surveys include questions related to mental illness, few provide prevalence estimates of *diagnosable mental illness* (e.g., major depressive disorder as opposed to feeling depressed, or generalized anxiety disorder as opposed to feeling anxious), and fewer still provide *national* prevalence estimates of diagnosable mental illness. This report briefly describes the methodology and results of three large surveys (funded in whole or in part by the U.S.

Department of Health and Human Services) that provide *national prevalence estimates of diagnosable mental illness*: the National Comorbidity Survey Replication (NCS-R), the National Comorbidity Survey Replication Adolescent Supplement (NCS-A), and the National Survey on Drug Use and Health (NSDUH). The NCS-R and the NCS-A have the advantage of identifying specific mental illnesses, but they are a decade old. The NSDUH does not identify specific mental illnesses, but it has the advantage of being conducted annually.

Between February 2001 and April 2003, NCS-R staff interviewed more than 9,000 adults aged 18 or older. Analyses of NCS-R data have yielded different prevalence estimates. One analysis of NCS-R data estimated that 26.2% of adults had a mental illness within a 12-month period (hereinafter called 12-month prevalence). Another analysis of NCS-R data estimated the 12- month prevalence of mental illness to be 32.4% among adults. A third analysis of NCS-R data estimated the 12-month prevalence of mental illness *excluding substance use disorders* to be 24.8% among adults. The 12-month prevalence of *serious* mental illness was estimated to be 5.8% among adults, based on NCS-R data.

Between February 2001 and January 2004, NCS-A staff interviewed more than 10,000 adolescents aged 13 to 17. Using NCS-A data, researchers estimated the 12-month prevalence of mental illness to be 40.3% among adolescents. Some have suggested that the current approach to diagnosing mental illness identifies people who should not be considered mentally ill. The 12- month prevalence of *serious* mental illness was estimated to be 8.0% among adolescents, based on NCS-A data.

The NSDUH is an annual survey of approximately 70,000 adults and adolescents aged 12 years or older in the United States. According to the 2012 NSDUH, the estimated 12-month prevalence of mental illness *excluding substance use disorders* was 18.6% among adults aged 18 or older. The estimated 12-month prevalence of *serious* mental illness (excluding substance use disorders) was 4.1% among adults. Although the NSDUH collects information related to mental illness (e.g., symptoms of depression) from adolescents aged 12 to 17, it does not produce estimates of mental illness for that population.

The prevalence estimates discussed in this report may raise questions for Congress. Should federal mental health policy focus on adults or adolescents with *any* mental illness (including some whose mental illnesses may be mild and even transient) or on those with *serious* mental illness? Should substance use disorders be addressed through the same policies as other mental illnesses? Members of Congress may approach mental health policy differently depending in part on how they answer such questions.

In: Mental Health and Rural America
Editor: Pamela Rhodes

ISBN: 978-1-63321-122-3
© 2014 Nova Science Publishers, Inc.

Chapter 1

MENTAL HEALTH AND RURAL AMERICA: 1994-2005 AN OVERVIEW AND ANNOTATED BIBLIOGRAPHY[*]

Office of Rural Health Policy

FOREWORD

It is with pleasure that we offer you this third edition of **Mental Health and Rural America**. This work, which provides a comprehensive overview and annotated bibliography, focuses upon the period of 1994-2005. The preceding editions of this work are some of the most cited in rural mental health.

What we see in these bodies of work are the challenges facing rural America in meeting the needs of its citizens with mental illnesses and substance use disorders. Beyond the challenges, the opportunities captured and unique solutions are also reported. **Mental Health and Rural America: 1994-2005** seeks to concisely present a comprehensive summary of the current knowledge base around mental health issues in rural and frontier America. This information, it is hoped, will be a valuable resource across the spectrum

---

[*] This is an edited, reformatted and augmented version of a document prepared under contract for the U.S. Department of Health and Human Services, Health Resources and Services Administration, Office of Rural Health Policy, released in 2005.

of rural mental health, from local community planning to national policy development.

This publication was developed by the Federal Office of Rural Health Policy, Health Resources and Services Administration in cooperation with the Mental Health Program of the Western InterState Commission for Higher Education (WICHE). Rural America is a diverse environment in every way, including its cultures, landscapes, and economies. There is "no one rural", but there are many rural myths. This chapter will provide the reader with an array of information to begin to help understand the facts of rural mental health today at the beginning of the 21st Century.

Marcia K. Brand, Ph.D.
Associate Administrator for Rural Health, HRSA

While many things have changed over the course of the 30 years since this series was first published, too many challenges facing rural mental health systems of care remain unresolved. Rural America suffers critical shortages of mental health professionals, and the percent of rural Americans who are underserved has remained unchanged across this span of time.

Financing for rural mental health services remains problematic today, with rural Americans too often being priced out of the health insurance marketplace, and the coverage that many rural Americans can afford does not provide benefits for mental health or substance use care.

It appears clear today, after decades of study that rural Americans suffer from mental illnesses and substance use disorders at rates similar to their urban peers. It is also clear, that while the prevalence and incidence rates may be evenly distributed and rurality does not in itself increase the possibility that rural Americans may be at significantly increased risk for poor health outcomes, the resources to address their mental health and substance use disorders are either not available or not accessible.

Mental Health and Rural America: 1994-2005, provides a solid resource to assist Federal, State, and local efforts to improve quality mental health and substance use policy and services for rural America.

Dennis F. Mohatt, Director
WICHE Mental Health Program

INTRODUCTION

Mental Health and Rural America:1994-2005 represents the third edition of a comprehensive overview and annotated bibliography focused on rural mental health. The previous editions (Flax, Wagenfeld, Ivens & Weiss, 1979; and Wagenfeld, Murray, Mohatt & DeBruyn, 1994) have been frequently cited in the rural mental health literature and have served as valuable sources of information relating to rural mental health in the United States.

The previous editions, and the current, have reviewed the environment of rural mental health at points-in-time over the past three decades. Not surprising to those engaged daily in the delivery of mental healthcare in rural America, much has changed and much has remained the same across this span of time. This new edition will examine both what is new and what remains unchanged.

Support for Mental Health and Rural America: 1994-2005 has been made available by the Federal Office of Rural Health Policy (ORHP) in the Health Resources and Services Administration (HRSA), U.S. Department of Health and Human Services (HHS). ORHP is the "focal-point" for coordination of rural health services for HHS. ORHP also supported the production of the second edition, in the early 1990s, and has provided strong leadership since its establishment in including mental health in its rural health vision. The Mental Health Program of the Western InterState Commission for Higher Education (WICHE) was selected to edit and coordinate its production. Since 1955, the WICHE mental health program has worked to support mental health system improvement and workforce development. It is fitting the publication of this Third edition coincides with the 50th anniversary of the WICHE mental health program.

In keeping with the style and content of the previous editions, the Third edition seeks to provide a single-source of current rural mental health information. The focus is upon the period of 1994- 2005. The volume is divided into two sections: the narrative overview and annotated bibliography. These two sections are integrated, however not all annotated references have been cited in the narrative section or vice versa. The material utilized in this document was discovered through electronic library searches of mental health and health related archives and indexes. The editors reviewed the enormous amount of material and selected those that together seemed to provide a clear and comprehensive picture of the rural mental health environment today. The electronic search was augmented by numerous colleagues who offered their insights, knowledge, and assistance.

In the midst of the "information age," the need for this work is even more important to provide a source of context, review, and analysis of the vast array of data and information that can sometimes be overwhelming and often more than a little confusing.

The development of the Mental Health and Rural America: 1994-2005, coincided with the WICHE Mental Health Program's work with the Rural Issues Subcommittee of the President's New Freedom Commission on Mental Health and the development of the Rural Issues Background Paper released for public access in 2005. The work of the President's Commission has truly created new momentum across the nation to transform mental healthcare, and has brought serious attention to rural mental health. The Commission's Rural Issues Subcommittee Chairperson, Nancy Speck, Ph.D., provided extraordinary guidance to these parallel review efforts.

Blanca Fuertes, from the staff of the Federal Office of Rural Health Policy, served as the project officer for the development of Mental Health and Rural America: 1994-2005 and provided both good counsel and technical advice. The support of ORHP was essential to making the notion of a third edition a reality. The leadership of ORHP Director, Marcia Brand, and Deputy Director, Tom Morris, was critical in making this project move from a good idea to a finished product. We also acknowledge the support and guidance of many colleagues from across the nation. Dr. Anthony Pollitt, from the National Institute of Mental Health (NIMH) Office of Rural Mental Health Research, was always prepared to field a research question and assist our efforts to identify key studies. Dr. David Lambert, past-President of the National Association for Rural Mental Health, and Steve Wilhide, former Executive Director of the National Rural Health Association, were always responsive to requests for information and policy analysis. Finally, Jenny Shaw, the WICHE mental health administrative and project coordinator provided the organizational focal point for putting it all together. Thank you for the hard work.

Transforming mental health in America is the battle cry today, as a result of the work of the President's New Freedom Commission on Mental Health. Other reports such as the Institute of Medicine Report Quality through Collaboration: The Future of Rural Health (2005) also emphasize the need for better coordination of care and collaboration among providers of services and their communities. Rural mental health is on the agenda, and the leadership within HRSA and SAMHSA are taking rural seriously. From rural mental health workforce development to scientific discovery, rural America has often simply not been taken into account, it is our hope that Mental Health and Rural

America: 1994- 2005 helps support those many individuals from across our vast nation make rural count.

Dennis F. Mohatt
Mimi M. Bradley
Scott J. Adams
Chad D. Morris

Western InterState Commission for Higher Education
Boulder, Colorado
January 2005

1. RURAL AMERICA TODAY

There is not one rural America. The rural United States is a place of great diversity, which is perhaps a surprise to many in the majority metropolitan population. Rural is many small places scattered across the vast landscape of America.

In the eastern half of the nation, rural is the green space between the large metropolitan areas from Maine to Florida, the little towns and villages off the InterState 95 corridor, the isolated places of Appalachia, the Deep South, the Ohio and Mississippi river valleys. This rural America is much more densely populated, with many small towns spread along the twisting two-lane highways and back roads that lace the region like a spider's web. The State with the largest rural population is Pennsylvania, with over 2.8 million rural residents, while in Vermont, over 60 percent of the population is rural.[1]

Crossing the Mississippi River marks the beginning of a different rural. The density begins to thin, the little towns and villages becoming increasingly spread apart. The twisting roads give way to a uniform grid of roads, which follow the checkerboard like section lines. Finally, out past the 100th meridian, precipitation becomes a welcome albeit infrequent event and the population becomes so lean and remote it is referred to by many as frontier. Large metropolitan areas exist like island fortresses, and rural dominates the landscape. While satellite pictures of the eastern U.S. at night emanate a glow,

---

[1] Source: Northeast-Midwest Institute calculations based on data from U.S. Department of Commerce, Census Bureau, 2000 Census, Summary File 3, Table P.5 Urban and Rural, data extracted via http://factfinder.census.gov.

much of the west is darkness. The west coast again emulates the pattern of the east, with the population density high along the InterState 5 corridor, and thinning proportionate to distance from it.

Rural America has always been a place of diversity. The picture many hold of a homogeneous agrarian hinterland is simply a myth. Even prior to European discovery, diversity was the norm with an indigenous population made up of hundreds of tribes speaking nearly as many different languages. Some farmed in settlements, while others were nomads. Small places may have been the norm, but even then these places were very different.

This section will provide a picture of the demographics and socioeconomic landscape of the United States and attempt to share what is clear about rural America at the close of the 20th and beginning of the 21st century. It cannot be a complete picture, but it will be a complex illustration.

What's Rural?

A myriad of methods for determining what physically constitutes rural versus non-rural areas of the United States is employed by the Federal government. No consistent definition is used across agencies or programs (HHS, 2002). For the purposes of this chapter, the terms *rural* and *nonmetro* will be used interchangeably, as will the terms *urban* and *metro*.

When programs are implemented to provide health services to rural areas, they immediately encounter the problem that there are no operational definitions of "rural areas" that precisely divide the population of the United States into "rural residents" and "urban residents."

The two most commonly used definitions are by the Office of Management and Budget (OMB) and the Census Bureau. All information for the following section was cited from OMB, Census Bureau and Economic Research Service data. Over the past 10 years, many sources encouraged the OMB to classify the entire United States into population categories and to not leave any regions outside urban areas as unclassifiable.

In June 2003, the OMB released a new classification system to define metropolitan (i.e., metro or urban) and nonmetropolitan (i.e., nonmetro, micropolitan, or rural) areas based on census data from 2000. The OMB previously defined metropolitan areas by central counties with one or more cities of at least 50,000 residents or with an urbanized area of 50,000 or more and total area population of at least 100,000. Counties surrounding these areas were included if they met two primary criteria: 1) they were both economically tied to the central county measured by daily commuting and 2) they showed a level of "metropolitan character" defined by population density, urbanization and population growth. However, a county with high "metropolitan character" would be included even though only 15 percent of it workers commute, but a county low in "metropolitan character" would be classified as nonmetro no matter how high the commuting percentage to the main county.

In the new "core-based statistical area" system, OMB defined metro by the following two characteristics: 1) central counties with one or more urbanized areas and 2) outlying counties that are economically tied to the core counties as measured by the amount of people who commute for work. Outlying counties are included in the metro classification if 25 percent of workers living in the county commute to the metro counties, or if 25 percent of the employment in the county consists of workers coming out from the metro counties (i.e., reverse commuting).

The OMB defines nonmetro as those counties outside the boundaries of metro areas. These nonmetro counties are then subdivided into two types: 1) micropolitan areas and 2) noncore counties. Micropolitan areas are defined by clusters of 10,000 or more persons. All remaining areas are classified as "noncore" counties.

The Census Bureau modified its measurement procedures for rural and urban areas in 2003 as well. An *urbanized* area is defined by a region with at least 50,000 people. The Census Bureau added the definition of *urban cluster*, measured by at least 2,500 people but no more than 50,000 people. *Rural* is still defined by small settlements of less than 2,500 people. However, the Bureau now identifies small towns and cities that have adjoining towns or suburbs. For example, if a town of 3,000 people has 300 residents living in thinly settled portions, the 300 are classified as rural and the 2,700 are classified as an urban cluster.

New classification parameters within the OMB and the Census Bureau have led to significant shifts in the description of rural geography and population data. These shifts highlight the diversity that exists in non-urban areas in America. New population measurement procedures will allow for better and more complete data collection in rural areas. Better data will ultimately lead to increased understanding of rural population trends and attention from policymakers and other interested parties.

Extensive discussions of the implications of this array of definitions to health and human services programs have been published by Hewitt (1989), Wagenfeld, Murray, Mohatt & DeBruyn (1994) and Ciarlo, Wagenfeld & Mohatt (1996).

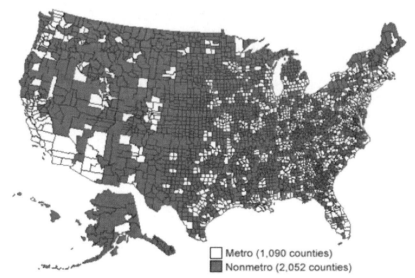

Source: Prepared by ERS using data from the Census Bureau.

Map 1. Nonmetropolitan and metropolitan countries, 2003.

Despite advances in making rural definitions more precise, the fact that the OMB and the Census Bureau categorize regions slightly differently leads to disparate population results. For example, according to the OMB definition, rural America comprises 17 percent (49 million) of the population, compared to 21 percent (59 million) by the Census definition. Researchers and policy makers need to be aware of which definition is used and that it is used consistently throughout a study or document.

According to the Census Bureau definitions, in 2000, 68 percent of Americans lived in *urbanized* areas, 11 percent lived in *urban clusters* and 21 percent in *rural* areas. In the OMB's recent population data (also from 2000), 298 formerly nonmetro counties are now classified as metro and 45 metro counties were reclassified as nonmetro. These recent statistics reflect the pattern of urban growth over the past decade as well as highlight the new system for metro and nonmetro classification.

Defining rural does make a difference in ensuring limited resources intended to address critical rural needs actually are transmitted to locations that have those needs. The President's *New Freedom Commission on Mental Health, Subcommittee on Rural Issues* (NFC-SRI, 2004) recommended DHHS adopt a single definition that was precise enough to capture the diversity of rural America as to enable focused targeting of Federal resources to address specific rural needs.

Rural Demographics

For rural America to be taken into account, it is essential that the reality of rural be understood instead of the myths. Many myths exist, and perhaps the most persistent is the notion of rural America being synonymous with agriculture and farms. There is a persistent image of rural areas being a patchwork of family farms surrounding tranquil communities. Today, less than 10 percent of the rural population live on farms and people in rural areas are engaged in a wide range of activities.

In 1992, only 7.6 percent of rural employment was in farming (ERS/USDA 1995:5). Service employment, on the other hand, accounted for 50.6 percent and has experienced the greatest growth over the past two decades. Even in areas of the U.S. with the greatest percentage of farm employment, nonfarm employment still accounts for nearly 80 percent of jobs. Simply Stated, most family farmers supplement their farm-based income with non-farm employment (ERS/USDA, 1995:12).

The family farm is fading from the rural landscape, with a continued decline in the number of family farms during the past decade, which continues a trend established for over a half-century. Family farms are broadly defined here to include family-held corporations and partnerships, as well as sole proprietorships. Census of agriculture data confirms that family-owned farms are not losing their share of U.S. farm product sales in relation to non-family corporations. Non-family corporations comprised a relatively stable and minor share (0.3 to 0.4 percent) of total U.S. farm numbers between 1978 and 1997, while their share of total farm product sales actually fell, from 6.5 percent in 1978 and 1982 to 5.6 percent in 1997.

Socio-economic factors play an important role in the accessibility of health and human services. Rural employment is dominated by low wages, and rural incomes are less than those in urban areas. In 1996, 23 percent of rural workers were employed in the service sector and were nearly twice as likely to earn the minimum wage as their urban peers (U.S. Congress, 2002). Compared to urban workers, rural citizens are more likely to be unemployed and less likely to move out of low wage jobs. Rural working families are more likely to be poor than working urban families.

More than 25 percent of rural workers over age 25 earn less than the Federal poverty rate of $18,390, and 600 (23 percent) rural counties are classified as persistent poverty counties by the U.S. Government. According to the Economic Research Service (ERS) website (http://www.ers.usda.gov/), the rural low-wage employment was 24 percent versus 16.6 percent in urban areas. The higher incidence of nonmetro poverty compared with metro poverty has existed since the 1960s when poverty rates were first formally recorded.

Rural economies benefited from the economic expansion during the 1990s. In addition, recent data on metro and nonmetro employment change shows substantial employment growth in nonmetro areas since mid-2002, based on the 2003 classification of metropolitan status. Micropolitan and noncore counties are now experiencing employment growth at a rate of more than 1 percent a year (ERS, 2005).

Over the last decade, nonmetro employment growth has generally been fastest in the West even in times of economic slowing. The slowdown had the greatest effect on nonmetro employment growth in the South and the Midwest (ERS, 2005).

Nonmetro unemployment rates were highest in *mining* counties during the 1990s, but this changed around the year 2001. After a relatively positive experience in the 1990s, *manufacturing* counties experienced a sharp increase in unemployment in 2001 and currently have the highest unemployment rate of any county economic type (ERS, 2005).

Child poverty is higher in rural areas, with more than half of all rural children (3.2 million) in female-headed households living in poverty. Children of color are particularly at risk, with 46.2 percent of rural African American, 43 percent of rural Native American, and 41.2 percent of rural Hispanic children living in poverty (U.S. Congress, 2002).

People of color constituted about 17 percent of the rural population in 1997, compared with about 25 percent of the overall U.S. population. A disproportionately large number of Native Americans—nearly half of the overall Native American population—live in rural areas. The rural white population is roughly proportional, with 23 percent of whites living in rural areas. The remaining major ethnic and racial groups are underrepresented in rural areas. Fifteen percent of African Americans, nine percent of Hispanics, and five percent of Asians and Pacific Islanders are rural.

Poverty rates by race indicate that non-Hispanic Black people have the highest incidence of rural poverty at a rate of approximately 30 percent. One out of every four Hispanics living in rural areas lived in poverty in 2003. The above statistics exceed the rate of poverty for non-Hispanic White people in rural areas, which was 11 percent in 2003. The high poverty level for Hispanic people is remarkable as their share of the rural population has been increasing in the past 10 years (ERS, 2005).

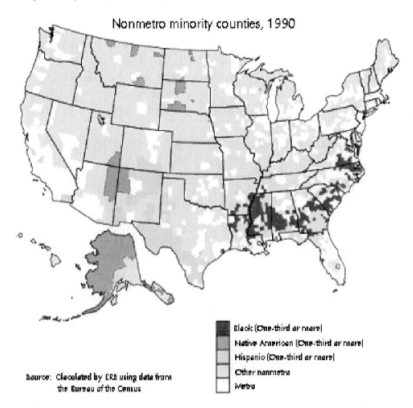

As for rural population, some places are growing, while many are not. During the 1990s, 2.2 million more people moved from the city to the country than vice versa, reversing a trend of rural outmigration established during the early 20th century. During this same time period, 70 percent of rural counties grew in population, but the pace of growth slowed during the end of the decade of the 1990s (U.S. Congress, 2002).

Since the mid-1990s, all rural counties (except rural commuter counties) have experienced reduced rates of population growth and the rural rate of growth is only half the rate of urban. The great plains has experienced the most significant population loss, and depopulation of some frontier counties (those counties with fewer than six persons per square mile). These population trends, especially population loss, strain the resources available to sustain comprehensive systems of health and human services (NFC-SRI, 2004).

Rural educational levels continue to be less than those in urban environments. Fewer rural adults have a college education than do urban adults (15 percent versus 28 percent), and the number of rural adults without a high school diploma is greater than in urban areas (20 percent versus 15 percent). Fewer young adults in rural areas seek higher education. Since the high school graduation levels match or exceed urban levels, clearly these graduates are leaving rural America more often than are their non-graduating peers, making the "best and brightest" a chief rural export (U.S. Congress, 2002).

This out-migration of capable young persons limits the pool of local persons available to train and staff health and human service systems. As a result many services are provided by persons who are not indigenous to the rural communities they serve, and often are only available on an itinerant basis (NFCSRI, 2004).

Immigration is changing rural America in some places. While most immigrants (about 95 percent) settle in large metro areas, those who move to rural areas concentrate in a few locations (Effland & Butler, 1997). For example, Texas is home to 17 percent of the total rural immigrant population of the United States. The West accounts for about seven percent of the nation's rural immigrants. Overall, immigrants to rural areas comprise only two percent of the total rural population. The single largest group of rural immigrants is Mexican, whose share in rural immigrants has increased from 48 percent in the 1980s to 57 percent in 1990s.

Rural America is home to numerous social, cultural, religious and language differences. These differences are a part of the reason why it is difficult to capture a cultural understanding of rural America as a whole. While there are many similarities (e.g., small community), rural areas also differ from region to region. For example, a rural community in the Northeast is likely very different culturally from a small town in Alaska. These differences are distinguished by the ethnicities that reside there, the political climate of the State and other economic and social factors that are indigenous to the area.

Data on homelessness in rural is limited and does not reflect the true number of homeless, as efforts to identify homeless persons often depend upon formal systems of support (e.g. shelters) and often miss rural homeless who may be outside of rural support systems. However, according to the National Coalition for the Homeless (1997), "studies comparing urban and rural homeless populations have shown that homeless people in rural areas are more likely to be white, female, married, currently working, homeless for the first time and homeless for a shorter period of time" (p. 1).

Rural Mental Health

Demographics, economics and cultural values have a dynamic impact upon mental health and mental health care. The prevalence and incidence of adults with severe mental illnesses and children with serious emotional disturbances are not significantly different in rural and urban areas. What differs in rural America is the experience of individuals with mental illnesses and their families (Wagenfeld et al., 1994). Too often, that experience seems to result in higher suicide rates for both rural adults with mental illnesses and children with serious emotional disturbances (George Mason University, 2000).

The different experiences that rural persons with mental illnesses face are influenced by three factors (variables) that may prevent them from receiving the mental health care they need:

- Accessibility
- Availability
- Acceptability

These variables lead rural residents with mental health needs to: enter care later in the course of their disease than do their urban peers; enter care with more serious, persistent and disabling symptoms and require more expensive and intensive treatment response (Wagenfeld et al., 1994).

Accessibility: The *New Freedom Commission on Mental Health, Subcommittee on Rural Issues* (2004) identified three significant components of access to mental health services that put rural residents at a significant disadvantage: knowledge, transportation and financing.

An essential element of access is *knowing when one needs care* and *where and what care options are available* to address needs. In both respects, the rural experience differs from the urban one. The frequently noted myth of an idyllic rural existence persists (HHS Rural Task Force, 2002). This myth, when widely held, becomes a barrier to creating an impetus for action to address rural mental health problems.

The perception of need for care is the first step in seeking care, and rural residents enter care later than do their urban peers due to a lower perception of need—a problem that is then compounded by their perceiving less access to care. Empirical studies show that lower access to mental health services is directly related to lower availability or supply of mental health providers (Lambert & Agger, 1995). The barrier to care posed by provider availability in rural areas is discussed further in the next section.

The ability to travel to services and to pay for those services if accessed is a significant barrier to rural persons. Physically and psychologically accessible and affordable transportation services may be unavailable, especially to rural children, people with disabilities and the elderly. Public transportation is often not an option to rural consumers of mental health services. As a result, many rural mental health providers operate some form of transportation service to bring consumers to care—an operational cost not often incurred by their urban counterparts. Rural consumers and families must often travel hundreds of miles weekly to access care available only in larger communities that serve as "regional centers of trade."

Employment-based health insurance covers a wide variety of health services for Americans, and is the most common form of health insurance coverage in the United States, covering 64.9 percent of the non-elderly population and 34.4 percent of the elderly population in 1998. Size matters; often small employers do not offer a full range of benefits and employers with 50 or fewer workers were exempt from the Mental Health Parity Act of 1996. Retiree health benefits have steadily declined over the past decade, with only 30 percent of employers offering retiree health benefits in 1998, as compared to 40 percent in 1993 (McDonnell & Fronstin, 1999). A similar dramatic decline occurred for mental health benefits, where per employee expenditures for behavioral health benefits have gone from $151.54 in 1988 to $69.61 in 1997 (The Hay Group, 1998).

For rural Americans, the cost of health services (only partially reimbursed by Medicare Part B; or at a discount by Medicaid) may be too expensive—especially prescription drugs. Small group and individual purchasers, who often cannot afford comprehensive policies, dominate the rural health insurance marketplace. As a result, these policies often have large deductibles, and limited or no behavioral health coverage (McDonnell & Fronstin, 1999). Rural residents also have longer periods of time without insurance than do their urban peers and, hence, a greater likelihood of pent-up demand. Also, they are more likely not to seek physician services when they cannot pay, both because of pride and limited opportunities for free or reduced-fee clinical care (Mueller, Kashinath & Ullrich, 1997).

Parents who have children with mental health problems but limited or no ability to pay for treatment may have to face a disturbing option: relinquishing custody of the child in order to obtain needed services. Multiple groups have commented on this practice, including the National Alliance for the Mentally Ill (NAMI), the Bazelon Center for Mental Health Law, and the Federation of Families for Children's Mental Health (FFCMH).[2]

It is beyond the scope of this document to present all the issues related to relinquishment of custody to receive services. However, a report by the FFCMH lists the consequences of relinquishment. They State:

"These public practices:

- Lead children to believe they have been abandoned by their family into the care of the State thus irreparably harming the bond between the child and family;
- Force parents to make an otherwise unthinkable choice between retaining responsibility for and a relationship with their children and giving over decision-making authority and control to a State agency in order to obtain the help their child desperately needs;
- Waste public funds by keeping children as wards of the State when their basic needs could otherwise be provided by families who love them; and
- Force children into expensive residential placements rather than promoting and supporting families with less costly community-based services.

The implications of these phenomena can have a significant bearing on rural mental health through limiting the:

1. Supply pool of skilled individuals to staff mental health programs;
2. Availability of natural supports for persons with serious mental illnesses and children with serious emotional disturbances;

---

[2] For more information on these organizations and the issue of relinquishing custody, please visit the following websites: http://www.bazelon.org/issues
http://www.ffcmh.org/New%20Site/factsheet_custody.htm;
http://www.nami.org/youth/custody.html.

3. Level of peer support and affiliations available to create and sustain an environment that supports professional recruitment and retention of mental health and allied staff; and,
4. Financial resources available to support a "continuum of mental health services" (Gamm, Tai-Seale & Stone, 2002).

Rural mental health systems can rarely operate without direct or indirect governmental subsidy; this is especially true for programs serving persons with serious mental illness (SMI) or children with severe emotional disturbances (SED) (Wagenfeld, 2000).

Availability: The availability of rural mental health services and providers is seriously limited in rural communities. Over 85 percent of the 1,669 Federally designated mental health professional shortage areas (MHPSAs) are rural (Bird, Dempsey & Hartley, 2001). According to the National Advisory Committee on Rural Health (1993), of the 3,075 rural counties in the United States, 55 percent had no practicing psychologists, psychiatrists, or social workers, and all of these counties identified were rural.

It is often difficult to recruit and keep professionals in rural areas. Although there have been government-subsidized programs (e.g., student loan repayment), they have only had a minimal effect in solving the mental health workforce shortage in rural areas. Furthermore, it is often difficult for mental health providers with spouses or partners to find work for both people. For those brought up or currently living in urban or suburban areas, the transition to life in a rural or frontier area can be difficult. Lower salaries and a more limited range of social and other outlets may be disincentives to move to such areas or motivators to return to urban centers.

Unlike the situation in general rural healthcare, specific Federal strategies for sustaining a rural mental health infrastructure do not exist (e.g., Community and Migrant Health Clinic Programs, Critical Access Hospitals). Finally, rural programs often operate in areas with disproportionately limited sources of financial resources to leverage as matching funds in seeking to compete for Federal and private foundations grant support.

Acceptability: Most Americans value self-reliance or utilizing family or other close relationships to solve problems. For this reason, many attach stigma to having or seeking help for mental health or substance abuse problems. However, this appears to be more of an issue in rural communities, as there is less anonymity in seeking help. That is, belief in self-reliance and limited anonymity combine to more significantly limit a rural person's likelihood of seeking services.

On the provider side, Roberts, Battaglia and Epstein (1999) described how rural caregivers face serious clinical ethical dilemmas every day. Rural clinicians commonly provide care without optimal supports, services and safeguards for their patients. It is necessary at times to ration care; to provide care outside of their usual areas of expertise and competence; to deal with patients' "noncompliance" related to access problems; to respond to complaints about colleagues' impairments and to make complex clinical decisions about reproductive, end-of-life and quality-of-life issues without the benefit of specialists.

Care requires addressing patients' potential for self-harm and violence; dealing with the heightened social stigma associated with mental disorders; protecting vulnerable patients from potential abuse or exploitation and grappling with care planning for individuals with impaired decision-making capacity. These ethical issues are often more acute in rural or isolated health care settings primarily because usual practices to ensure ethical conduct are narrowed by the scarcity of health care resources.

References

Bird, D.C., Dempsey, P. & Hartley, D. (2001). *Addressing mental health workforce needs in underserved rural area: Accomplishments and challenges.* Portland, ME: Maine Rural Health Research Center, Muskie Institute, University of Southern Maine.

Ciarlo, J.A., Wackwitz, J.H., Wagenfeld, M.O. & Mohatt, D.F. (1996). *Focusing on "frontier": Isolated rural America. Letter to the Field No. 2.* Boulder, CO: Frontier Mental Health Resource Network, WICHE Mental Health Program, http:/www.wiche/edu/mentalhealth.

Effland, A. B. W. & Butler, M. A. (1997). Fewer immigrants settle in nonmetro areas and most fare less well than metro immigrants. *Rural Conditions and Trends*, 8(2), 60-65.

Economic Research Service; United States Department of Agriculture. (Information accessed in 2005) http://www.ers.usda.gov/

ERS/USDA (1995). *Understanding Rural America.* Agricultural Information Bulletin No. 710. Washington, D.C.: Economic Research Service, U.S. Department of Agriculture.

Gamm, L., Tai-Seale, M. & Stone, S. (2002). *Meeting the mental health needs of people living in rural areas.* Rockville, MD: Center for Mental Health Services, SAMHSA, U.S. Department of Health and Human Services.

Lambert, D. & Agger, M. (1995). Access of rural Medicaid beneficiaries to mental health services. *Health Care Financing Review*, 17(7), 133-145.

McDonnell, K. & Fronstin, P. (1999). *EBRI health benefits data book* (1st ed.). Washington, D.C.: Employee Benefit Research Institute.

Mueller, K., Patil, K. & Ullrich, F. (1997). Lengthening Spells of Uninsurance and their Consequences. *The Journal of Rural Health, 13*(1).

National Advisory Committee on Rural Health (1993). *Sixth annual report on rural health.* Rockville, MD: Office of Rural Health Policy, Health Resources and Services Administration, HHS.

National Coalition for the Homeless (1997). *Rural homelessness (NCH Fact Sheet No. 13).* Also available: http://nch.ari.net/rural.html (1998, November 10).

Office of Management and Budget (1990). OMB Circular A-11. Preparation and Submission of Budget Estimates.

Office of Management and Budget (2003). OMB Bulletin No. 03- 04. http://www.whitehouse.gov/omb/bulletins/b03-04.html

Roberts, L. W., Battaglia, J., & Epstein, R. S. (1999). Frontier ethics: Mental health care needs and ethical dilemmas in rural communities. *Psychiatric Services, 50*(4), 497-503.

The Hay Group. (1998). *Health care plan design and trends.* Arlington, VA: The Hay Group.

The President's New Freedom Commission on Mental Health (2004). *Achieving the Promise: Transforming Mental Health Care in America. A final report.* DHHS Pub. No. SMA-03-3832. Rockville, MD.

The President's New Freedom Commission on Mental Health (2004). *Subcommittee of Rural Issues: Background Paper.* DHHS Pub. No. SMA-04-3890. Rockville, MD.

U.S. Census Bureau (2003). http://www.ers.usda.gov/Briefing/Rurality/New Definitions/.

U.S. Congress (2002). Why rural matters. In *Fast Facts* [Electronic Version]. Washington, DC: Congressional Rural Caucus. U.S. House of Representatives.

U.S. Health and Human Services Rural Task Force. (2002). *One department serving rural America* (Report to the Secretary). Washington, DC: U.S. Department of Health and Human Services.

Wagenfeld, M.O. (2000). Organization and delivery of mental health services to adolescents and children with persistent and serious mental illness in frontier areas. *Journal of the Washington Academy of Sciences, 86*(3), 81-88.

Wagenfeld, M.O., Murray, J.D., Mohatt, D.F., and DeBruyn, J.C. (1994). *Mental Health and Rural America 1980-1993: An Overview and Annotated Bibliography.* Rockville, Md. Office of Rural Health Policy, HRSA, and Office of Rural Mental Health Research, NIMH, NIH, 1994. NIH Publication No. 94-3500.

2. EPIDEMIOLOGICAL OVERVIEW OF MENTAL HEALTH IN RURAL AMERICA

This section will review the epidemiologic evidence for the prevalence of mental health disorders in rural areas of the United States since the last publication of this chapter. In addition, this section will address some of the clinical, social and policy implications for rural communities as a result of the epidemiologic data.

Historically, rural America has lacked the necessary political influence to promote effective rural mental health policy agendas (Ahr & Halcomb, 1985; Danbom, 1995; Dyer, 1997; Kimmel, 1992). Recent survey results indicate that rural health centers and State organizations for rural health rated mental health as a top priority (Gamm, Tai-Seale & Stone, 2002). Several Federal projects including Rural Healthy People 2010, the President's *New Freedom Commission, Subcommittee on Rural Issues* and the 1990 Surgeon General's report on Mental Health indicate the existence of underserved mental health issues in rural communities.

Recommendations from these various reports are described throughout this section.

Prevalence

The most comprehensive and recent data indicate that the prevalence and incidence of mental health problems are similar between rural and urban populations (Kessler et al., 1994). Current prevalence rates show that approximately 20 percent of the United States population is affected by mental health issues each year (Kessler et al., 1994). Additionally, although this chapter presents mental health and substance abuse disorders in separate sections, it is important to keep in mind that these disorders often co-occur. A study by Gogek (1992), found that approximately 40 percent of mentally ill individuals in rural populations were using illegal substances. This illustrates the importance of integrating services through formal and informal collaboration and including substance abuse statistics when discussing mental health.

The overall prevalence of substance abuse among adults has frequently been shown to be comparable between rural and urban areas. According to the Epidemiological Catchment Area (ECA) Study, which compared rural and urban prevalence rates for a large variety of psychiatric disorders, the rural lifetime prevalence rate of these combined disorders was 32 percent, only slightly lower than the 34 percent rate in urban areas (Robins & Reiger, 1991).

In a review of studies investigating the prevalence of psychiatric disorders in rural primary care settings, Sears and colleagues (2003) found that 34 to 41 percent of patients had a mental health disorder. Additionally, results of studies of seriously mentally ill individuals indicate that rural residents have poorer outcomes (e.g., reliance on inpatient services, increased symptom severity) when compared to urban residents, especially if there are co-occurring substance abuse issues (Fisher, Owen & Cuffel, 1996; Rost et al., 1998).

One striking difference between rural and urban populations is the higher rate of suicide in rural communities, which has been a consistent trend for more than a decade (*New Freedom Commission Subcommittee on Rural Issues*; NFC-SRI, 2004; Institute of Medicine, 2002; Stack, 1982; Wagenfeld et al., 1994). Specifically, the suicide rate for older adult (elderly) males and Native American youth in rural populations is significantly higher than in urban populations (Eberhardt, Ingram & Makuc, 2001).

Adults suffering from depression, who live in rural areas, tend to make more suicide attempts than their urban counterparts (Rost et al., 1998).

However, Rost and colleagues (2002) suggest that it is difficult to attribute these elevated suicide rates to rurality per se because suicide comparisons have not been adjusted for other variables such as income and education.

Women & Families

Rural families often experience stress because of the high poverty rates, high unemployment rates and low educational opportunities (Champion, 2002; Human & Wasem, 1991). Women living in rural areas are particularly affected by these barriers of rural culture and are at a higher risk for abuse (Boyd, 2000; Champion, 1999; Champion, 2002; Dimmitt, 1995). Because of the small size of rural communities and a lack of anonymity, it may be very difficult for women to leave abusive or dangerous relationships, which is compounded by a lack of mental health and other community services. Health providers, especially in rural communities, need to be aware of the complex emotional repercussions of abuse (emotional or physical), such as depression and other mood disturbances. Studies have found additional factors associated with depression in rural women, including isolation, declining farm economy (making income unpredictable) and the lack of social, educational and childcare resources (Bushy, 1993; Hauenstein & Boyd, 1994).

Rural women are more likely to seek mental health treatment than rural men, but both are more likely to utilize mental health care services if they have previously sought mental health treatment in the past (Kenkel, 2003). Hauenstein and Boyd (1994) found that 41 percent of their sample of rural women reported depressive symptoms, which contrasts with the typical urban prevalence rates of 13 to 20 percent. Several factors including age, employment status (i.e., unemployed) and lack of education were associated with more depressive symptoms (Hauenstein & Boyd, 1994). Despite the fact that depression is common in rural areas (i.e., 40 percent of all patient visits to primary care physicians), rural doctors detect 50 percent less depression in their patients than their urban counterparts (Rost et al., 1995). The implication of this lower detection rate is the need for increased training for general medical professionals and improved collaborative relationships between medical and mental health professionals.

Children

Approximately one-third of American youths live in rural areas (Cutrona, Halvorson & Russell, 1996). Epidemiologic studies of rural youths are not common, but existing results have consistently found comparable rates of psychiatric disorder, controlling for income (Angold et al., 2002).

Rural children have some different characteristics when compared to urban children. Nordal, Copans and Stamm (2003) report that although drug abuse rates are lower overall, rural teenagers tend to drink more alcohol and have higher rates of risky sexual behavior (i.e., two times as likely to be sexually active, have an earlier first sexual experience and report more alcohol-related sexual intercourse). Twenty percent of teen pregnancies occur in rural communities (Yawn & Yawn, 1993). It is not uncommon for adolescents who engage in risky sexual behavior or who have substance abuse problems to also be struggling with emotional issues that contribute to or increase the odds of engaging in such behaviors.

Rural areas often have difficulty meeting the needs of children with serious mental health problems (Holzer, 1998). A study by Angold and colleagues (2002), which compared psychiatric disorder, impairment and service use among rural African American and White youth, found that despite equal access to mental health services (i.e., school-based mental health services), African American youth were only half as likely as White youth to use specialty mental health services. This study also reported that only one in three youth with a current psychiatric diagnosis had received any mental health care from any professional during the previous three months (Angold et al., 2002).

Youths in the United States who are in need of mental health services are not receiving care traditionally offered by outpatient service agencies (Flaherty, Weist & Warner, 1996; Weist, 1997). Possible reasons for this trend include a lack of trained mental health providers, transportation issues, family disorganization, or stigma linked to mental health issues (Kelleher, Taylor & Rickert, 1992). However, there is a significant lack of providers specializing in providing treatment to children and adolescents (Nordal et al., 2003).

Students with mental health issues are most commonly seen in school-based clinics, which reduce some barriers to accessing care (Welsh, Domitrovich & Bierman, 2003). These authors describe a school program initiated in rural Pennsylvania in which several mental health programs were integrated into their current services. Specifically, the referral process for mental health services was directly connected with the Student Assistance Program (SAP), a State-regulated program that identified and provided interventions to students with emotional or behavioral problems. School-based mental health professionals participated on the SAP team and were able to conduct assessments, provide case management when necessary and act as a link to the community mental health care system, which increased access and helped streamline care.

Elderly

Rural elders may perceive or interpret the need for mental health services differently than their urban counterparts. Rural elderly often encounter the same or increased health needs as urban elderly. However, they often face unique geographic and economic factors (e.g., transportation difficulties, inadequate housing and limited availability of health care services) that influence the environment in which they grow older (Chalifoux et al., 1996; Lubben, Weiler, Chi & De Jong, 1988). The literature indicates that rural elderly persons with mental health issues are often underserved (Dellasega, 1991; Gamm, Stone & Pittman, 2003).

It is estimated that 15 to 25 percent of individuals 65 years or older have significant mental health problems. However, roughly 85 percent do not receive needed treatment (Dorwart, 1990). This is troubling, as rural areas typically have a higher number of older adults than urban areas, a ratio that continues to increase. This increase, which began in the 1950s, is partly attributable to the aging of the population in general, the immigration of older persons from urban areas and the outmigration of younger adults (Rogers, 1999; Rowland & Lyons, 1989).

The rural elderly also have complex mental health needs (e.g., Alzheimer's and other dementias) that are compounded by fragmented and inaccessible services (Buckwalter, Smith & Caston, 1994), fears of institutionalization and geographic isolation. Although there are national data on the prevalence of dementia in the general population, there are no data on the specific prevalence of dementia in rural areas (Buckwalter, Smith & Caston, 1994).

It has been noted that the misdiagnosis of Alzheimer's disease may have serious repercussions for the elderly in rural areas, who often have less access to diagnostic expertise (Rathbone-McCuan & Fabian, 1992). Only approximately five percent of patients at Community Mental Health Centers and less than two percent of private psychiatric patients in rural areas are elderly, which is most likely attributable to transportation issues and stigma regarding mental health in general. In rural areas, the criminal justice system and nursing homes are frequently responsible for the mentally ill rural elderly (Buckwalter et al., 1994).

Despite some of the barriers encountered by rural elderly, there are some positive attributes as well, including a strong sense of community and social support. In addition, despite isolation and evidence of diminished health status for rural elders, they do not differ much in life satisfaction compared to urban elders. While there are some value differences between urban and rural areas, some authors (Buckwalter et al., 1994; Harbert & Ginsberg, 1990) caution against categorizing rural elders as a homogenous group, as cultural differences exist even in predominately white farmlands.

Area Agencies on Aging (AAA) can be influential in mobilizing informal community resources to provide support during crises and prevent unnecessary institutionalization (RathboneMcCuan, 1993). In addition, increased outreach efforts directly targeting the rural elderly, as well as increased home visitation programs may be helpful in increasing education and utilization of mental health services for this group. Psychiatric nurses and other mid-level providers with adequate training in geriatric mental health may be instrumental in providing services for the rural elderly.

A higher percentage of rural elderly live below 200 percent of the Federal poverty level compared to their urban counterparts (52.3 percent vs. 41.2 percent) (Agency for Healthcare Research and Quality, 2000). Rural elderly comprise almost 25 percent of the Medicare population, but not all beneficiaries may be offered a plan that covers prescription drugs. In 2003, rural beneficiaries on average spent more out-of-pocket on prescription drugs compared to urban beneficiaries (Caplan & Brangan, 2004).

In 2003, Medicare beneficiaries either obtained drug coverage from some other public or private source, or paid for their drugs out of pocket. Prescription drugs for all Medicaid beneficiaries in 2003 were the largest single out-of-pocket expense on health care, with the exception of the costs of health care premiums. Sixty percent of rural beneficiaries had some type of prescription drug coverage in 2003, compared to almost three quarters (72 percent) of urban beneficiaries. In addition, rural beneficiaries were more likely to have Medigap and were less likely to be in a private health plan, regardless of drug coverage status. Prescription drug coverage under Medigap generally provides a limited benefit, with higher coinsurance (50 percent) and annual benefit limits that are not commonly found in employer-provided plans. Consequently, the majority of beneficiaries with Medigap do not have any drug coverage (Caplan & Brangan, 2004).

The drug benefit established by the Medicare Prescription Drug, Improvement, and Modernization Act (MMA) of 2003 will be effective in 2006. The goals of the new benefit are to change the spending characteristics of the Medicare population, increase utilization, decrease drug prices and lower out-of-pocket spending for Medicare beneficiaries (Stell & Rodgers, 2004). This new legislation (MMA) will add prescription drug coverage to Medicare beginning in 2006. The availability of new coverage may provide a critical source of drug coverage for individuals in rural areas (Caplan & Brangan, 2004).

Veterans

In the late 1980s, veterans in rural areas did not have access to specialized Post-Traumatic Stress Disorder (PTSD) treatment unless they traveled long distances to larger Veteran's Administration hospitals (Sandrick, 1990). Research indicated that veterans are more likely to access PTSD treatment through the Veteran's Health Administration (VHA) than through non-VA mental health services (Rosenheck & Fontana, 1995). By the late 1990s, the

VHA opened 141 inpatient and outpatient PTSD treatment programs across the nation (Fontana et al., 1999). However, a commission that reviewed the methodology used to identify new clinic locations indicated that the selection process was disadvantageous to veterans living in rural areas. In response to these findings, the VHA revised its Community Based Outpatient Clinic (CBOC) planning criteria to include more emphasis on the importance of access to care for rural veterans. The purpose of these clinics was to improve access to primary care and mental health services for veterans in rural communities.

Refugees

Refugee communities from a variety of racial and ethnic backgrounds are increasing in rural areas (Marsella et al., 1994) in search of safety and job opportunities (Markstrom et al., 2003). Between five and 35 percent of refugees are survivors of torture (Baker, 1992) and often struggle with emotional difficulties (e.g., Post-Traumatic Stress Disorder, social adjustment problems) (U.S. Committee for Refugees, 1997). This is important for mental health professionals working in rural areas and implies the need for increased knowledge and training in working with refugee populations and survivors of trauma. The information regarding refugee mental health in rural communities is significantly inadequate. While there is some information regarding refugee mental health in general that may be useful and applicable to rural refugees, there is a significant need for further research in this area. Language and cultural barriers also sometimes prevent refugees from receiving mental health services.

Barriers to Mental Health Treatment in Rural Communities

There are numerous barriers that contribute to disparities in access to care, utilization of services and treatment of mental health disorders for rural residents. Fox, Merwin and Blank (1995) and the *New Freedom Commission on Mental Health, Subcommittee on Rural Issues* (2004) indicate that obstacles to service use generally fall into three categories: availability, accessibility and acceptability.

Availability refers to the presence or absence of services and service providers. Accessibility refers to whether or not people can reach the services they need. Acceptability indicates a person's attitude to mental health issues, willingness to seek services and enter treatment.

Whether individuals with mental health issues received treatment has been predicted by availability (Fortney, Rost & Zang, 1998) and accessibility (Fortney, Rost & Warren, 2000). Hoyt and colleagues (1997) indicated that perceived acceptability predicts the willingness to initiate an evidence-based treatment regimen.

The mental health service system in rural areas is often described as de facto and is comprised of a loosely organized and fragmented array of services and providers (Fox, Merwin & Blank, 1995; Rost et al., 2002). Rural residents with mental health issues often do not seek treatment until the problem has worsened and is currently impeding functioning in multiple areas of life (e.g., relationships, work). Delays in seeking treatment are often due to financial barriers (Schur & Franco, 1999). In this way, rural mental health, generally speaking, is not preventive, but is often reactive to mental health issues that have been exacerbated by crises.

Availability

There is clear evidence that the availability of mental health services and the number of mental health providers in rural areas is severely inadequate. Rural America has been underserved by mental health professionals for the past 40 years. Over 85 percent of the 1,669 Federally designated mental health professional shortage areas (MHPSAs) are rural (Bird, Dempsey & Hartley, 2001). According to the National Advisory Committee on Rural Health (1993), of the 3,075 rural counties in the United States, 55 percent had no practicing psychologists, psychiatrists, or social workers, and all of these counties identified were rural (NFC-SRI, 2004). In the past 10 years, many rural hospitals have closed or been converted to Critical Access Hospitals due to financial and other economic reasons (NFC-SRI, 2004). Although Critical Access Hospitals provide a more limited array of services than full-service hospitals, they still serve an important function in the service system in rural areas.

It is estimated that approximately two-thirds of individuals with symptoms of mental illness receive no care at all. Of those who do receive treatment in rural areas, approximately 40 percent receive care from a mental health specialist and 45 percent from a general medical practitioner (Regier et al., 1993). There are approximately 605 rural counties in the U.S. without a medical health care provider, and approximately 1,600 rural counties that do no have accredited mental health care providers (Rosmann & Van Hook, 1998).

Primary care physicians and other general medical practitioners are often the first-line mental health providers for rural residents. However, primary care physicians may not be adequately trained to identify and treat mental illness and behavioral disorders (Ivey, Scheffler & Zazzali, 1998; Little et al., 1998; Susman, Crabtree & Essink, 1995). In addition to training concerns, primary care physicians may also lack the time and resources to diagnose mental health disorders adequately.

The public mental health system is frequently the only provider in rural areas that serves individuals with serious mental health issues. In the absence of a formal safety net of providers (e.g., public hospital systems, Federal, State and locally supported Community Health Centers and local public health departments), the "informal" safety net (e.g., private professionals and organizations that provide free or low-cost care) is forced to bear the responsibility of treating the majority of mental health issues in rural communities (Taylor, et al., 2003; Hartley & Gale, 2003). Additionally, informal safety net providers utilize lay community health workers (also known as indigenous paraprofessionals) as providers of mental health care in rural communities (Hollister et al., 1985; Wagenfeld et al., 1994).

As a result of the lack of mental health services in rural areas, law enforcement is often responsible for responding to mental health emergencies (Larson, Beeson & Mohatt, 1993). Other first responders include fellow community members who, as with law enforcement, generally do not have the training or experience recognizing mental illness and/or providing triage or stabilization assistance to individuals in immediate crisis. Identifying mental illness, especially if substance abuse issues are also present, is often complicated and requires specialized knowledge and experience to handle these situations effectively.

There are significant differences in the distribution of rural Community Health Centers (CHCs). Many Eastern and Southern States have approximately 30 to 40 rural CHC sites, but many Midwestern and Mountain States (e.g., Iowa, Minnesota, Nebraska, Kansas) have few or none (e.g., North Dakota) (National Advisory Committee on Rural Health, 2000; Hartley & Gale, 2003). The Farm Bill of 1987 included the Rural Crisis Recovery Act which helped support direct funding of rural mental health services. However, community efforts are often limited by the lack of long-term funding to ensure sustainability.

The recruitment and retention of certified mental health professionals is of major concern in rural communities (Kimmel, 1992). In addition, Medicare reimbursement rates are often lower in rural areas, which affect the earning potential for rural mental health professionals (Meyer, 1990). The shortage of mental health professionals prompted the National Health Service Corps (NHSC) to offer loan repayment in exchange for service in MHPSAs. From 1995 to 1999, the NHSC placed 244 mental health professionals in rural areas (Bird et al., 2001).

The availability of specialty mental health services (e.g., neuropsychology, geriatric) is even lower than that of general mental health services. Most specialty mental health services are available through larger trade centers or locally by periodic visits made by providers (Wagenfeld et al., 1994). Rural areas also contain fewer hospital-based inpatient and outpatient services for both psychiatric and substance abuse (Hartley et al., 1999). Often when individuals are released from inpatient care to the community, there are few social services and rehabilitation agencies to provide follow-up care.

Although there has been increased National attention and support for evidence-based practices, there have been only minor efforts to increase workforce development activities to enable rural mental health providers and systems to initiate such practices. In fact, there has been a steady decline in the number of training programs that specifically target rural mental health professionals (NFC-SRI, 2004; Wagenfeld et al., 1994).

Accessibility

Despite comparable prevalence rates for mental disorders among rural and urban residents, rural residents are much less likely to have access to services or providers (Lambert & Agger, 1995). As discussed in Section 1, there are three significant components of access to mental health services for rural residents: knowledge, transportation and financing. These issues will be briefly expanded upon here.

Mohatt and Kirwan (1995) found that rural residents lacked an awareness of the need for mental health care, which leads to seeking care later in the course of their disorders. Perceived need for treatment is often hindered by acute symptoms that obscure an individual's understanding of the need for immediate treatment (Rost et al., 2002). Current research suggests that perceived need for care is so low that even minimal barriers in other areas can prevent a person from seeking assistance (Rost et al., 2002).

One response to overcoming these barriers is a marketing effort to enhance rural knowledge of mental illnesses, treatment options/best practices and local resources. However, administrators and providers of rural mental health services have expressed their apprehension about creating an increased demand when current resources are often over-utilized. Nevertheless, consumers, noting "they couldn't go because they didn't know," believe public education/marketing efforts should be among the top priorities for enhancing the rural mental health care system (Ralph & Lambert, 1999). Many outreach interventions in rural areas have failed to convince mentally ill individuals that they need to seek care (Fox et al., 1999).

The ability to travel to mental health services is a significant barrier for rural Americans (NFC-SRI, 2004). Transportation barriers for people living in rural communities include the lack of personal transportation to travel to service providers, limited, inefficient, or inconvenient public transportation (Schauer & Weaver, 1993; U.S. Senate, 1992) and the use of catchment areas, which can complicate access to services for rural residents. The catchment area system may require individuals to seek services in an area that they do not usually frequent due to the allocation of funding streams (Mulder et al., 2002).

Inability to pay further hinders accessibility to mental health services, either because of insufficient insurance coverage or high co-payments for appointments (Zevenbergen & Buckwalter, 1991). Of the people living in rural areas who do have health insurance, many do not have comprehensive benefits and do not have coverage for psychotherapy (NIMH, 2000). Many rural residents are self-employed or are employed by a small business and, thus, may not have employer-based health insurance. In response to increased insurance premiums (by an average of 16.4 percent in 2001), many small businesses are either discontinuing insurance coverage for their employees, dropping coverage for dependents, increasing the employee's contribution to the premium and deductibles, or not providing health insurance at all (Levitt, Holve & Wang, 2001; Hartley & Gale, 2003). As a result, more rural residents are paying out-of-pocket for basic primary care services (Hartley & Gale, 2003).

Two-thirds of those uninsured living in rural areas are poor or near-poor, meaning their family income is less than 200 percent of the poverty level (Kaiser Commission, 2003). Low-income adults, who comprise almost half of the rural uninsured, only qualify for Medicaid if they are disabled, pregnant, elderly, or have dependent children (Kaiser Commission, 2003). Approximately one-fourth of the rural poor qualify for Medicaid, compared to 43 percent of low-income urban residents.

The cost of health services that are only partially reimbursed by Medicare and Medicaid may be too expensive for some rural residents. Further complicating the cost issue is the lack of Federal strategies for sustainable mental health services (NFC-SRI, 2004). In addition, rural programs often operate in areas with limited sources of financial resources to leverage as matching funds for other grant support (NFC-SRI, 2004). Finally, although the actual numbers of individuals with serious mental illness in rural areas may be relatively small (Gale & Deprez, 2003), the geographic limitations and fragmented delivery of mental health services make it difficult for this population to access appropriate services.

Lack of insurance can be especially tragic for families with children with severe emotional disturbances (SED). Too often, parents face the unthinkable choice of relinquishing custody of their child to obtain mental health treatment because they cannot pay for care. It has been estimated that more than 25 percent of families in the nation face this crisis each year (Bazelon Center, 2000; NAMI, 1999). While the data are not extensive in this area, the available data would suggest that rural families with lower rates of insurance coverage and lack of provider availability may be at greater risks of facing this horrible dilemma.

The emergence of telehealth strategies over the past decade has opened a new access point for many rural consumers, families and systems. The use of telecommunication in the delivery of health services, consultation and training in mental health is expanding rapidly. The field is very broad, spanning audio-only telephone or radio consultation and crisis intervention to very sophisticated interactive audio-video linkages between distant clinical and training sites.

A recent review and survey of current grantees under the Federal Office for the Advancement of Telehealth (LaMendola, Mohatt & McGee, 2002) found mental health was listed as the most often service being delivered. However, closer examination found that telehealth mental health care was a major component of less than a dozen projects, and few noted any formal link to the systems of care for adults with SMI or children with SED. Frequently, these projects are organized around hospital and primary care networks that may lack strong collaborative traditions with the systems of care for adults with SMI and children with SED.

The study also found little data on telehealth mental health care performance beyond consumer satisfaction surveys and process measures.

Telehealth mental health care has been held forth as a significant tool in improving the chronic lack of access to mental health services among rural populations. However, there simply are not enough data available to measure the ability of such telehealth strategies to enhance access for adults with SMI or children with SED.

Acceptability

The acceptability of mental health services in rural areas is hindered by stigma, cultural beliefs and values (Intermill & Rathbone-McCuan, 1991). Rural residents tend to value self-reliance and view help-seeking behavior in a more negative light than urban residents (Rost et al., 2002). Other cultural attitudes often observed in rural communities include the fear that fellow rural community members will discover they are in treatment for emotional issues (Berkowitz & Helund, 1979; Bushy, 1993; Wagenfeld et al., 1994). Many rural individuals may be fearful of being labeled "insane," of being shunned by friends and other community members, or of being institutionalized (Buckwalter et al., 1994).

According to Rost, Smith and Taylor (1993), the more negative the labeling of a rural individual struggling with depression, the less likely they are to seek treatment.

A survey of rural mental health outreach programs by the National Association for Rural Mental Health (NARMH) found that even the best programs felt unprepared to meet the cultural and clinical needs of recent immigrants to rural areas (NFC-SRI, 2004; Lambert et al., 2001). Many ethnic minority individuals are unable to access providers who are of similar ethnic or cultural background, speak their native language, or are knowledgeable about their particular culture (Martin, 1997; NFCSRI, 2004; U.S. Public Health Services Office of the Surgeon General, 2001). Because of this barrier, ethnic minority individuals may be more hesitant to enter treatment based on fear that the provider may not understand their culture and traditions.

It is common for public mental health programs and services to be based on urban models and experiences, and are merely applied to fit rural communities (Beeson et al., 1998; Bergland & Dixon, 1988; Gamm et al., 2002; Larson et al., 1993; Mohatt, 2000; NFC-SRI, 2004). Mental health professionals are generally trained with urban-centered standards that often do not directly apply to rural communities (Wagenfeld & Buffum, 1983).

Mental health providers in rural areas need an understanding of and appreciation for cultural similarities and differences within, among and between groups (NRHA, Issue Paper, 1999). The American Psychological Association (1995) identified five important goals of cultural competence: 1) identifying social, economic, political and religious influences affecting rural communities 2) understanding the importance of ethnic and cultural influences in rural communities and the importance of the oral tradition 3) understanding the impact of the interaction between social institutions and ethnicity on the delivery of mental health services 4) recognizing the impact of the provider's own culture, sensitivity and awareness as it affects his or her ability to deliver mental health care and 5) understanding alternative treatment sources in the ethnic minority culture.

Reducing the stigma against mental disorders and encouraging individuals to seek treatment when needed may be accomplished by increasing educational campaigns and enhancing social and professional network referrals (Kenkel, 2003). Understanding and utilizing the work of indigenous healers or other natural supports could be particularly helpful in this regard (Neese, Abraham & Buckwalter; 1999; Buckwalter, 1992).

Summary

As Roberts, Battaglia and Epstein (1999) wrote, "The mental health needs of rural America are immense, and it is increasingly recognized that implementation of adequate psychiatric services in nonmetropolitan areas is a critical national health imperative." Rural mental health has emerged as a priority area for policy makers, mental health professionals and rural community-based service providers. The literature on mental health in rural communities clearly defines areas of unmet need for individuals with mental health issues including a lack of availability of services, a lack of access to these services and a lack of acceptability by rural residents due to the ever-present stigma around mental illness.

Suggestions for improvement include increasing the number of training programs focused on rural issues while simultaneously promoting recruitment and retention efforts for students interested in working in rural areas. Other recommendations include increasing training for primary medical providers about mental health issues and increasing collaborative relationships between medical providers and mental health professionals. The most recent Institute of Medicine report *Quality through Collaboration: The Future of Rural Health* (2005) also emphasizes the need for better coordination of care and collaboration. This report offers many suggestions on increasing partnerships and is a guide for service agencies and policymakers on the benefits of such collaboration in rural America. Policy reform at the legislative level is also critical to increasing public attention to rural mental health issues and to increasing funding streams for providers and agencies working in rural communities. New technology, such as telemedicine, can also help to fill some of the service gaps in rural communities. Lastly, continued research is necessary to further define rural mental health issues and the service needs that result from those issues.

References

Ahr, P.R. & Halcomb, W.R. (1985). State mental health directors' priorities for mental health care. *Hospital and Community Psychology, 36,* 39-45.

Agency for Healthcare Research and Quality (2000). Medical Expenditure Panel Survey: MEPS HC-011, 1996 Preliminary Person Level Expenditure File. [Electronic data file].

American Psychological Association (1995). *Caring for the rural community: An interdisciplinary curriculum.* Washington, DC: Office of Rural Health.

Angold, A., Erkanli, A., Farmer, E., Fairbank, J., Burns, B., Keeler, G., Costello, J. (2002). Psychiatric disorder, impairment, and service use in rural African American and White youth. *Archives of Genereal Psychiatry, 59,* 893-901.

Anthony, W., Rogers, E.S. & Farkas, M. (2003). Research on evidence-based practices: Future Directions in an Era of Recovery. *Community Mental Health Journal, 39*(2), 101- 114.

Baker R. (1992). Psychosocial consequences for tortured refugees seeking asylum and refugee status in Europe. In M. Basoglu (Ed.), *Torture and its consequences: Current treatment approaches* (pp. 83–101). Cambridge: Cambridge University Press.

Bazelon Ceneter (2000). *Relinquishing Custody: The Tragic Result of Failure to Meet Children's Mental Health Needs.* http://www.bazelon.org

Beeson, P.G., Britain, C., Howell, M.L., Kirwan, D. & Sawyer, D.A. (1998). Rural mental health at the millennium. In R.W. Manderscheid & M.J. Henderson (Eds.), *Mental Health United States 1998* (pp. 82-97). Rockville, MD: Center for Mental Health Services, SAMHSA, U.S. Department of Health and Human Services.

Bergland, B. (1988). Rural mental health : Report of the National Action Commission on the Mental Health of Rural America. *Journal of Rural Community Psychology, 9,* 2, 29.

Berkowitz, A. & Hedlund, D. (1979). Psychological stress and role congruence in farm families. *Cornell Journal of Social Relations, 14,* 47-58.

Bird, D.C., Dempsey, P. & Hartley, D. (2001). *Addressing mental health workforce needs in underserved rural area: Accomplishments and challenges.* Portland, ME: Maine Rural Health Research Center, Muskie Institute, University of Southern Maine.

Boyd, M.R. & Mackey, M.C. (2000). Running away to nowhere: Rural women's experiences of becoming alcohol dependent. *Archives of Psychiatric Nursing,14*(3), 142-149.

Buckwalter, K. (1992). Mental and social health of the rural elderly. Paper presented at the Health and Aging in Rural America: A National Symposium, San Diego, CA.

Buckwalter, K., Smith, M. & Caston, C. (1994). Mental and social health of the rural elderly. In R. Coward, N. Bull, G. Kulkulka, and J. Gallager (Eds.), *Health services for rural elders* (pp. 203-232). New York: Springer Publishing Co.

Bushy, A. (1993). Rural women: Lifestyles and health status. *Nursing clinics of North America, 28*(1), 187-197.

Caplan, C. & Brangan, N. (November, 2004). *Prescription Drug Spending and Coverage Among Rural Medicare Beneficiaries in 2003.* AARP Public Policy Institute: Washington, D.C., Available online: http://www.aarp.org/ppi

Chalifoux, Z., Neese, J., Buckwalter, K., Litwak, E., Abraham, I. (1996). Mental health services for rural elderly: Innovative Service Strategies. *Community Mental Health Journal, 32, 5,* 463-480.

Cutrona, C.E., Halvorson, M.B.J & Russell, D.W. (1996). Mental health services for rural children, youth, and their families. In: Heflinger, C.A., Nixon, C.T. (Eds). *Families and the mental health system for children and adolescents: Policy, services, and research. Children's mental health services*, Vol. 2. (pp. 217-237).

Danbom, D. (1995). Born in the country: A history of rural America. Baltimore: Johns Hopkins University Press.

Dekraai, M. (2004). Web-cast/Powerpoint Presentation. Welcome to Building Child and Family Systems of Care in Rural Areas. WICHE.

Dellasega, C. (1991). Meeting the mental health needs of elderly clients. *Journal of Psychosocial Nursing, 29*(2): 10-14.

Dimmitt, J. & Davila, Y. (1995). Group psychotherapy for abused women: A survivor group prototype. *Applied Nursing Research, 8,* 3-8.

Doniger, M, Tempier, R., Lalinec-Michaud, M. & Meunier, D. (1986). Telepsychiatry: Psychiatric consultation through two-way television. A controlled study. *Canadian Journal of Psychiatry, 31*(1) 32-34.

Dorwart, R.A. (1990). "Managed Mental Health Care: Myths and Realities in the 1990s." *Hospital & Community Psychiatry* 41: 1087-1091.

Dyer, J. (1997). Harvest of rage: Why Oklahoma City is on the beginning. Boulder, CO: Westview Press.

Eberhardt, M.S., Ingram, D.D & Makuc, D.M. (2001). *Urban and rural health chartbook: Health United States 2001.* Hyattsville, MD: National Center for Health Statistics.

Fischer, E.P., Owen, Jr., R.R. & Cuffel, B.J. (1996). Substance abuse, community services use, and symptoms severity of urban and rural residents with schizophrenia. *Psychiatric Services, 47*(9), 980-984.

Flaherty, L.T., Weist, M.D. & Warner, B.S. (1996). School-based mental health services in the United States: History, current models and needs. *Community Mental Health Journal, 32,* 341-352.

Fontana, A., Ronsenheck, R., Spencer, H., Gray, S. & DiLella, D. (1999). *The long journey home VII: Treatment of posttraumatic stress disorder in the Department of Veterans Affairs: Fiscal year 1998 service delivery and performance.* West Haven, CT: U.S. Department of Veterans Affairs Northeast Program Evaluation Center.

Fortney, J., Rost, K. & Warren, J. (2000). Comparing alternative methods of measuring geographic access to health services. *Health Services and Outcomes Research Methodology, 1*(2), 173-184.

Fortney, J., Rost, K. & Zhang, M. (1998). A joint choice model of the decision to seek depression treatment and choice of provider sector. *Medical Care, 36*(3), 307-320.

Fox, J., Merwin, E. & Blank, M. (1995). Defacto mental health services in the rural south. *Journal of Health Care for the Poor and Underserved, 6*(4), 434-468.

Fox, J., Blank, M., Berman, J. & Rovnyak, V.G. (1999). Mental disorders and help seeking in a rural impoverished population. *International Journal of Psychiatry in Medicine, 29*(2), 181-195.

Gale, J.A. & Deprez, R.D. (2003) A public health approach to the challenges of rural mental health service integration. Rural behavioral health care: An interdisciplinary guide. B.H. Stamm. Washington, DC, American Psychological Association: 95-108.

Gamm, L.G., Stone, S. & Pittman, S. (2003). Mental Health and Mental Disorders – A Rural Challenge. Rural Health People 2010: A companion document to Health People 2010. Volume 1. College Station, TX: The Texas A&M University System Health Science Center, School of Rural Public Health, Southwest Rural Health Research Center.

Gamm, L., Tai-Seale, M. & Stone, S. (2002). *Meeting the mental health needs of people living in rural areas.* Rockville, MD: Center for Mental Health Services, SAMHSA, U.S. Department of Health and Human Services.

Gogek, L.B. (1992). Letters to the editor. American Journal of Psychiatry 149: 1286.

Hartley, D., Bird, D. & Dempsey, P. (1999). Mental health and substance abuse. In Ricketts, T. (Eds). Rural Health in the United States. New York: Oxford University Press.

Hartley, D. & Gale, J. (2003). Rural Health Care Safety Nets. In Weinick, Robin M. and John Billings, Eds. *Monitoring the Health Care Safety Net. Book III: Tools for Monitoring the Health Care Safety Net.* (AHRQ Pub. No. 03-0027). Rockville, MD: Agency for Healthcare Research and Quality.

Hauenstein, E.J. & Boyd, M.R. (1994). Depressive symptoms in young women of the Piedmont: Prevalence in rural women. *Women and Health, 21*(2/3), 105-123.

Hollister, W., Edgerton, J., and Hunter, R. (1985). Alternative services in community mental health: programs and processes. Chapel Hill, North Carolina. University of North Carolina.

Hoyt, D.R., Conger, R.D., Valde, J.G. & Weihs, K. (1997). Psychological distress and help seeking in rural America. *American Journal of Community Psychology, 25*(4), 449-470.

Human, J. & Wasem, C. (1991). Rural mental health in America. *American Psychologist, 46,* 3, 232-239.

Institute of Medicine (2005). *Quality Through Collaboration: The Future of Rural Health.* The Committee on the Future of Rural Health Care; Board on Health Care Services. The National Academies Press: Washington, D.C.

Institute of Medicine (2002). *Reducing Suicide: A National Imperative.* Goldsmith, S.K., Pellmar, T.C., Kleinman, A.M. & Bunney, W.E. (Eds). Washington, D.C.: National Alchemy Press.

Intermill, N.L. & Rathobone-McCuan, E. (1991). *Mental health services for elders in rural America.* Kansas City, MO: National Resource Center for Rural Elderly.

Ivey, S.L., Scheffler, R. & Zazzali, J.L. (1998). Supply dynamics of the mental health workforce: Implications for health policy. *Milbank Quarterly, 76,* 25-58.

Kaiser Commission on Medicaid and the Uninsured (2003). The uninsured in rural America. Publication Number: 225202. Available online: http://www.kff.org/uninsured/kcmu225202factsheet.cfm

Kelleher, K.J., Taylor, J.L. & Rickert, V.I. (1992). Mental health services for rural children and adolescents. *Clinical Psychology Review, 12,* 841-852.

Kenkel, M.B. Rural women: Strategies and resources for meting their behavioral health needs. Stamm, B. Hudnall (Ed). (2003). Rural behavioral health care: An interdisciplinary guide. (pp. 181-192). Washington, DC, US: American Psychological Association. Xiv, 250pp.

Kessler, R.C., McGonagle, K.A., Zhao, S., et al. (1994). Lifetime and 12-month prevalence of DSM-III-R psychiatric disorders in the United States: Results from the national comorbidity survey. *Archives of General Psychiatry, 51*(1), 8-19.

Kimmel, W.A. (1992). Rural mental health policy issues for research: A pilot exploration. Rockville, MD: National Institute of Mental Health, Office of Rural Mental Health Research.

Lambert, D. & Agger, M. (1995). Access of rural Medicaid beneficiaries to mental health services. *Health Care Financing Review, 17*(1), 133-145.

Lambert, D., Donahue, A., Mitchell, M. & Strauss, R. (2001). *Mental Health Outreach in Rural Areas: Promising Practices.* Rockville, MD: Center for Mental Health Services, Substance Abuse and Mental Health Services.

LaMendola, W. F., Mohatt, D. F. & McGee, C. (2002). *Telemental health: Delivery models and performance measurement.* Boulder, CO: WICHE Mental Health Program Administration.

Larson, M.L., Beeson, P.G. & Mohatt, D.F. (1993). *Taking rural into account: A report of the National Public Hearing on Rural Mental Health.* St. Cloud, MN: National Association for Rural Mental Health and the Federal Center for Mental Health Services.

Levitt, L., Holve, E., Wang, J. (2001). *Employer Health Benefits 2001 Annual Survey.* Menlo Park: Henry J. Kaiser Family Foundation.

Lewis, S.H. (2003). Unspoken crimes: Sexual assault in rural America. National Sexual Violence Resource Center.

Little, D.N., Hammond, C., Kollisch, D., Stern, B. & Dietrich, A.J. (1998). Referrals for depression by primary care physicians. A pilot study. *Journal of Family Practice, 47,* 375-377.

Lubben, J.E., Weiler, P.G., Chi, L. & De Jong, F. (1988). Health promotion for the rural elderly. *Journal of Rural Health, 4*(3), 85-96.

Markstrom, C.A., Stamm, B.H., Stamm, H.E., Berthold, S.M. & Running Wolf, P. (2003). Ethnicity and rural status in behavioral health care. In:

Stamm, B.H. (Ed). *Rural behavioral health care: An interdisciplinary guide.* Washington, DC, US: American Psychological Association.

Marsella, A.J., Bornemann, T., Ekblad, S. & Orley, J. (Eds.) (1994). *Amidst peril and pain: The mental health and wellbeing of the world's refugees.* Washington, D.C.: American Psychological Association.

Martin, P. (1997). Immigration and the changing face of rural America. In *Increasing understanding of public problems and policies* (pp. 201-212). Oak Brook, IL: Farm Foundation.

Medicare Payment Advisory Committee. (2001). Report to the Congress: *Medicare in rural America.* Washington, DC: Medicare Payment Advisory Committee. Available at: http://www.medpac.gov/publications/congressional_reports/J un01%20Entire%20report.pdf. Accessed May 7, 2003.

Meyer, H. (1990). Rural American: Surmounting the obstacles to mental health care. *Minnesota Medicine, 73,* 24-31.

Mohatt, D.F. (2000). Access to mental health services in frontier areas. *Journal of the Washington Academy of Sciences, 86*(3), 35-48.

Mohatt, D.F. & Kirwan, D. (1995). *Meeting the challenge: Model programs in rural mental health.* Rockville, MD: Office of Rural Health Policy.

Mulder, P.L., Shellenberger, S., Kenkel, M., Constantine, M. G., Jumper-Thurman, P., et al., (2000). *The behavioral health care needs of rural women.* Washington, D.C.: American Psychological Association, Committee on Rural Health. Available online: http://www.apa.org/rural/ruralwomen.pdf.

NAMI (July 1999). *Families on the brink: The impact of ignoring children with serious mental illness.* Washington, DC: National Alliance for the Mentally Ill.

National Advisory Committee on Rural Health (1993). *Sixth annual report on rural health.* Rockville, MD: Office of Rural Health Policy, Health Resources and Services Administration, HHS.

National Economic Council/Domestic Policy Council. (2000). Prescription drug coverage & rural Medicare beneficiaries: A critical unmet need. June 13, 2000. Available online: clinton4.nara.gov/WH/New/html/20000613.html

National Institute of Mental Health (2000). Rural mental health research at the National Institute of Mental Health. Available online: http://www.nimh.nih.gov/publicat/ruralresfact.cfm.

National Rural Health Association (1999). Mental health in rural America: An issue paper prepared by the National Rural Health Association. Available online: http//www.nrharural.org/dc/issuepapers/ipaper14.html.

Neese, J.B., Abraham, I.L., Buckwalter, K.C. (1999). Utilization of mental health services among rural elderly. *Archives of Psychiatric Nursing, (13)*1, 30-40.

Nordal, K.C., Copans, S.A. & Stamm, B.H. (2003). Children and adolescents in rural and frontier areas. In: Stamm, B.H. (Ed). *Rural behavioral health care: An interdisciplinary guide.* Washington, D.C., US: American Psychological Association.

Ralph, R.O. & Lambert, D. (1999). Best practices in rural Medicaid Managed Behavioral Health: Consumer Issues. In *Working Papers Series.* Portland, ME: Muskie Institute, University of Southern Maine.

Rathbone-McCuan, E. Rural geriatric mental health care: A continuing service dilemma. Bull, C. Neil (Ed). (1993). *Aging in rural America.* Sage focus editions, 162, 146-160.

Regier, D.A., Narrow, W.E, et al. (1993). The de facto United States mental and addictive disorders services system. *Archives of General Psychiatry, 50,* 85-94.

Roberts, L.W., Battaglia, J., Epstein, R.S. (1999). Frontier ethics: Mental health care needs and ethical dilemmas in rural communities. *Psychiatric Services, 50*(4), 497-503.

Robins, L.N. & Reiger, D.A. (Eds). (1991). Psychiatric disorders in America: The Epidemiologic Catchment Area Study. New York: The Free Press.

Rogers, C.C. (1999). Growth of the oldest old population and future implications for rural areas. *Rural Development Perspectives, 14,* 3, 22-26.

Rosenheck, R. & Fontana, A. (1995). Do Vietnam era veterans who suffer from posttraumatic stress disorder avoid VA mental health services? *Military Medicine, 160,* 136-142.

Rosmann, M. & Van Hook, M..P. (1998). Changes in rural communities in the past twenty-five years: Policy implications for rural mental health. Available online: http://www.narmh.org/pages/refone.html.

Rost, K., Smith, R. & Taylor, J. (1993). Rural-urban differences in stigma and the use of care for depressive disorders. *Journal of Rural Health, 9,* 57-62.

Rost, K., Williams, C., Wherry, J. & Smith, Jr., G.R. (1995). The process and outcomes of care for major depression in rural family practice settings. *The Journal of Rural Health, 11*(2), 114-121.

Rost, K.M., Owen, R.R., Smith, J. & Smith, Jr., G.R. (1998). Rural-urban differences in service use and course of illness in bipolar disorder. *Journal of Rural Health, 14*(1), 36-43.

Rost, K., Fortney, J., Fischer, E., Smith, J. (2002). Use, quality and outcomes of care for mental health: The rural perspective. *Medical Care Research and Review, 59*(3), 231- 265.

Rowland, D, & Lyons, B. 1989. Triple Jeopardy: Rural, Poor, and Uninsured. *Health Services Research,* 23, (6): 975-1004. Sandrick, K. (1990). Expanded delivery system needed for post-traumatic stress. *Hospitals, 64*(11), 44-45.

Sawyer, D. & Beeson, P. (1998). Rural Mental Health: Vision 2000 and Beyond. Available online: http://www.narmh.org/pages/future.html.

Schauer, P.M. & Weaver, P. (1993). Rural elder transportation. In J.A. Krout (Ed.), *Providing Community-Based Services to the Rural Elderly* (pp. 42-64). Thousand Oaks, CA: Sage.

Schur, L, Franco, S. Access to health care. In: Ricketts T, editor, *Rural health in the United States.* New York: Oxford University Press; 1999. p 25-37.

Sears, S.F. & Evans, G.D. et al. (2003). Rural social services systems as behavioral health delivery systems. Rural behavioral health care: An interdisciplinary guide. B.H. Stamm. Washington, D.C., American Psychological Association: 109-120.

Stack, S. (1982). Suicide: A decade of review of the sociological literature. *Deviant Behavior: An Interdisciplinary Journal, 4,* 41-66.

Stell, J. & Rodgers, J. (2004). *The Medicare Presecription Drug Benefit: Potential Impact on Beneficiaries.* AARP Public Policy Institute: Washington, D.C.. Available online: http://www.aarp.org/ppi.

Susman, J.L., Crabtree, B.F. & Essink, G. (1995). Depression in rural family practice. Easy to recognize, difficult to diagnose. *Archives of Family Medicine, 4,* 427-431.

Taylor, P, Blewett, L, Brasure, M, et al. (2003). Small town health care safety nets: report on a pilot study. *J Rural Health, 19*(2):125-34.

Wagenfeld, M.O. & Buffum, W.E. (1983). Problems in, and prospects for, rural mental health services in the United States. *International Journal of Mental Health, 12*(1-2), 89- 107.

Wagenfeld, M.O., Murray, J.D., Mohatt, D.F. & DeBruyn, J.C. (Eds.). (1994). *Mental health and rural America: 1980 – 1993* (NIH Publication No. 94-3500). Washington, D.C.: US Government Printing Office.

United States Committee for Refugees (1997). A cry for help: Refugee mental health in the United States. *Refugee Reports, 19,* 9.

United States Public Health Service Office of the Surgeon General (2001). *Mental health: Culture, race, and ethnicity.* Rockville, MD: Department of Health and Human Services

United States Senate, Special Committee on Aging. (1992). *Common beliefs about the rural elderly: Myth or fact?* Serial No. 102-N. Washington, D.C.: U.S. Government Printing Office.

Weist, M.D. (1997). Expanded school mental health services: A national movement in progress. *Advances in Clinical Child Psychology, 19,* 319-352.

Welsh, J., Domitrovich, C.E. & Bierman, K. (2003). Promoting Safe schools and health students in rural Pennsylvania. *Psychology in the Schools, 40*(5), 457-472.

Yawn, B.P. & Yawn, R.A. (1993). Adolescent pregnancies in rural America: A review of the literature and strategies for primary prevention. *Family and Community Health, 16*(1), 36-45.

Zevenbergen, P. & Buckwalter, K.C. (1991). The mental health of rural elderly outreach project: Then and now. Paper presented at the Gerontological Society of American Annual Conference, San Francisco, CA.

3. EPIDEMIOLOGICAL OVERVIEW OF SUBSTANCE ABUSE IN RURAL AMERICA

Since the last publication of this chapter, research regarding substance abuse in rural America has grown significantly. A wide variety of publications have addressed issues such as substance abuse in a rural context from a developmental perspective; specific populations that include youth, elderly, women, inmates and ethnic minority groups; prevention and service delivery.

Findings described in previous sections regarding the similarity in prevalence rates for both mental health and substance use disorders, as well as the widely documented spread of such drugs as methamphetamine, have undoubtedly contributed to the increased attention paid to substance abuse in rural areas. Additionally, the recent release of the President's *New Freedom Commission on Mental Health, Subcommittee on Rural Issues* report will continue to propel rural America to the forefront of research foci.

As discussed in Section 2, an increasingly important issue is the co-occurrence of mental and substance abuse disorders for both adults and children (Regier et al., 1990). The interrelationship of mental health and substance abuse problems has been well-documented, and efforts have occurred to address this fact. For instance, the Substance Abuse and Mental Health Services Administration (SAMHSA) has released grants that promote integrated mental health and substance abuse services through State or tribal agencies. Furthermore, some States (e.g., Alaska) have integrated their substance abuse and mental health service divisions into single entities, usually called a "Division of Behavioral Health."

Evidence-based practices have been established for treating co-occurring disorders (Drake et al., 2001; SAMHSA, 2004), but there is little research on the incidence, prevalence, and etiology of co-occurring disorders in rural populations. Thus, the field lacks an understanding of current needs, as well as ways to tailor evidence-based practices to treat persons with co-occurring disorders in rural areas. Furthermore, because there is not one rural America, research findings are still very difficult to generalize across the manifold places and variety of people that live in these areas.

This section will discuss each of the topic areas indicated above, but it should be viewed as only a snapshot of a process that is in continual motion.

Substance Abuse in a Rural Context

The National Institute on Drug Abuse (USDHHS, 1997) published a monograph series titled "Rural Substance Abuse: State of Knowledge Issues." In that publication, Conger (1997) reviewed the literature on substance abuse in rural America and provided a context in which to understand the process that underlies the development of substance use disorders. Synthesizing work from a number of authors and researchers, he described five major themes that characterize the relationships among social context, individual dispositions and syndromes of problem behaviors that include substance use and abuse. The five themes are:

i. Substance abuse is part of a developmental progression from relatively minor to more serious antisocial activities (Elliot et al., 1989; Loeber & LeBlanc, 1990; Patterson, 1993).
ii. Placing substance abuse within a developmental progression of antisocial behaviors that begin with relatively minor deviant acts during childhood underscores the need for social-contextual models of substance abuse that include explanatory variables existing early in

the life course (Gottfredson & Hirschi, 1990; Hawkins et al., 1992; Moffitt, 1993; Patterson, 1993; Simons et al., 1994a).
iii. The realization that the early manifestations of problem behaviors likely become apparent before adolescence has placed new emphasis on the role of the family in explanations of antisocial tendencies (Akers, 1994; Conger et al., 1992, 1993, 1994a; Gottfredson & Hirschi, 1990; Hawkins et al., 1992; Loeber & Stouthhamer-Loeber, 1986; Patterson et al., 1992; Moffitt, 1993; Simons et al., 1994a, 1994b; Thornberry, 1987).
iv. Family interactions involve reciprocal influences in parent and child behaviors that affect both the probability of child misconduct and also disruptions in effective child-rearing practices (Conger & Rueter, 1995; Lytton, 1990; Thornberry et al., 1991; Vuchinich et al., 1992).
v. Reciprocal influences exist not only within the family but also between the behaviors of individual family members and the other social contexts important to the development or restraint of adolescent misconduct (Conger & Rueter, 1995; Elliott et al., 1989; Hawkins et al., 1992; Melby et al., 1993; Richters & Martinez, 1993; Sampson & Groves, 1989; Thornberry et al., 1991).

In other words, substance abuse problems do not "just happen"; they develop over time and are foreshadowed by early childhood behavioral problems, which are often the result of particular interactions between parents and their children, as well as individual family member interactions with other social contexts (e.g., jobs, school, friends, law).

Aspects of individuals who develop substance abuse disorders include genetic, biological and/or neuropsychological factors, emotional responses, and cognitive factors that interact with social-contextual issues.

For instance, Moffitt (1993) discussed how genetically or environmentally-induced biological deficits may reduce overall competence or exacerbate behavioral problems. Estimates of heritability for substance use and abuse are consistent with the degree to which delinquency is heritable (Hawkins et al., 1992; Plomin et al., 1994). Furthermore, based on adoption studies, Conger (1997) concludes "the genetic component of a biological predisposition to substance abuse and related conduct problems appears to become manifest largely in disrupted social environments; and social-contextual variables (poverty) affect biological development, which... affects antisocial substance use behaviors" (p. 16).

Chassin and colleagues (1993) reported that negative emotional responses can include antisocial behavior and predict involvement with alcohol and other drugs. Environmental issues can exacerbate a child or adolescent's emotional characteristics and make him or her more vulnerable to substance abuse, as can biologically-based emotional dispositions. Several dimensions of delinquency, such as behavior under-control, poor emotional regulation and impulsive, risky behaviors, both predict and are predicted by substance use (Elliott et al., 1989; Hawkins et al., 1992; Sher et al., 1991).

Additionally, in terms of cognitive issues, when models (e.g., family members, family friends) for substance use are plentiful, consumption is defined as acceptable and enjoyable, and use is encouraged in social settings, youths will likely adopt these beliefs and practices, which increases risk for later substance use problems (Akers, 1994; Conger & Rueter, 1995). Thus, the conclusion is that the social-contextual approach to understanding substance use and abuse provides a framework for identifying the dynamic through which social settings combine with the individual attributes that impact "developmental trajectories of risk or resilience to substance abuse and related conduct problems" (Conger, 1997, p. 17).

Youth and Adolescent Substance Abuse

In 1999, *Mental Health: A Report of the Surgeon General* was released and addressed youth and adolescent substance use and abuse. According to the report, the early 1990s was the beginning of a "sharp resurgence" in the misuse of alcohol and other drugs by adolescents (Johnston et al., 1996). Kessler and colleagues (1996) reported results from the National Comorbidity Study, indicating that about 51 percent of those with one or more lifetime mental disorders also had a lifetime history of at least one substance use disorder, with the rates being highest in the 15 to 24 year-old age group (Kessler et al., 1994).

The National Center on Addiction and Substance Abuse (CASA; 2000) analyzed national data and reported that the prevalence of tobacco, alcohol, marijuana, amphetamine and cocaine use among eighth-graders to be higher in rural areas (defined as counties with no city over 50,000 inhabitants) than in urban areas. Rural eighth-graders were reported to be more than twice as likely to smoke cigarettes, 70 percent more likely to have been drunk, 34 percent more likely to smoke marijuana, 104 percent more likely to use amphetamines, and 50 percent more likely to have used cocaine than their urban counterparts.

Johnston, Bachman and O'Malley (2000) found the alcohol use prevalence rate among rural eighth-graders to be 57 percent, compared with 50 percent among their urban peers.

Substance abuse rates in rural areas were reported to exceed those in urban areas for every drug except ecstasy and marijuana among 10th graders (CASA; 2000). In addition, the monthly prevalence rate of alcohol use among youth (6th, 8th, and 11th graders) in a rural Midwestern State was 26 percent (Iowa Consortium on Substance Abuse and Research Evaluation, 1999), compared with 21 percent in a national sample of adolescents (USDHHS, SAMHSA, Office of Applied Studies, 1999).

Despite these data, Edwards (1997) warned against using national level data to characterize rural drug use, as rural community variability is significant. For instance, communities similar in size and geographic location can have very different youth drug use profiles. Also, consistent with the need for research based on a continuum of rurality, data illustrate that there is a lower aggregate level of drug use among youth in very small, rural communities (population <2,500) than among those in larger rural and metropolitan communities. Edwards (1997) reported that problems related to drug use are much higher for metro than nonmetro and rural youth. For example, the percent of metropolitan youth who have tried marijuana is reportedly almost twice that of small rural community youth and significantly higher than that of other nonmetropolitan youth. Thus, the differences in data represent the ongoing problems of researching certain rural populations and then generalizing these findings across diverse rural areas.

Youth and Adolescent Risk and Protective Factors

Underlying the prevalence of substance abuse by rural youth are risk and protective factors. Although studies of specific individual and family risk factors in the 1980s and beginning of the 1990s indicated that there were higher levels of risk in urban areas (especially risk associated with peer influence), more recent research has found some risk factors to be more prevalent among adolescents in rural areas (e.g., family history of drug involvement, early initiation of problem behavior and low school achievement) (Becker et al., 1999a, 1999b).

Oetting and colleagues (1997) surveyed a total of 2,861 students in the 7th, 8th, 11th and 12th grades in nine rural communities (population range 451 to 18,400) in nine States. The surveys included a drug use questionnaire, *The*

American Drug and Alcohol Survey, and the *Prevention Planning Survey*. Youth were classified into high, moderate, or no drug involvement groups. The results indicated that risk factors for rural and urban youth are similar; adolescent drug use is chiefly a social behavior rather than a response to the addictive properties of drugs. Additionally, families can have either a direct or indirect influence on substance use, particularly alcohol and tobacco. For instance, a direct influence identified was that a smoking parent doubles the risk of a child's smoking, and quadruples the risk if the parent's attitude is conducive toward the child's smoking. Indirect influence on increasing drug use was seen when young people believe their families are unconcerned about it and when there is family conflict (Oetting et al., 1997).

Children with relational problems at home are more likely to select friends who also have problems, and their peers are more likely to get involved with drugs and reinforce drug use. Nonusers typically have friends who would try to stop them (Oetting et al., 1997). Young women who are depressed and/or have low self-esteem may find that drug use relieves negative feelings, which increases their susceptibility to drug-using peers. Angry youth and adolescents with high need for excitement or risk-taking interact with similar youth, which drug use may satisfy.

Studies of the accumulation of risk factors show that there is an almost linear relationship; the greater the number of risk factors, the greater the chances of drug use (Swaim, 1991). Although personal and social risk factors are generally the same for urban and rural youth, there is likely to be more variability in risk factors across rural towns. This is supported by the work of Spoth and colleagues (2001), who evaluated rural-urban differences in cumulative risk for youth substance abuse using a cumulative risk index. The index included family-related (e.g., parent-child bonding or conflict, family financial stress, parental marital status, parental education, etc.) and individual-related (items from the Child Behavior Checklist that ask about youth problem behaviors) risk and protective variables.

The results of the study indicated that parent-reported cumulative risk for young adolescence substance use was significantly higher for rural youth than urban youth, although differences were small to medium in magnitude (Spoth et al., 2001). However, comparing these findings to others in the literature is difficult due to differences in cohorts, rural-urban classification schemes and measures. The studies also differ in sampling methods and related sample characteristics across studies. Nevertheless, consistent with the CASA (2000) report, there is evidence to indicate that risk factors for youth substance use may be changing for rural and urban populations. Also, factors that have protected rural youth against developing substance abuse problems may be eroding, and the literature generally suggests a higher level of cumulative risk for rural youth (Spoth et al., 2001).

One aspect of protective factors that has gained attention in the literature is the role of spirituality and/or religious participation in youths' lives. For instance, Hodge, Cardenas and Montoya (2001) examined the relationship between spirituality and religious participation and substance use in a multicultural (Hispanic, Native American, non-Hispanic white and African-American) sample of rural youths. The authors viewed spirituality and religion as distinct but overlapping concepts— spirituality was defined as "an experiential relationship with God," and religion was defined as "a formal set of rituals, beliefs, and practices that expresses an internal, commonly held, spiritual reality in a community context" (p. 154).

The results indicated that the higher the level of religious participation, the higher the probability that an adolescent never used alcohol. Also, the higher an adolescent's level of spirituality, the higher the probability the youth had not used marijuana. Finally, the higher the level of spirituality, the greater the likelihood of abstaining from hard drugs. Spirituality was not significantly related to alcohol use, while participation in religious activities was not significantly related to marijuana use or to hard drug use. More research in this area is needed to corroborate, clarify, or generalize these findings.

Prevention of Substance Abuse for Rural Youth

The use of prevention programs to curb rising rates of substance abuse has proliferated since the last edition of this chapter. Although there is no distinctively rural prevention program, D'Onofrio (1997) described two general categories: 1) school-based and 2) community-based.

School-Based Programs
Prevention programs conducted by rural school districts and communities without outside sponsorship are often not theoretically-based, but reflect reasoned assumptions about what is needed, using available resources creatively, and are more limited in scope (D'Onofrio, 1997). Programs sponsored by local service organizations usually try to coordinate referrals and treatment resources. Those organized by civic groups seek to develop youth leadership or provide youth with new options for recreation and employment.

Reviews of existent school-based programs indicated that most rural districts provide at least three types of drug education for students, which may include classroom instruction, extracurricular activities and drug-free social events, student intervention services, peer-managed self-monitoring, as well as parent and/or community involvement (D'Onofrio, 1997). Classroom instruction was a program component in nearly all districts, augmented by extracurricular activities, drug-free social events and intervention services. There were also training programs for teachers and staff, parent programs, and educational programs in the community.

Having multiple components in school-based prevention programs apparently increases their effectiveness (NIAAA, 1994). It has been recommended that such programs provide factual information about the harmful effects of drugs; support and strengthen students' resistance to using drugs; carry out collaborative drug abuse prevention efforts with parents and other community members; be supported by strong school policies and provide services for confidential identifications, assessment, and referral to treatment and support groups for users.

Community-Based Programs

Community-based prevention programs are typically organized in rural areas by professionals in schools and agencies, local business leaders, service clubs, local activists, and external sponsors (D'Onofrio, 1997). Different types include community programs for youth; media campaigns; community coalitions; community team-building and networking; community development; grassroots movements and participation in statewide coalitions. Many include young people and other members of the community in assessing issues of alcohol use and generating possible solutions. Most complement or substitute for school-based programs.

Characteristics of Other Programs

D'Onofrio (1997) also described characteristics of the various programs that existed at the time of that writing, but pointed out that very few rural programs focus solely on the prevention of youthful drinking; goals and objectives tend to be general rather than specific and vary with program sponsorship. For instance, at SAMHSA, the Center for Substance Abuse Prevention (CSAP) programs are required to endorse a philosophy of youth abstinence from substance use. Almost all of these projects are based on a risk factor model and try to reduce at least two risk factors from different domains (as of 1993: individual = 70 percent, family = 50 percent, school = 50 percent, peer = 40 percent, neighborhood/community = 40 percent).

The few rural prevention programs organized by university researchers are based on social normative theory, with most being implemented in school classrooms using diverse instructional and skill-building techniques. These programs seek to delay the onset of smoking and drinking and to reduce the prevalence of tobacco, alcohol, and sometimes marijuana use among youth in particular grades (usually seventh).

Popular Prevention Programs

Two of the most popular and researched prevention programs are *Preparing for the Drug Free Years (PDFY)* and *Drug Abuse Resistance Education (DARE)*. The PDFY program is theoretically based on the social development model, which is an integration of social control theory (Hirschi, 1969) and social learning theory (Akers, 1977). The former views prosocial bonding as a protective factor against adolescent substance use and delinquency, while the latter specifies processes by which bonding develops. The social development model hypothesizes that bonding is determined by the levels of 1) opportunities provided to the child for proactive involvement in the family, 2) the child's skills for participating, problem-solving, and positive interaction with other family members and 3) the rewards and punishments received from parents for appropriate and inappropriate behaviors. Thus, the quantity and quality of parent-child communication or family discipline style are hypothesized to affect family bonds, which in turn affect children's behavior.

The core objectives of PDFY include conveying information about the risks and dangers of childhood substance use, increasing opportunities for family involvement and teaching the necessary skills to ensure that such involvement is rewarding and enhances parent-child bonds.

DARE is an early prevention program that promotes youths' resiliency to later problem behaviors, including drug use, by co-training parents and children to enhance self-efficacy, effective child rearing, and problem-solving. It has historically focused on youth 5 to 18 years old, their parents, and/or community professionals who work with this age group. The community team component includes a curriculum that is delivered through 15-18 hours of training for multi-agency teams who provide services to youth. This training, from which the parent workshops evolved, emphasizes four areas: 1) decision-making and problem-solving skills, 2) assertiveness in communication and conflict management, 3) responsibility for one's behavior, and 4) esteem for oneself (e.g., self-efficacy) and others.

Research on the PDFY and DARE Programs

It was noted that the PDFY and DARE programs have been fairly well researched. However, among these studies, a relatively limited number have been concerned specifically with rural areas. Thus, this section will present findings from the available literature, but will primarily focus on research conducted on these programs in rural areas.

PDFY Program: The PDFY program has been found to have a significant, positive impact on parenting skills (e.g., proactive communication, child-management, protective behaviors,) and/or the parent-child relationship (e.g., reducing negative interactions) (Kosterman et al., 1997, 2001; Rueter, Conger & Ramisetty-Mikler, 1999; Spoth et al., 1995; Spoth, Redmond & Shin, 1998); protective factors (e.g., parent-child attachment, peers with prosocial norms) (Park et al., 2000; Spoth et al., 1996a, 1996b); initiation of substance use (Guyll et al., 2004; Mason et al., 2003; Park et al., 2000; Spoth et al., 1999, 2004; Spoth, Redmond & Shin, 2001); and delinquency (Ellickson, 1996; Mason et al., 2003). However, one study did not find significant effects of PDFY regarding the ability of parents to proactively manage their families, reduce family conflict, or help their children learn skills to resist antisocial peer influences (Park et al., 2000).

DARE Program: Burke (2002) notes that although DARE is the most widely implemented youth drug prevention program in the United States, research studies indicate poor results of this program. Multiple studies could not find any significant effects of the program on use of a number of substances (e.g., alcohol, cigarettes, marijuana, inhalants) (Becker, Agopian & Yeh, 1992; Britt & Jachym, 1996; Harmon, 1993; Thombs, 2000; Wysong, Aniskiewicz & Wright, 1994) for students ranging from fifth-grade to undergraduate college students or on such things as attitudes about police, coping strategies, attachment and commitment to school, resistance to peer pressure, delay of experimentation with drugs, rebellious behavior, or self-esteem (Dukes, Ullman & Stein 1996; Harmon, 1993). Seventh-graders in an "All Stars" program, developed to address four mediators of high-risk behaviors, had significantly better outcomes on each mediator compared to seventh-graders who received the DARE program (Hansen, 1996). Hansen and McNeal (1997) found that the primary effect of DARE on eighth- then ninth-graders was a change in commitment not to use substances, but the magnitude of the effect was relatively small.

On the positive side, Miller-Heyl, MacPhee and Fritz (1998) found DARE to have result in significant, persistent increases in parental self-appraisals and democratic child-rearing practices, parent satisfaction with social support, enhanced children's developmental levels, with a corresponding decrease in harsh discipline and oppositional behavior. Furthermore, Donnermeyer and Wurschmidt (1997) found that 286 fifth- and sixth-grade educators highly rated overall DARE program quality and the impact it had on students. Rural, suburban and urban parents' views of DARE indicated that parent involvement and knowledge of the program was high, and generally, parents were very positive about it, especially when they viewed the DARE officer as an effective educator (Donnermeyer, 2000). Finally, in comparing 341 fifth-grade DARE students to 367 non-DARE students, Harmon (1993) found significant differences for alcohol use in the last year, belief in prosocial norms, association with drug-using peers, positive peer association, attitudes against substance use, and assertiveness. Thus, it appears that individuals' views of the DARE program, as well as some results, are in conflict with significant data indicating that the actual effectiveness of the program is limited or non-existent, depending on what is being measured.

Other Programs

The current literature contains information on a number of other prevention programs that typically share similar goals to PDFY or DARE. These will be briefly summarized here. Pilgrim and colleagues (1998) evaluated a program called "Families in Action — Meeting the Challenge of Junior High and Middle School" (FIA) that was designed to increase positive attachment to family, schools and peers; use of counseling services as necessary and appropriate attitudes toward substance use by minors. The results indicated that girl- and boy-program graduates were more willing to seek counseling services at the follow-up, as were their parents. Program participation was more beneficial for boys than for girls, and increased parent activities at their child's school compared to non-participants. Short-term program effects found for parent graduates only included greater curriculum knowledge, higher family cohesion, and an increase in the age considered appropriate for alcohol consumption. The FIA program goals were slightly altered for students and parents, with results indicating that student participants, as compared to nonparticipants, had higher family cohesion, less family fighting, greater school attachment, higher self-esteem and believed that alcohol should be consumed at an older age at the one year follow-up (Abbey et al., 2000).

Miano, Forest and Gumaer (1997) evaluated a university and school collaborative project that provided individual counseling, group counseling, couples counseling and family counseling, as well as a day and evening program to a secondary school population and the larger community of a rural locality in Southwest Virginia. The purpose was to reduce the dropout rate and improve at-risk students' attendance and school achievement. Over approximately six years, the dropout rate went from 7.09 percent to 3.32 percent.

Johnson and colleagues (1996) evaluated the *Creating Lasting Connections,* a five-year demonstration project, designed to delay onset and reduce frequency of alcohol and other drug use among high-risk 12 to 14 year old youth by positively impacting resiliency factors in church community, family and individual (youth). Results showed that the program successfully engaged church communities in substance abuse prevention activities and produced positive direct effects on family and youth resiliency, as well as moderating effects on onset and frequency of alcohol and other drug use.

Results from the Community Health Demonstration Project (CHDP), which was organized to develop, implement, and evaluate substance abuse prevention programming in a resource-poor rural Appalachian area, included increased awareness and knowledge of problems associated with alcohol, tobacco and other drug (ATOD) use during pregnancy and postpartum; new services adopted by local agencies and organizations; more cooperative efforts to provide presentation programs for all ages throughout the community; a range of new or expanded programs to enhance development and a reduction in ATOD use during and after pregnancy by women in this rural area (Vicary et al., 1996).

Stevens, Mott and Youells (1996) tested two approaches to substance prevention in The New Hampshire Substance Abuse Prevention Study, which included a cohort of 4,406 rural public school children in elementary school, junior high school, or in the 10th grade. It included a comprehensive school curriculum implemented in grades 1 through 12, a parent communication course, a community task force, and delayed intervention control. Some positive prevention results were achieved for cigarettes, marijuana, other illicit drugs and spitting tobacco, but no effects were found for any of the three levels of alcohol use (initiation, drinking, drunkenness) at 36 months follow-up.

Rural Substance Abuse Prevention Strategies

Karim (1997) offers an interdisciplinary approach to prevention in rural areas. First, the local context should drive the design and development of prevention programs. Specifically, there must be an investigation into the nature of substance abuse in a particular place, including a needs assessment and development of a prevention curriculum that is based (in part) on an evaluation of how community members view substance use and abuse issues. This information will help make the prevention message meaningful. Second, prevention practitioners must disseminate materials that are significant, relevant, and interesting to youth. This includes using the most effective instruction methods and ways in which young people learn best.

Karim (1997) argues that the traditional prevention paradigm needs to abandon program-driven approaches (i.e., those based on risk/resiliency, risk and protective factors, self-esteem and health models) in favor of a broad, unified, research-based understanding of substance abuse issues that is woven into an overall school- reform or school-improvement plan. Stand-alone programs will be unsuccessful if the bulk of the prevention responsibility is based on their successful implementation. For further information on substance abuse prevention strategies, see Biglan and colleagues (1997).

Service Delivery & Treatment Issues

Treating substance abuse in rural America involves many of the same complications noted for mental health treatment generally, especially regarding co-occurring disorders. These include 1) rural substance abuse programs seem to be based on urban models, 2) a fragmented system of services, 3) centralized services in a large geographic area, 4) overly restrictive regulations, 5) conceptual differences in treatment approaches, 6) different value-orientations between providers and clients 7) confidentiality and stigma in a rural culture and 8) academic and professional isolation of mental health workers, leading to high turnover and a shortage of staff having appropriate training and experience to work with persons with dual diagnoses (Howland, 1995; Wagenfeld et al., 1997).

This last point is buttressed by results from a survey of licensed psychologists in Idaho about their training and provision of substance abuse services. Of 144 respondents, nearly all (89 percent) had contact with substance abusers, yet most rated their graduate training as inadequate preparation for practice. Rural psychologists reported seeing a high percentage of substance abusers, but many limited their treatment to self-help group referral (Celluci & Vik, 2001).

Using 1994-1996 indicator data, McAuliffe and colleagues (2003) estimated State substance abuse treatment needs and service gaps. There were large inter-state variations in the rates of drug and alcohol deaths, arrests and treatment services, which appeared to reflect real and substantial differences among State populations in their alcohol and drug treatment needs. Maps of the indexes showed that drug treatment needs were greatest in the urban Northeast, on the West Coast and in States bordering Mexico. Moderately high levels of drug treatment needs were also found in southern States (Mississippi, South Carolina, Georgia and Louisiana). The lowest levels of relative drug treatment needs were clustered in rural States of the northern plains and in New England. Alcohol treatment needs were greatest in the West; North Carolina had the highest alcohol needs in the East. The lowest alcohol treatment needs were in Hawaii, selected southern and Midwestern States and urban East Coast States.

Comparison of Substance Abuse Treatment index scores with the Substance Abuse Need index scores revealed that States varied substantially in the extent to which current treatment needs are being met. The States with the greatest relative treatment gaps were clustered in the South (Mississippi, Georgia, Arkansas, Tennessee, North Carolina and West Virginia), Southwest (Arizona, Nevada, Texas and New Mexico), and the most northern tier of plains and mountain States (Idaho, Montana, North Dakota, Minnesota and Wisconsin). The States with the most favorable combined service rates relative to substance abuse need were also mostly in two clusters: 1) New York, Massachusetts, Rhode Island, Connecticut, Maryland, Maine and Delaware and 2) Colorado, Utah, Nebraska, Kansas, and Iowa.

Anderson and Huffine (2003) studied treatment needs and service use of 177 rural adolescents with mental and substance use disorders who were served in community-based settings. The results indicated that two-thirds of adolescents with co-occurring disorders did not receive the recommended treatment based on widely supported guidelines, leaving this group's service needs unmet.

Regarding the location of services, VaughanSarrazin, Hall and Rick (2000) evaluated effects of the Iowa Case Management Project (ICMP) for Rural Drug Abuse on the utilization of substance abuse, medical and mental health services by rural substance abuse treatment clients subsequent to initiating residential treatment. Clients who volunteered for the program were randomly assigned to one of four case management conditions: 1) an ICMP case manager located at the substance abuse treatment facility, 2) an ICMP case manager located at a facility independent of the substance abuse agency, 3) an ICMP case manager who provided case management through a computer-based telecommunication system, or 4) standard substance abuse treatment.

Results indicated that ICMP participants assigned to case managers housed in the treatment facility used more aftercare, outpatient services and medical services upon completion of the residential program than clients with no case manager, suggesting that key components to the success of a case management program are integration of case managers into the treatment organization and accessibility to clients (Vaughan-Sarrazin, Hall and Rick, 2000). However, the authors note that these results should be interpreted with caution, as the study relied on self-report data, difficulty defining specific types of services (e.g., physician contact, surgical procedure), missing data and attrition. Furthermore, they did not have data regarding the treatment styles of case managers.

Farrell and associates (1999) report the results of a comprehensive study of predictors influencing continuity of care for individuals discharged from State hospitals to communities. The results indicate that although someone discharged from a State hospital to a rural CMHC is twice as likely to have continuity of care compared to those discharged to an urban CMHC, a primary diagnosis of substance abuse strongly predicts low continuity of care.

In terms of particular kinds of treatment and their effectiveness, a meta-analysis and literature review concluded that family-oriented therapies were superior to other treatments and enhanced the effectiveness of other treatments (Stanton & Shadish, 1997). Multisystemic family therapy in particular was found to be effective in reducing alcohol, substance use and other severe behavioral problems among adolescents (Pickrel & Henggeler, 1996).

Killeen and Brady (2000) report outcome data from a study of a residential substance abuse treatment program for women and young children in rural South Carolina. Data were collected regarding addiction severity, parenting and child emotional and behavioral development at six and twelve months following discharge from the program. Results showed that women who completed treatment had better scores on addiction severity and parental stress, and their children had improved behavioral and emotional functioning at the six- and twelve-month follow-ups. Additionally, program completion and longer length of stay may be associated with improvement in the women's ability to function as parents.

Leukefeld and colleagues (2002) developed a therapy for rural drug and alcohol users that incorporated social skills training, motivational interviewing, case management and thought mapping. A primary basis for this type of therapy was that, in rural areas, there is a strong emphasis on independence and self-sufficiency, which makes it difficult to talk about substance abuse problems, especially with strangers. Additionally, fatalism (the belief that one must cope with unsolvable problems) persists. Thus, social skills training was taught in the context of cognitive-behavioral therapy via structured stories. The stories provided context, highlighted difficulties, and served as a starting point for describing negative thinking patterns and substituting positive for negative self-talk as described by cognitive-behavioral therapy.

Clark, Leukefeld, and Godlaski (1999) presented a model of case management with rural clients entering drug and alcohol treatment. As part of a larger treatment protocol called Structured Behavioral Outpatient Rural Therapy, behavioral contracting was combined with strengths perspective case management to help rural clients motivate themselves to engage and complete drug and alcohol treatment. This approach was designed to continually communicate and teach an "A-B-C" cognitive-behavioral approach to problems-solving and change. The Strengths Perspective of Case Management was developed to help clients identify resources despite the view that few exist, and to help clients overcome attitudes that feed denial as well as avoid change (Rapp et al., 1996).

Monti and colleagues (1997) adapted coping skills training (CST), a promising treatment approach for alcoholics, for use with cocaine abusers and evaluated the effects on outcomes. The cocaine-specific CST intervention was conducted in individual sessions and involved CST based on functional analysis of high risk situations. Clients who received CST had significantly fewer cocaine-use days, and the length of their longest binge was significantly shorter at the three-month follow-up period compared to clients in the control condition. CST did not affect relapse rates or use of other substances.

Methamphetamine

Starting in the 1990s, methamphetamine abuse and dependence has risen to near-epidemic levels in some parts of the country (Cunningham & Thielemier, 1995); therefore, it requires special attention in this section. A startling statistic indicates that emergency room admissions due to methamphetamine increased 261 percent from 1991 to 1994 (Drug Abuse Warning Network, 1997). While State substance abuse or behavioral health divisions have increased efforts to identify the prevalence of methamphetamine use, the task is difficult for several reasons, especially in rural areas.

For instance, Montana and Hawaii exemplify the difficulties found in large isolated or geographically separated areas, which have limited health care services, privacy issues related to disclosure of illicit drug use, lack of drug testing capability and failure of patients to report the problem (Freese et al., 2000). However, available data in Hawaii indicated that treatment agencies were reporting methamphetamine as the primary drug of abuse at entry for 38 percent of clients (ONDCP, 1997). An average of 55 percent of clients at treatment entry used the drug, and a significant number are single women with dependent children, half of whom were receiving public assistance (Joe, 1995).

Freese and colleagues (2000) note that determining key elements for effective treatment of methamphetamine abuse and dependence is complex, as use patterns are variable, the drug can be taken in multiple ways, and triggers for cravings and use vary widely. While specific populations affected by abuse of this substance can be identified according to a continuum of geography, culture, sexual orientation, and other circumstances leading to treatment, treatment programs must be accessible and understanding of these particular clients. The authors suggest that the *Matrix Model Treatment Program* (Rawson et al., 1991), a standardized relapse prevention treatment format that provides a comprehensive framework to learn recovery skills and facilitates participation in recovery activities, may be the means through which providers can identify key elements for successful treatment.

Special Populations

Despite the growth in literature regarding specific populations, such as ethnic minority groups, women and the elderly, an ongoing problem is the limited research regarding these populations in rural areas. Nevertheless, this section will cover literature produced since the last publication of this chapter regarding the populations noted, as well as jail inmates and prisoners.

Ethnic Minority Populations

African Americans

Dawkins and Williams (1997) review literature on substance abuse in rural African American populations and note that most of the research has focused on alcohol problems. Among the small proportion of studies regarding rural black populations, three areas covered are 1) ethnographic studies describing the integration of alcohol in rural black culture, 2) community surveys of blacks and whites to determine racial differences in drinking behavior, attitudes and problems and 3) regional and national survey findings for areas of the country where rural blacks are concentrated. In general, existing literature suggests that patterns of use for substances such as alcohol and cigarettes are either similar between rural blacks and whites or somewhat lower for blacks, but health and social consequences are worse for rural blacks. Also, problems associated with use of illicit drugs, such as heroin, marijuana, and cocaine persist (Dawkins & Williams, 1997).

Albrecht, Amey and Miller (1996) used data from the most recently available Monitoring the Future survey to examine the role of race and residence in affecting substance abuse patterns among 12,168 high school seniors self-described as black or white. Between the two groups, blacks had substantially lower reported use of all types of drugs compared to whites in both urban and rural settings. Indeed, rural versus urban residence differences were modest, but access and opportunity were important for facilitating drug use. Also, family factors, self-esteem and involvement in activities such as church attendance play important protective roles.

Dawkins (1996) examined the extent to which substance use perceptions and behavior of African American youth and adolescents are influenced by social environmental contexts. The findings indicated that there are both similarities and differences in perceptions and patterns of substance use, as well as the prediction of alcohol and marijuana use in metropolitan (urban and suburban) and nonmetropolitan (rural) social contexts.

The major similarities were that 1) alcohol or illegal drugs were rated among the top three problems at school by youth in early adolescence (eighth-grade) in both metropolitan and nonmetropolitan settings; 2) by the time these youth reached 12th grade, patterns of marijuana use were similar across social contexts; and 3) there was a relatively strong influence of peers and early substance use on later substance use within each of the three settings.

The major differences were that 1) rural eighth-graders were more likely than metropolitan youth to perceive alcohol use as a problem at school and, as

12th-graders, were more likely to exhibit patterns of heavy alcohol involvement and more frequent current use; 2) in the rural setting, the strong direct effect of being male on alcohol use is consistent with previous research on drinking patterns of black men.

However, being recognized for receiving good grades operated as a protective factor which decreased alcohol use in the rural setting only; 3) the urban context may provide a setting where substance use is more likely to be linked to violation of conventional norms and family, school and community values; 4) prior cigarette use was the most powerful predictor of marijuana use among rural youth.

Mexican Americans

Castro & Gutierres (1997) provide an overview of the literature regarding Mexican American substance use and abuse. They note that little research exists, but that studies of alcohol use in rural Mexico found that men were most likely to be heavy alcohol consumers, whereas women were most likely to be abstinent. Rural Mexican men who move to cities tend to reduce their alcohol consumption, which is the opposite pattern from that of the United States. The authors indicate that research regarding substance use for rural Mexican American youth is mixed, as some has shown similar use rates between these and white youth, whereas others have shown higher drug use rates for Mexican-American females. Issues of traditionalism and acculturation are thought to potentially influence different use rates.

Vega and colleagues (1998) report data from the Mexican American Prevalence and Services Survey, which presents lifetime prevalence rates for 12 DSMIII-R psychiatric disorders in a sample of 3,012 adults (non-institutionalized persons aged 18 to 59 years of age) of Mexican origin. Comparing these results with those of population surveys conducted in the United States and Mexico, Mexican immigrants had lifetime rates similar to those of Mexican citizens, while rates for Mexican-Americans were similar to those of the national population of the United States. A higher prevalence for any disorder was reported in urban (35.7 percent) compared with town (32.1 percent) or rural (29.8 percent) areas. Despite very low education and income levels, Mexican Americans had lower rates of lifetime psychiatric disorders compared with rates reported for the U.S. population by the National Comorbidity Survey.

Native Americans

Rural Native Americans do not differ from urban Native American populations in rates of alcohol abuse, which are higher than the population at large. However, rural Native Americans tend to have more episodes of binge drinking (National Rural Health Association, 1999).

Based on interviews with 212 children (115 boys and 97 girls) from three American Indian reservations located in the upper Midwest, Whitbeck and colleagues (2002) identified a profile among the fifth- to eighth-grade American Indian adolescents who report gang involvement. The profile is that of a male or female who engages in delinquent behaviors and/or substance abuse and lives in a single-mother household where the mother has a history of antisocial behavior. The adolescent is probably not doing well academically and has experienced multiple life transitions or losses in the past year.

Rowe (1997) reported results from a five-year CSAP-funded community substance abuse prevention program that was launched in a small (550 member), rural Native American communities in Washington State that had a history of serious alcohol and drug problems. The Chi-e-thee ("workers") grass-roots program sought to address substance abuse by using community collaboration between tribal agencies, community empowerment and education, cultural enhancement and development of support networks and services for people engaged in healing and recovery.

This program was successful in sponsoring over 215 cultural and educational events, and resulted in 96 community members making a commitment to sobriety, a community-wide change in norms about wellness and substance abuse, the creation of new networks of communication and collaboration and new tribal policies and enforcement practices to curtail drug and alcohol abuse. The number of clean and sober individuals was determined to have increased from 25 percent of the adult population in 1992 to 40 percent of the adult population in 1996.

Asian-Americans

Despite growing literature addressing mental health and substance use issues among the many populations that have Asian origin, the authors could find no research regarding substance use issues for Asians in mainland rural areas. This is likely due, at least in part, to very limited numbers of Asians in most rural areas of America. However, Waitzfelder, Engel and Gilbert (1998) studied substance abuse in Hawaii, including 1) the magnitude of the statewide substance abuse problem, 2) the unmet needs of the State's substance abuse treatment system and 3) the features of the problem unique to Hawaii's many ethnic and other subgroups.

The study targeted 55 human service organizations most burdened by the substance abuse problem. Respondents perceived the magnitude of the Hawaii substance abuse problem to be at least comparable to that of the mainland United States. Although most respondents viewed the problem using a medical model, the problem was generally thought to be exacerbated by a community context in which substance abuse is accepted, excused or denied. Increasing use of crystal methamphetamine and heroin were cited as the most worrisome trends.

Systems issues identified were similar to those of rural areas (e.g., unstable funding, lack of services, transportation, outreach). Cultural alienation, exacerbated by the State's prevailing multiculturalism, was thought to contribute to the substance abuse problem among all ethnic groups, but especially among Native Hawaiians. Cultural factors were thought to have a major impact on seeking care and subsequent acceptance of such care.

Women

Boyd (2000) conducted a study to identify risk factors that predict substance abuse and primary comorbid psychiatric disorders in rural women. Two factors—alcohol beliefs and threats of minor violence—correctly identified substance abusing women from nonsubstance abusing women, and women with nonsubstance use psychiatric disorders from those with no psychiatric disorder. Women who abuse alcohol, as well as those who predominately abuse drugs, have significantly more positive expectations for alcohol use than those who do not drink or abuse alcohol. Victimization and other forms of traumatic experiences affect women's beliefs in personal invulnerability, perceptions of a meaningful world and positive self-views. The assault on these important beliefs often leads to symptoms of hopelessness, helplessness, self-defeating coping strategies and alienation. Boyd and Mackey (2000) found that factors contributing to women's sense of alienation included a background of emotional, physical, and sexual abuse.

Boyd and Hauenstein (1997) describe efforts to diagnose co-occurring disorders in rural women. They used the Michigan Alcoholism Screening Test (MAST; Selzer, 1971), Center for Epidemiologic Studies Depression Scale (CES-D; Radloff, 1977) and the National Institute of Mental Health (NIMH) Diagnostic Interview Schedule, Version III (DIS; Robins, Helzer, Croughan & Ratcliff, 1981). The results indicate that the MAST and CES-D are effective screening tools for alcoholism and depression among rural women, and because these instruments are relatively short, they can be easily incorporated into regular health screening.

Prisoners/Inmates

Warner and Leukefeld (2001) examined differences between urban and rural drug use patterns and treatment utilization among chronic drug abusers to determine whether, and in what ways, rurality may affect substance abuse and treatment seeking. Findings showed that chronic drug abusers from rural and very rural areas have significantly higher rates of lifetime drug use, as well as higher rates of drug use in the 30 days prior to their current incarceration than chronic drug abusers from urban areas. However, being from a very rural area decreased the likelihood of having ever been in treatment.

Using interview data collected at seven county jails in both urban and rural areas of Ohio, Lo and Stephens (2002) examined factors associated with arrestees' subjective perception of substance treatment needs and evaluated whether relationships between these factors and perceived needs for treatment were identical in urban and rural areas.

Results indicated that motivation for substance-specific treatment differed among urban and rural arrestees only regarding perceived treatment needs for cocaine, with urban arrestees more likely to see a need for treatment. However, respondents identified as currently dependent on alcohol, cocaine, opiates or marijuana were more likely than nondependent respondents—across the urban–rural spectrum—to show motivation for substance-specific treatment. The results show that having a romantic partner was linked to perceived needs for marijuana treatment. In addition, being employed full time increased perceived needs for cocaine treatment among urban arrestees. In contrast, full-time employment decreased this perception among rural arrestees.

Stohr and colleagues (2002) evaluated residential substance abuse and treatment (RSAT) programs developed to address the drug and alcohol treatment needs of inmates in prisons. Typically, such programs range from six to twelve months, have an Alcoholics Anonymous and/or Narcotics Anonymous component, occur in a therapeutic community environment and some programs include a cognitive self-change component. Inmate participation in their programming is crucial to the success of a therapeutic community treatment environment. Participants in two RSAT programs were generally positive in their perceptions of most of the program components. However, those who were in the program longest were less positive about several aspects of it, whereas those who were heavy alcohol users were more positive about other aspects.

Godley and colleagues (2000) described a case management model for individuals involved with the criminal justice system who had significant, co-occurring mental illness and substance abuse disorders. During the three-year project, 54 out of 115 screened were accepted into the project. Of the clients accepted into the program, 44 (81 percent) were terminated from the program (61 percent successfully, 39 percent unsuccessfully) and 10 (19 percent) remained active at the end of the pilot period.

Program evaluation data indicated that six months after entering the program, clients had fewer legal problems and appeared to have symptom relief. However, measures did not reveal significant improvements in drug or alcohol composite scores. Clients perceived themselves as better off in most areas than the previous year, were generally satisfied with the case-management program, but had some dissatisfaction in the area of employment.

Qualitative reviews from two probation officers and a judge who referred to the project were positive.

Elderly

The Surgeon General's Report on Mental Health (1999) included a section on alcohol and substance use disorders in older adults. The report Stated that older people are not immune to the problems associated with improper use of alcohol and drugs, but *misuse* of alcohol and prescription medications appears to be more common than *abuse* of substances. However, few studies have focused on incidence and prevalence of substance abuse for older adults, and these studies had methodological problems, suggesting that this popular perception may be misleading.

A persistent research problem has been that diagnostic criteria for substance abuse were developed and validated on young and middle-aged adults. For example, DSM-IV criteria include increased tolerance to the effects of the substance, which results in increased consumption over time. However, changes in pharmacokinetics and physiology may alter drug tolerance in older adults— decreased tolerance to alcohol for older individuals may lead to decreased consumption of alcohol with no apparent reduction in intoxication. Criteria that relate to the impact of drug use on typical tasks of young and middle adulthood (e.g., school and work performance) may be largely irrelevant to older adults. Thus, abuse and dependence among older adults may be underestimated (Ellor & Kurz, 1982; Miller et al., 1991; King et al., 1994).

Seriously Mentally Ill (SMI)

In a cross-sectional study of 1,551 clients receiving care in 10 community-based rural mental health care systems, Barry and colleagues (1996) assessed problem behaviors and psychiatric symptoms among three groups of SMI clients: those with a current substance abuse problem, those with a history of substance abuse but no current problem and those with no history of substance abuse problems. Results indicated that clients with a current substance abuse problem were younger, had more 1) symptoms of anger, 2) trouble with the law and 3) suicidal threats than clients in the other two groups.

Mueser and colleagues (2001) evaluated the differences between two cohorts of patients with SMI (schizophrenia-spectrum or bipolar disorder) and co-occurring substance-use disorders, living in either predominantly rural (New Hampshire) or urban areas (two cities in Connecticut). The two study groups were compared on demographic characteristics, housing, legal problems, psychiatric and substance use diagnoses, substance use and abuse, psychiatric symptoms and quality of life. The urban group had higher rates of cocaine-use disorder, more involvement in the criminal justice system, more homelessness and was more likely to have a minority background. This group also had a higher proportion of patients with schizophrenia, more severe symptoms, as well as lower rates of marriage, educational attainment and work. Alcohol-use disorder was higher in the rural group.

Summary

The growing literature on substance abuse in rural America reflects data indicating increases in substance use disorders in these areas. Co-occurring mental health and substance abuse disorders for both children and adults has become a major focus of providers, administrators and policy makers in the 21st Century. We now have a better understanding of the developmental pathways toward substance abuse, but are still limited in our knowledge of the larger social context in which such disorders are cultivated. Part of the difficulty is the wide variability from one rural area to the next across the country and outlying States (i.e., Alaska and Hawaii). There are many different kinds of people, living in vastly different geographical and geological places, each with unique cultures.

Attempts to prevent the development of substance abuse disorders have had mixed results, but some programs, such as *Preparing for the Drug Free Years*, have been shown to have positive effects for parents and children.

Other programs that adopt similar principles and objectives have also demonstrated success, but the long-term effects of all such programs still require more research.

Treating substance abuse in rural America involves the same problems noted for mental health, such as rural programs based on urban models, fragmented service systems, large geographic areas, confidentiality and stigma in a rural culture, to name just a few. Research regarding specific populations in rural areas, such as ethnic minorities, women and the elderly are still lacking. However, initiatives such as the President's *New Freedom Commission on Mental Health* have rural America as a primary area of focus, and will undoubtedly impel our knowledge and effectiveness forward.

References

Abbey, A., Pilgrim, C., Hendrickson, P. & Buresh, S. (2000). Evaluation of a family-based substance abuse prevention program targeted for the middle school years. Journal of Drug Education, 30(2), 213-228.

Akers, R. L., (1977). *Deviant behavior: A social learning approach* (2nd ed.). Belmont, CA: Wadsworth Press.

Akers, R. L., (1994). *Criminological Theories: Introduction and Evaluation.* Los Angeles: Roxbury Publishing.

Albrecht, S.L., Amey, C. & Miller, M.K. (1996). Patterns of substance abuse among rural black adolescents. Journal of Drug Issues, 26, 751-781.

Anderson, R.L., & Huffine, C. (2003). Child & adolescent psychiatry: Use of community-based services by rural adolescents with mental health and substance use disorders. Psychiatric Services, 54, 1339-1341.

Barry, K.L., Fleming, M.F., Greenley, J.R., Kropp, S.; et al. (1996). Characteristics of persons with severe mental illness and substance abuse in rural areas. Psychiatric Services, 47, 88-90.

Becker, H.K., Agopian, M.W. & Yeh, S. (1992). Impact evaluation of Drug Abuse Resistance Education (DARE). Journal of Drug Education, 22, 283-291.

Becker, L., Barga, V., Sandberg, M., Stanley, M. & Clegg, D. (1999a). 1999 county profile on risk and protection for substance abuse prevention planning in Ferry County. Olympia, WA: Division of Alcohol and Substance Abuse, Research and Data Analysis, Department of Social and Health Services.

Becker, L., Barga, V., Sandberg, M., Stanley, M. & Clegg, D. (1999b). 1999 county profile on risk and protection for substance abuse prevention planning in King County. Olympia, WA: Division of Alcohol and Substance Abuse, Research and Data Analysis, Department of Social and Health Services.

Biglan, A., Duncan, T., Irvine, A.B., Ary, D., Smolkowski, K. & James, L. (1997). A drug abuse prevention strategy for rural America. In: Roberson, E.B., Sloboda, Z., Boyd, G.M., Beatty, L, and Kozel, N.J., eds. *Rural Substance Abuse: State of Knowledge and Issues*. National Institute on Drug Abuse; U.S. Department of Health and Human Services; National Institutes of Health: NIH Publication No. 97-4177. Rockville, MD.

Boyd, M.R. (2000). Predicting substance abuse and comorbidity in rural women. Archives of Psychiatric Nursing, 14, 64-72.

Boyd, M.R. & Hauenstein, E.J. (1997). Psychiatric assessment and confirmation of dual disorders in rural substance abusing women. Archives of Psychiatric Nursing, 11, 74-81.

Boyd, M.R. & Mackey, M.C. (2000). Alienation from self and others: The psychosocial problem of rural alcoholic women. Archives of Psychiatric Nursing, 14, 134-141.

Britt, M.A. & Jachym, N.K. (1996). Cigarette and alcohol use among 4th and 5th graders: Results of a new survey. Journal of Alcohol & Drug Education, 43, 44-54.

Burke, M.R. (2002). School-based substance abuse prevention: Political finger-pointing does not work. Federal Probation, 66, 66-71.

Castro, F.G. & Gutierres, S. (1997). Drug and alcohol use among rural Mexican Americans. In: Roberson, E.B., Sloboda, Z., Boyd, G.M., Beatty, L, and Kozel, N.J., eds. *Rural Substance Abuse: State of Knowledge and Issues*. National Institute on Drug Abuse; U.S. Department of Health and Human Services; National Institutes of Health: NIH Publication No. 97-4177. Rockville, MD.

Cellucci, T. & Vik, P. (2001). Training for substance abuse treatment among psychologists in a rural State. Professional Psychology - Research & Practice, 32, 248-252.

Chassin, L., Pillow, D.R., Curran, P.J., Molina, B.S.G & Barrera, M., Jr. (1993). Relations of parental alcoholism to early adolescent substance use: A test of three mediation mechanisms. Journal of Abnormal Psychology, 102, 3-19.

Clark, J.J., Leukefeld, C. & Godlaski, T. (1999). Case management and behavioral contracting: Components of rural substance abuse treatment. Journal of Substance Abuse Treatment, 17(4), 293-304.
Conger, R.D. (1997). The social context of substance abuse: A developmental perspective. In: Roberson, E.B., Sloboda, Z., Boyd, G.M., Beatty, L, and Kozel, N.J., eds. *Rural Substance Abuse: State of Knowledge and Issues*. National Institute on Drug Abuse; U.S. Department of Health and Human Services; National Institutes of Health: NIH Publication No. 97-4177. Rockville, MD.
Conger, R.D., Conger, K.J., Elder, Jr., G.H., Lorenz, F., Simons, R. & Whitbeck, L. (1992). A family process model of economic hardship and adjustment of early adolescent boys. Child Development, 63, 526-541.
Conger, R.D., Conger, K.J., Elder, Jr., G.H., Lorenz, F., Simons, R. & Whitbeck, L. (1993). Family economic stress and adjustment of early adolescent girls. Developmental Psychology, 29, 209-219.
Conger, R.D., Ge, X., Elder, Jr., G.H., Lorenz, F.O. & Simons, R.L. (1994). Economic stress, coercive family process, and developmental problems of adolescents. Child Development, 65, 541-561.
Conger, R.D. & Rueter, M.A. (1995). Siblings, parents, and peers: A longitudinal study of social influences in adolescent risk for alcohol use and abuse. In: Brody, G., ed. *Sibling Relationships: Their Causes and Consequences*. Norwood, NJ: Ablex Publishing.
Cunningham, J.K. & Thielemier, M.A. (1995). *24 Trends and Regional Variations in Amphetamine-Related Emergency Admissions*: California, 1984-1993. Irvine, CA: Public Statistics Institute.
Dawkins, M.P. (1996). The social context of substance use among African American youth: Rural, urban and suburban comparisons. Journal of Alcohol & Drug Education, 41, 68- 85.
Dawkins, M.P. & Williams, M.M. (1997). Substance abuse in rural African-American populations. In: Roberson, E.B., Sloboda, Z., Boyd, G.M., Beatty, L, and Kozel, N.J., eds. *Rural Substance Abuse: State of Knowledge and Issues*. National Institute on Drug Abuse; U.S. Department of Health and Human Services; National Institutes of Health: NIH Publication No. 97-4177. Rockville, MD.
Donnermeyer, J.F. (2000). Parents' perceptions of a school-based prevention education program. Journal of Drug Education, 30, 325-342.
Donnermeyer, J.F. & Wurschmidt, T.N. (1997). Educators' perceptions of the D.A.R.E. program. Journal of Drug Education, 27, 259-276.

D'Onofrio, C.N. (1997). The prevention of alcohol use by rural youth. In: Roberson, E.B., Sloboda, Z., Boyd, G.M., Beatty, L, and Kozel, N.J., eds. *Rural Substance Abuse: State of Knowledge and Issues*. National Institute on Drug Abuse; U.S. Department of Health and Human Services; National Institutes of Health: NIH Publication No. 97-4177. Rockville, MD.

Drake, R. E., Essock, S. M., Shaner, A., Carey, K. B., Minkoff, K., Kola, L., Lynde, D., Osher, F. C., Clark, R. E., & Rickards, L. (2001). Implementing dual diagnosis services for clients with severe mental illness. *Psychiatric Services*, 52, 469-476.

Drug Abuse Warning Network (1997). *Number of Methamphetamine and Amphetamine-Related Episodes: 1988-1995*. Substance Abuse and Mental Health Services Administration,//http:www.samhsa.gov/oas/dawn/ar 17_013.htm.

Dukes, R.L., Ullman, J.B & Stein, J.A. (1996). Three-year follow-up of drug abuse resistance education (D.A.R.E.). Evaluation Review, 20, 49-66.

Edwards, R.W. (1997). Drug and alcohol use among youth in rural communities. In: Roberson, E.B., Sloboda, Z., Boyd, G.M., Beatty, L, and Kozel, N.J., eds. *Rural Substance Abuse: State of Knowledge and Issues*. National Institute on Drug Abuse; U.S. Department of Health and Human Services; National Institutes of Health: NIH Publication No. 97-4177. Rockville, MD.

Elliot, D.S., Huizinga, D. & Menard, S. (1989). *Multiple Problem Youth: Delinquency, Substance Use, and Mental Health Problems*. New York: Springer-Verlag.

Ellor, J. R. & Kurz, D. J. (1982). Misuse and abuse of prescription and nonprescription drugs by the elderly. *Nursing Clinics of North America, 17,* 319–330.

Farrell, S.P., Blank, M., Koch, J.R., Munjas, B. & Clement, D.G. (1999). Predicting whether patients receive continuity of care after discharge from State hospitals: Policy implications. Archives of Psychiatric Nursing, 13, 279-285.

Freese, T.E., Obert, J., Dickow, A., Cohen, J. & Lord, R.H. (2000). Methamphetamine abuse: Issues for special populations. Journal of Psychoactive Drugs, 32, 177-182.

Godley, S.H., Finch, M., Dougan, L., McDonnell, M., McDermeit, & M., Carey, A. (2000). Case management for dually diagnosed individuals involved in the criminal justice system. Journal of Substance Abuse Treatment, 18, 137-148.

Gottfredson, M.R. & Hirschi, T. (1990). *A General Theory of Crime*. Stanford, CA: Stanford University Press.

Guyll, M., Spoth, R.L., Chao, W., Wickrama, K. & Russell, D. (2004). Family-focused preventive interventions: Evaluating parental risk moderation of substance use trajectories. Journal of Family Psychology, 18, 293-301.

Hansen, W.B. (1996). Pilot test results comparing the All Star program with seventh grade D.A.R.E.: Program integrity and mediating variable analysis. Substance Use & Misuse, 31, 1359-1377.

Hansen, W.B. & McNeal Jr., R.B. (1997). How D.A.R.E. works: An examination of program effects on mediating variables. Health Education & Behavior, 24, 165-176.

Harmon, M.A. (1993). Reducing the risk of drug involvement among early adolescents: An evaluation of Drug Abuse Resistance Education (DARE). Evaluation Review, 17, 221- 239.

Hawkins, J.D., Catalano, R.F. & Miller, J.Y. (1992). Risk and protective factors for alcohol and other drug problems in adolescence and early adulthood: Implications for substance abuse prevention. Psychological Bulletin, 112, 64-105.

Hays, R. D. & Ellickson, P. L. (1996). Associations between drug use and deviant behavior in teenagers. Addictive Behaviors, 21, 291–302.

Hirschi, T. (1969). *Causes of Delinquency*. Berkeley, CA: University of California Press.

Hodge, D.R., Cardenas, P. & Montoya, H. (2001). Substance use: Spirituality and religious participation as protective factors among rural youths. Social Work Research, 25, 153-162.

Howland, R.H. (1995). The treatment of persons with dual diagnoses in a rural community. Psychiatric Quarterly, 66, 33-49.

Joe, K.A. (1995). Ice is strong enough for a man but made for a woman: A social cultural analysis of crystal methamphetamine use among Asian Pacific Americans. Crime, Law, and Social Change, 22, 269-289.

Johnson, K., Bryant, D., Strader, T., Bucholtz, G., et al. (1996). Reducing alcohol and other drug use by strengthening community, family, and youth resiliency: An evaluation of the Creating Lasting Connections Program. Journal of Adolescent Research, 11, 36-67.

Johnston, L. D., O'Malley, P. M. & Backman, J. G. (1996). *National survey results on drug use from the Monitoring the Future study, 1975–1995. Vol. I: Secondary school students*. (NIH Pub. No. 97-4139). Rockville, MD: National Institute on Drug Abuse.

Johnston, L., O'Malley, P. & Bachman, J. (2000). *Monitoring the future: National survey results on drug use, 1975–1999: Vol. 1. Secondary school students* (NIH Publication No. 00- 4802). Washington, D.C.: U.S. Department of Health and Human Services.

Karim, G. (1997). In living context: An interdisciplinary approach to rethinking rural prevention. In: Roberson, E.B., Sloboda, Z., Boyd, G.M., Beatty, L, and Kozel, N.J., eds. *Rural Substance Abuse: State of Knowledge and Issues.* National Institute on Drug Abuse; U.S. Department of Health and Human Services; National Institutes of Health: NIH Publication No. 97-4177. Rockville, MD.

Kessler, R. C., Berglund, P. A., Zhao, S., Leaf, P. J., Kouzis, A. C., Bruce, M. L., Friedman, R. M., Grosser, R. C., Kennedy, C., Narrow, W. E., Kuehnel, T. G., Laska, E. M., Manderscheid, R. W., Rosenheck, R. A., Santoni, T. W. & Schneier, M. (1996). The 12-month prevalence and correlates of serious mental illness (SMI). In R. W. Manderscheid & M. A. Sonnenschein (Eds.), *Mental health United States, 1996* (DHHS Publication No. SMA 96-3098, pp. 59–70). Washington, D.C.: Superintendent of Documents, U.S. Government Printing Office.

Kessler, R.C., McGonagle, K.A., Zhao, S., Nelson, C.B., Hughes, M., Eshleman, S., Wittchen, H., and Kendler, K.S. (1994). Lifetime and 12-month prevalence of DSM-III-R psychiatric disorders in the United States: Results from the national comorbidity study. Archives of General Psychiatry, 51, 81- 89.

Killeen, T. & Brady, K.T. (2000). Parental stress and child behavioral outcomes following substance abuse residential treatment: Follow-up at 6 and 12 months. Journal of Substance Abuse Treatment, 19, 23-29.

King, C. J., Van Hasselt, V. B., Segal, D. L. & Hersen, M. (1994). Diagnosis and assessment of substance abuse in older adults: Current strategies and issues. Addictive Behaviors, 19, 41–55.

Kosterman, R., Hawkins, J.D., Haggerty, K.P., Spoth, R. & Redmond, C. (2001). Preparing for the drug free years: Session-specific effects of a universal parent-training intervention with rural families. Journal of Drug Education, 31, 47-68.

Kosterman, R., Hawkins, J.D., Spoth, R., Haggerty, K.P., et al. (1997). Effects of a preventive parent-training intervention on observed family interactions: Proximal outcomes from preparing for the drug free years. Journal of Community Psychology, 25, 337-352.

Leukefeld, C.G., Godlaski, T., Clark, J., Brown, C. & Hays, L. (2002). Structured stories: Reinforcing social skills in rural substance abuse treatment. Health & Social Work, 27, 213- 217.

Lo, C.C. & Stephens, R.C. (2002). Arrestees' perceived needs for substance-specific treatment: Exploring urban-rural differences. American Journal of Drug & Alcohol Abuse, 28, 623-642.

Loeber, R. & LeBlanc, M. (1990). Toward a developmental criminology. In: Tonry, J. and Morris, N., eds. *Crime and Justice.* Vol. 12. Chicago: University of Chicago Press.

Loeber, R. & Stouthhamer-Loeber, M. (1986). Family factors as correlates and predictors of juvenile conduct problems and delinquency. In: Tonry, J. and Morris, N., eds. *Crime and Justice.* Vol. 7. Chicago: University of Chicago Press.

Lytton, H. (1990). Child and parent effects in boys' conduct disorder: A reinterpretation. Developmental Psychology, 26, 683-697.

Mason, W.A., Kosterman, R., Hawkins, J.D., Haggerty, K.P., Spoth, R.L. (2003). Reducing adolescents' growth in substance use and delinquency: Randomized trial effects of a parent-training prevention intervention. Prevention Science, 4, 203-212.

McAuliffe, W.E., LaBrie, R., Woodworth, R., Zhang, C. & Dunn, R.P. (2003). State substance abuse treatment gaps. American Journal on Addictions, 12(2), 101-121.

Melby, J.N., Conger, R.D., Conger, K.J. & Lorenz, F.O. (1993). Effects of parental behavior on tobacco use by young adolescent males. Journal of Marriage and Family, 55, 439- 454.

Miano, G., Forest, A. & Gumaer, J. (1997). A collaborative program to assist at-risk youth. Professional School Counseling, 1, 16-20.

Miller, N. S., Belkin, B. M. & Gold, M. S. (1991). Alcohol and drug dependence among the elderly: Epidemiology, diagnosis, and treatment. Comprehensive Psychiatry, 32, 153–165.

Miller-Heyl, J., MacPhee, D. & Fritz, J.J. (1998). DARE to be you: A family-support, early prevention program. Journal of Primary Prevention, 18, 257-285.

Moffitt, T.E. (1993). Adolescence—limited and life-course- persistent antisocial behavior: A developmental taxonomy. Psychology Review, 100, 674-701.

Monti, P.M., Rohsenow, D.J., Michalec, E., Martin, R.A. & Abrams, D.B. (1997). Brief coping skills treatment for cocaine abuse: Substance use outcomes at three months. Addiction, 92, 1717-1728.

Mueser, K.T., Essock, S.M., Drake, R.E., Wolfe, R.S. & Frisman, L. (2001). Rural and urban differences in patients with a dual diagnosis. Schizophrenia Research, 48, 93-107.

National Center on Addiction and Substance Abuse (CASA) at Columbia University (2000). *No place to hide: substance abuse in mid-size cities and rural America.* New York: Author.

National Institute on Alcohol Abuse and Alcoholism (1994). *Alcohol and Health.* Eighth Special Report to the U.S. Congress, September. NIH Publication No. 94-3699. Rockville, MD: U.S. Department of Health and Human Services.

Oetting, E.R., Edwards, R.W., Kelly, K. & Beauvais, F. (1997). Risk and protective factors for drug use among rural American youth. In: Roberson, E.B., Sloboda, Z., Boyd, G.M., Beatty, L, and Kozel, N.J., eds. *Rural Substance Abuse: State of Knowledge and Issues.* National Institute on Drug Abuse; U.S. Department of Health and Human Services; National Institutes of Health: NIH Publication No. 97-4177. Rockville, MD.

Office on National Drug Control Policy, Executive Office of The President (ONDCP) (1997). Pulse Checdk, Summer 1997: Special Report—Methamphetamine Trends in Five Western States and Hawaii, 1997. (Order # NCJ-164261). Available at: www.whitehousedrugpolicy.gov/drugfact/pulsechk/pcappa.htm.

Park, J., Kosterman, R., Hawkins, J.D., Haggerty, K.P., Duncan, T.E., Duncan, S.C. & Spoth, R. (2000). Effects of the "Preparing for the Drug Free Years" curriculum on growth in alcohol use and risk for alcohol use in early adolescence. Prevention Science, 1, 125-138.

Patterson, G.R. (1993). Orderly change in a stable world: The antisocial trait as a chimera. Journal of Consulting and Clinical Psychology, 61, 911-919.

Patterson, G.R., Reid, J.B. & Dishion, T.J. (1992). *Antisocial Boys.* Eugene, OR: Castalia Publishing.

Pickrel, Susan G; Henggeler, Scott W. (1996). Multisystemic therapy for adolescent substance abuse and dependence. Child & Adolescent Psychiatric Clinics of North America, 5, 201-211.

Pilgrim, C., Abbey, A., Hendrickson, P. & Lorenz, S. (1998). Implementation and impact of a family-based substance abuse prevention program in rural communities. Journal of Primary Prevention, 18, 341-361.

Plomin, R., Chipuer, H.M. & Neiderhiser, J.M. (1994). Behavioral genetic evidence for the importance of nonshared environment. In: Heatherington, E.M., Reiss, D, and Plomin, R., eds. *Separate Social Worlds of Siblings:*

The Impact of Nonshared Environment on Development. Hillsdale, NJ: Erlbaum, pp. 1-31.

Rapp, R.C., Kelliher, C.S., Fisher, J.H. & Hall, J.F. (1996) Strengths-based case management: A role in addressing denial in substance abuse treatment. In H.A. Siegal & R.C. Rapp (Eds.), *Case management and substance abuse treatment: Practice and experience* (pp. 21–36). New York: Springer Publishing Co.

Rawson, R.A., Obert, J.L., McCann, M.J. & Ling, W. (1991). *The Matrix Model for Outpatient Treatment for Alcohol Abuse and Dependency.* Beverly Hills, CA: Matrix.

Regier, D.A., Farmer, M.E., Rae, D.S., Locke, B.Z., Keith, S.J., Judd, L.L., & Goodwin, F.K. (1990). Comorbidity of mental disorders with alcohol and other drug abuse: Results from the Epidemiologic Catchment Area Study. *Journal of the American Medical Association, 264,* 2511-2518.

Richters, J.E. & Martinez, P.E. (1993). Violent communities, family choices, and children's chances: An algorithm for improving the odds. Developmental Psychopathology, 5, 609-627.

Roberts, L.W., Battaglia, J. & Epstein, R.S. (1999). Frontier ethics: Mental health care needs and ethical dilemmas in rural communities. Psychiatric Services, 50, 497-503.

Rowe, W.E. (1997). Changing ATOD norms and behaviors: A Native American community commitment to wellness. Evaluation & Program Planning, 20, 323-333.

Rueter, M.A., Conger, R.D. & Ramisetty-Mikler, S. (1999). Assessing the benefits of a parenting skills training program: A theoretical approach to predicting direct and moderating effects. Family Relations: Interdisciplinary Journal of Applied Family Studies, 48, 67-77.

Sampson, R.J. & Groves, W.B. (1989). Community structure and crime: Testing social-disorganization theory. American Journal of Sociology, 94, 774-802.

Sher, K.J., Walitzer, K.S., Wood, P.K. & Brent, E.E. (1991). Characteristics of children of alcoholics: Putative risk factors, substance use and abuse, and psychopathology. Journal of Abnormal Psychology, 100, 427-488.

Simons, R.L., Whitbeck, L.B., Beaman, W.J. & Conger, R.D. (1994b). The impact of mother's parenting, involvement by nonresidential fathers, and parental conflict on the adjustment of adolescent children. Journal of Marriage and Family, 56, 356-374.

Simons, R.L., Wu, C., Conger, R.D. & Lorenz, F.O. (1994a). Two routes to delinquency: Differences between early and late starters in the impact of parenting and deviant peers. Criminology, 32, 247-276.

Spoth, R., Goldberg, C., Neppl, T., Trudeau, L. & Ramisetty-Mikler, S. (2001). Rural-urban differences in the distribution of parent-reported risk factors for substance abuse among young adolescents. Journal of Substance Abuse, 13, 609-623.

Spoth, R., Redmond, C., Haggerty, K. & Ward, T. (1995). A controlled parenting skills outcome study examining individual difference and attendance effects. Journal of Marriage & the Family, 57, 449-464.

Spoth, R., Redmond, C., Hockaday, C. & Yoo, S. (1996). Protective factors and young adolescent tendency to abstain from alcohol use: A model using two waves of intervention study data. American Journal of Community Psychology, 24, 749-770.

Spoth, R., Redmond, C. & Shin, C. (1998). Direct and indirect latent-variable parenting outcomes of two universal family-focused preventive interventions: Extending a public health-oriented research base. Journal of Consulting & Clinical Psychology, 66, 385-399.

Spoth, R.L., Redmond, C. & Shin, C. (2001). Randomized trial of brief family interventions for general populations: Adolescent substance use outcomes 4 years following baseline. Journal of Consulting & Clinical Psychology, 69, 627-642.

Spoth, R., Redmond, C., Shin, C. & Azevedo, K. (2004). Brief Family Intervention Effects on Adolescent Substance Initiation: School-Level Growth Curve Analyses 6 Years Following Baseline. Journal of Consulting & Clinical Psychology, 72, 535-542.

Spoth, R., Reyes, M.L., Redmond, C. & Shin, C. (1999). Assessing a public health approach to delay onset and progression of adolescent substance use: Latent transition and log-linear analyses of longitudinal family preventive intervention outcomes. Journal of Consulting & Clinical Psychology, 67, 619-630.

Spoth, R., Yoo, S., Kahn, J.H. & Redmond, C. (1996). A model of the effects of protective parent and peer factors on young adolescent alcohol refusal skills. Journal of Primary Prevention, 16, 373-394.

Stanton, M.D. & Shadish, W.R. (1997). Outcome, attrition, and family-couples treatment for drug abuse: A meta-analysis and review of the controlled, comparative studies. Psychological Bulletin, 122, 170-191.

Stevens, M.M., Mott, L.A. & Youells, F. (1996). Rural adolescent drinking behavior: Three year follow-up in the New Hampshire Substance Abuse Prevention Study. Adolescence, 31, 159-166.

Stohr, M.K., Hemmens, C., Shapiro, B., Chambers, B. & Kelley, L. (2002). Comparing inmate perceptions of two residential substance abuse treatment programs. International Journal of Offender Therapy & Comparative Criminology, 46, 699-714.

Swaim, R.C. (1991). Childhood risk factors and adolescent drug and alcohol abuse. Educational Psychology Review, 3(4), 363-398.

Thombs, D.L. (2000). A retrospective study of DARE: Substantive effects not detected in undergraduates. Journal of Alcohol & Drug Education, 46, 27-40.

Thornberry, T.P. (1987). Toward an interactional theory of delinquency. Criminology, 25, 863-891.

Thornberry, T.P., Lizotte, A.J., Krohn, M.D., Farnworth, M. & Jang, S.J. (1991). Testing interactional theory: An examination of reciprocal causal relationships among family, school, and delinquency. Journal of Criminal Law and Criminology, 82, 3-35.

U.S. Department of Health and Human Services, Substance Abuse and Mental Health Services Administration, Office of Applied Studies (1999). *National household survey on drug abuse*, 1997 [Computer file; ICPSR version]. Ann Arbor, MI: Inter-university Consortium for Political and Social Research (Distributor).

U.S. Department of Health and Human Services (DHHS), *Mental Health: A Report of the Surgeon General*, (Rockville, MD: National Institute of Mental Health, 1999) chap. 3; accessed on February 10, 2004 at www.surgeongeneral.gov/library/mentalhealth/pdfs/c3.pdf.

Vaughan-Sarrazin, M.S., Hall, J.A. & Rick, G.S. (2000). Impact of case management on use of health services by rural clients in substance abuse treatment. Journal of Drug Issues, 30, 435-464.

Vega, W.A., Kolody, B., Aguilar-Gaxiola, S., Alderete, E., Catalano, R. & Caraveo-Anduaga, J. (1998). Lifetime prevalence of DSM-III-R psychiatric disorders among urban and rural Mexican Americans in California. Archives of General Psychiatry, 55, 771-778.

Vicary, J.R., Swisher, J.D., Doebler, M.K., Yuan, J., Bridger, J.C., Gurgevich, E.A. & Deike, R.C. (1996). Rural community substance abuse prevention and intervention. Family & Community Health, 19, 59-72.

Vuchinich, S., Bank, L. & Patterson, G.R. (1992). Parenting, peers, and the stability of antisocial behavior in preadolescent boys. Developmental Psychology, 28, 510-521.

Wagenfeld, M.O., Murray, J.D., Mohatt, D.F. & DeBruyn, J.C. (1997). Mental health service delivery in rural areas: Organizational and clinical issues. In: Roberson, E.B., Sloboda, Z., Boyd, G.M., Beatty, L, and Kozel, N.J., eds. *Rural Substance Abuse: State of Knowledge and Issues*. National Institute on Drug Abuse; U.S. Department of Health and Human Services; National Institutes of Health: NIH Publication No. 97-4177. Rockville, MD.

Waitzfelder, B.E., Engel Jr., C.C. & Gilbert Jr., F.I. (1998). Substance abuse in Hawaii: Perspectives of key local human service organizations. Substance Abuse, 19, 7-22.

Warner, B.D. & Leukefeld, C.G. (2001). Rural-urban differences in substance use and treatment utilization among prisoners. American Journal of Drug & Alcohol Abuse, 27, 265-280.

Whitbeck, L.B., Hoyt, D.R., Chen, X. & Stubben, J.D. (2002). Predictors of gang involvement among American Indian Adolescents. Journal of Gang Research, 10, 11-26.

Wysong, E., Aniskiewicz, R. & Wright, D. (1994). Truth and DARE: Tracking drug education to graduation and as symbolic politics. Social Problems, 41, 448-472.

4. MENTAL HEALTH SERVICE DELIVERY IN RURAL AMERICA: ORGANIZATIONAL AND CLINICAL ISSUES

Earlier sections have provided a context for a discussion of mental health service delivery issues in rural America. "Rural America comprises 2,305 counties, contains 83 percent of the nation's land, and is home to just over 60 million Americans, 25 percent of this country's total population" (McCabe & Macnee, 2002). Rural communities must address an equivalent prevalence of serious mental illnesses and clinical complexities in comparison to urban areas. The overall numbers of individuals with serious mental illnesses may be small (Gale & Deprez, 2003), but these individuals often live across vast areas, making coordinated service delivery challenging.

At the same time, rural communities generally have fewer services and mental health professionals than their urban counterparts. In many areas the number of mental health professionals is actually decreasing (Kane & Ennis, 1996), further exacerbating the issue of limited core services, such as case management, inpatient service, crisis response and continuity of care (Kane & Ennis, 1996; Rohland et al., 1998; Shelton & Frank, 1995). Limited resources are usually directed toward acute care needs, as opposed to prevention and health promotion (Gale & Deprez, 2003). In fact, Shelton and Frank (1995) found that rural community general hospitals provide more emergency psychiatric services than do their urban counterparts. Clearly, barriers to workforce development, as well as funding shortages are ever-present challenges.

To not only survive but also provide quality care, rural mental health systems are required to become increasingly creative in the assessment and provision of services. There has been little research done on what organizational structures and partnerships are most effective in meeting rural need (Amundson, 2001). Local decision-makers are struggling with how to transform fragmented care into coordinated service delivery systems (Gale & Deprez, 2003). Specialty practices are often not feasible, pushing communities to explore cross-system partnerships to meet consumers' individualized needs.

Mental health consumers generally seek services through the path of least resistance, which is often emergency rooms, primary care physicians, schools, the criminal justice system and natural support systems (e.g., faith-based organizations). These various service sectors may become components of a community's integrated mental health system. More specifically, many communities are establishing partnerships with primary care and schools, establishing multidisciplinary teams using assertive community treatment (ACT) or ACT-like models and utilizing paraprofessionals on treatment teams (Gale & Deprez, 2003; Kane & Ennis, 1996).

As indicated in previous sections, rural areas are often perceived as homogeneous. However, there is actually a rich diversity among rural communities in terms of geography and culture. In this sense, service delivery systems need to match the unique history and qualities of different communities (Mulder et al., 2003). Some rural communities are able to optimize the natural strengths and supports they possess (Kane & Ennis, 1996).

Culturally, rural communities may rely much more on institutions outside of the traditional mental health system for mental health issues (Sears et al., 2003). Funding levels are typically anemic for mental health care, but dollars are not the only driver of services in many communities. Talents, infrastructure and even geographical features can be community assets over and above general funding levels (Mulder et al., 2003). However, there has been little work done on how rural communities may most effectively scan and then optimize these local assets.

Calls for the integration of service sectors and community assets are frequent, but a number of potential hurdles exist. Different professional groups may have conflicting philosophies and practices, communication may be ineffective, there may be disagreement regarding roles and regulations may discourage service flexibility (Van Hook & Ford, 1998). Rural successes and barriers are presented below as information for communities exploring service delivery alternatives for mental health.

Community Mental Health Centers

The Community Mental Health Centers Act of 1963 and amendments in 1975 created CMHCs in many rural areas. These CMHCs were required to provide a range of services, including outpatient, inpatient, consultation and education, partial hospitalization and emergency/crisis intervention. Federal regulations also required linkages to the community and other community agencies.

For many, this brought a mental health service presence to areas that had previously been lacking. In some cases, this service presence appears stronger in rural areas than it does in urban localities. For example, Farrell and colleagues (1999) found that persons discharged from State hospitals to rural CMHCs were twice as likely to have continuity of care compared to urban areas. In this study, continuity of care was operationalized as demonstrating sufficient communication and planning between CMHCs and hospitals and services offered within two weeks of discharge.

Although rural communities have benefited from the CMHC system, traditional centers are unable to sufficiently address the level of current need. CMHCs are considering ways to form relationships with other health services to leverage resources to adequately meet this need (Hargrove & Keller, 1997).

Alternative Service Models and Treatment Settings

Multidisciplinary Teams

Urban case management models may not be viable in rural areas due to inconsistent and inappropriate training, restrictions regarding the roles of paraprofessionals and other healthcare workers and general limited service availability. Alternative models are necessary. Some rural communities are developing multidisciplinary healthcare teams comprised of case managers, mental health professionals, social workers, health educators and/or community outreach workers and a primary care clinician (Amundson, 2001).

Mental health service teams require the participation of existing community provider organizations and agencies. This model has had initial positive results, but full utilization and systems outcome evaluations are in early stages of development. Early findings suggested that these multidisciplinary teams can be established by utilizing the existing range of mental health professionals within fairly simple community organizational structures, while optimizing community predispositions to integrated services (Amundson, 2001).

Assertive Community Treatment (ACT), an evidence-based practice (EBP) for persons with serious mental illness, is one example of using multidisciplinary treatment teams. While communities have been importing models of multidisciplinary care that have varying levels of fidelity to ACT, historically, ACT and other EBPs have been created and tested in urban, predominantly White treatment environments, and the availability of these service models have varied greatly.

EBP programs and policy are routinely based upon urban models and experiences, and scaled-down to fit rural settings (Gamm, 2002; Mohatt, 2000). Although ACT has been in existence for many years, there are only a small number of studies that have explored whether or not ACT can be effectively integrated into rural settings and across race/ethnicity. Accordingly, the challenges and pitfalls of adapting this EBP have been well documented (Lachance, 1996; McDonel, 1997; Santos, 1993).

Several studies provide emerging data regarding ACT models in rural America. Lachance and Santos (1995) discuss how to modify ACT models for use in rural areas and suggest the need to keep six basic elements: 1) multi-service teams, 2) 24-hour service availability, 3) small caseloads that do not vary in composition, 4) ongoing and continuous services, 5) assertive outreach and 6) in-vivo rehabilitation.

McGrew, Pescosolido & Wright (2003) evaluated 73 ACT teams' ratings on the benefit of 16 activities and importance of 27 possible critical ingredients of the ideal team. Having a full-time nurse on the team was rated as the most important ingredient, and medication management was rated as the most beneficial clinical activity. The ratings of teams from urban and rural settings were highly correlated. The most under-implemented critical elements included the presence of a full-time substance abuse specialist, a psychiatrist's involvement on the team, team involvement with hospital discharge and working with a client support system.

Santos and colleagues (1993) evaluated the effect of an ACT program on rates of hospital utilization and cost of care and found a 79 percent decrease in hospital days per year, a 64 percent decrease in the number of admissions per year, a 75 percent decrease in the average length of stay per admission, and a 52 percent reduction in estimated direct cost of care.

Fekete and colleagues (1998) assessed the effectiveness of ACT compared to traditional mental health services in four rural communities regarding hospitalization use, quality of life, level of functioning, attitudes toward medication and residential, vocational and legal involvement. Experimental differences on staff rating of quality of life, level of functioning and symptoms favored ACT clients. There were no experimental differences in hospital use, but ACT clients exhibited less residential stability than control clients.

In a three-year controlled comparison between urban and rural integrated service agencies in California, communities utilized interdisciplinary teams similar to those in ACT programs within a capitated service delivery system (Chandler et al., 1996). The study found that those receiving the intervention had less hospital care, greater workforce participation, fewer group and institutional housing arrangements, less use of conservatorship, greater social support, more leisure activity, less family burden and greater client and family satisfaction. It is noteworthy that urban participants also faired better than rural participants in financial stability, personal well-being and friendship.

School-Based Programs

Across the nation, there is a focus on school-based and school-linked initiatives. The value of schools to mental health care includes access to youth, geographic proximity and linkage to local policymakers and health professionals (Sears et al., 2003). These initiatives usually take the form of multidisciplinary approaches within school settings.

For example, more than 20 pilot schools in largely rural areas in South Carolina created integrated school-based mental health services models (Motes et al., 1999). One study surveyed 62 school administrators from rural, suburban and urban and found that suburban and rural schools provided more health and mental health services than urban schools. Even so, across all sites, physical health services still far outnumbered mental health services (Weist et al., 2000).

Partnerships between higher education and rural mental health systems have been successfully implemented in several States through Cooperative Extension Programs (Sears et al., 2003). The Institute for Social and Behavioral Research at Iowa State University has collaborated with Iowa State University Extension Services since the early 1990s in the creation and delivery of the Strengthening Families Program, a parenting skills and substance use prevention program that has shown promising results. This collaborative effort has supplied training and dissemination of the Strengthening Families Program to 30 counties.

A second collaborative model of mental health service delivery is found in Florida. In response to the psychological effects of Hurricane Andrew in 1992, the University of Florida Rural Psychology Program collaborated with the Department of Clinical and Health Psychology and the North Florida Area Health Education Center to improve access of mental health education and services for rural residents. The collaborative also sought to train health practitioners who in turn might foster local sustainability. There is growing evidence in support of these collaborative models of mental health service delivery (Sears et al., 2003).

The Physical and Behavioral Health Linkage

Primary care physicians (PCPs) provide most mental health treatment in rural areas (Badger et al., 1999), as they are usually the first medical professionals to encounter patients' mental health problems (Bray et al., 1997). Sears and colleagues (2003) reviewed studies investigating prevalence of psychiatric disorders in rural primary care settings and found that 34 to 41 percent of patients had a mental health disorder. Other authors have suggested that more than half of all people suffering from mental disorders seek help through primary care, yet the majority of their conditions remain inappropriately diagnosed (Badger et al., 1999).

Integration of behavioral and physical health matches many patients' preferences for the environment in which they wish to receive mental health services. From a resource management perspective, integrated models also reduce or eliminate duplicated assessment and treatment efforts (Badger et al., 1999). Integrated services allow a multidisciplinary team to efficiently treat the comorbid conditions that the majority of mental health consumers present.

Because most PCPs do not have the training to adequately diagnose mental health issues, a large number of individuals are not receiving appropriate or adequate treatment. Rural areas need to determine what proportion of mental health consumers are served through primary care and what particular integrated care models might be efficiently incorporated into local community health infrastructures. There is a wide spectrum of integrated models ranging from full onsite integration (almost always housed in a primary care setting) to more formalized linkage and referral systems (Badger et al., 1999; Bird et al., 1998).

McCabe and Macnee (2002) found that communities implementing integration plans moved through a series of stages, from parallel behavioral and physical health systems, to overlapping services, and finally to a synthesized system. Bird and colleagues (1998) studied 53 primary care organizations in 22 States and found that four integration models were identified: 1) diversification, 2) linkage, 3) referral and 4) enhancement, with communities typically using a combination of these strategies.

Although a number of viable alternatives exist, linking primary care and mental health care in rural areas remains difficult. A persistent problem is that primary care and mental health providers differ in terms of their patients, reimbursement and treatment philosophies (Lambert & Hartley, 1998). Additionally, primary care and mental health professionals may have long-standing modes of communication that are not advantageous to integrated care models. For instance, PCPs may be accustomed to consults at a distance (e.g., telephone), and they may receive little information back when referring out to mental health specialists. In part, this ineffective feedback loop is due to historical concerns regarding the balance between confidentiality and treatment partnerships (Little et al., 1998). In theory, integrated models are applauded by both the behavioral and physical health sectors, while in practice there are a multitude of details that must be worked through as communities forge innovative treatment partnerships.

Among the 53 successfully linked (i.e., integrated) programs Lambert and Hartley (1998) identified nationally, efforts ranged from small, local projects to sophisticated multi-county networks. The authors found that organizations cooperate with each other when it is in their self-interest and that motivation to integrate cannot be mandated. To overcome natural avoidance of change, community champions will need to identify and market the value-add that integrated models hold for all involved service sectors.

An essential element of outreach and marketing will be the clear message that integrated services are either cost neutral or, in the best case scenarios, lead to cost savings. At the same time, cost benefits will not be sufficient (Lambert & Hartley, 1998). There are inherent disadvantages to integrated care that must be addressed. For example, benefits to mental health consumers and cost savings may lead to individual organizations losing some autonomy. Also, sites may no longer enjoy the same levels of independence regarding budgets and accountability.

The Linkages Project is an example of a demonstration project that addresses many integration issues. The project trained psychologists and family physicians for collaborative practice and also focused on cultural differences between professional practices; differences between medical specialties and strategies for success, such as practice styles and issues, confidentiality and sharing patient records between the professions, stereotypes and emotional factors that impede collaborative practice, linkage and referrals, financial arrangements, methods for developing collaborative practice and nontraditional mental health practice (Bray et al., 1997).

Another study looked at the results of placing 28 mental health staff in general rural health care settings (Van Hook & Ford, 1998). The study found that benefits of the model included increased access and coordination and promotion of an integrated vision of health care. Barriers were also apparent. The partnering organizations needed to surmount space limitations, differences among health disciplines and administrative logistical problems. These and other studies of integrated care models will be instructive as communities tackle rural service delivery concerns such as healthcare professional shortages and the prevalence of mental health issues seen in primary care settings.

Safety Net Providers in Rural Areas

Various provider types (i.e., public hospitals and Community Health Centers) are often mentioned when discussing safety net providers. These two providers are responsible for a large portion of the safety net care in underserved communities (Hartley & Gale, 2003). The Community Mental Health Centers Act of 1963 provided Federal funding to develop satellite clinics in rural or remote areas (Geller et al., 1997). The number of these clinics has declined since 1981 due to shifts in government funding and with the growth of managed care systems (Geller et al., 1997).

Rural hospitals are more likely to be government-owned than urban hospitals (Mohr et al., 1999). Other differences exist between rural and urban hospitals. According to the Medicare Payment Advisory Committee (2001), rural hospitals, in general, have a lower Medicare inpatient margin (4.1 percent in 1999) when compared to urban hospitals (13.5 percent). Rural hospitals tend to be more dependent on Medicare and have a smaller percentage of patients who pay with private insurance (Medicare Payment Advisory Committee, 2001). Although urban hospitals have a large, publicly-funded patient base, they have a larger tax-base and have more clinicians to deliver the care (Hartley & Gale, 2003).

Federally Qualified Health Centers (FQHCs) are another type of safety net provider. According to Farley and colleagues (2002), as of 1998, 42 percent of the 1,890 FQHCs were located in rural counties.

A third type of safety net provider is public mental health departments. However, certain specialty services (e.g., prenatal care and HIV/AIDS treatment) are often not available in rural areas (Hartley & Gale, 2003; Ricketts, Slifkin & Silberman, 1998).

The Federal Government has established providers designed specifically for rural areas, including Rural Health Clinics (RHC) and Critical Access Hospitals (CAH) (Hartley & Gale, 2003). RHCs were created in 1977 to help recruit medical practitioners to rural communities (Gale & Coburn, 2003). RHCs are mandated to serve Medicaid patients but are not obligated to serve all uninsured patients (Hartley & Gale, 2003). CAHs were created by the Medicare Rural Hospital Flexibility Act (1997), which allows hospitals in rural areas to offer more acute inpatient services. A CAH facility must meet the following criteria: 1) be located in a State that has an approved rural health plan; 2) be located in a rural area more than a 35-mile drive from any other hospital or CAH (15 miles in mountainous terrain or in areas with only secondary roads) and 3) maintain an average acute care length of stay of 96 hours or less; limit their bed size to 25 acute care beds (Hagopian & Hart, 2001).

Programs Supporting Rural Health Care

Hartley and Gale (2003) delineate several Federal programs that support the delivery of health care services in rural areas.

1. **The National Health Service Corps (NHSC)** provides for assignments of Federally employed and/or service-obligated physicians, dentists and other health professionals. The program provides scholarship and loan repayments to health professionals who

agree to serve in the NHSC in Health Professions Shortage Areas (HPSAs).[3]

2. **The Area Health Education Center Program** addresses the maldistribution of health professionals in medically underserved areas by linking communities with academic health centers to promote cooperative solutions to local health problems.[4]

3. 3. **The Rural Health Clinics Program** provides enhanced Medicare and Medicaid reimbursement for services provided by physicians, physician assistants, nurse practitioners, certified nurse midwives, clinical social workers and clinical psychologists practicing in clinics in rural HPSAs, Medical Underserved Areas (MUAs), or Governor Designated Shortage Areas (GDSAs).[5]

4. **Medicare Incentive Payment for Physician Services Furnished in HPSAs** gives a 10 percent bonus payment to physicians providing Medicare-reimbursable services within geographic HPSAs.[6]

5. **Medicare Reimbursement for Teleconsultations** are provided for teleconsultations originating in nonmetropolitan counties or primary care geographic HPSAs in metropolitan areas.[7]

6. **Public Health Service Grant Programs** support innovations and targeted expansions in health professions, education and training. They emphasize increasing the diversity of the health care workforce and preparing providers to serve diverse populations and to practice in the Nation's 3,000 medically underserved communities.[8]

7. **Community Health Center** grant funds support the development and operation of health centers that provide preventive and primary health

8. services to medically underserved areas or populations. Priorities are focused on providing services in the most medically underserved areas and maintaining existing centers that are serving high-priority populations.[9]

9. **Federally Qualified Health Centers (FQHCs)** qualify systems of care as FQHCs, if they meet the definition of a community health

---

[3] http://nhsc.bhpr.hrsa.gov
[4] http://bhpr.hrsa.gov/ahec/
[5] http://www.cms.hhs.gov/manuals/27_rhc/rh00.asp
[6] http://www.cms.hhs.gov/manuals/pm_trans/r788ho.pdf
[7] http://www.cms.hhs.gov/manuals/pm_trans/r1885A3.pdf
[8] http://bhpr.hrsa.gov/Grants/Default.htm
[9] http://cfda.gov/static/93224.htm

center contained in Section 330 of the Public Health Service Act, but are not funded under that section, and are serving a designated MUA or MUP. This designation provides cost-based reimbursement of services to qualifying facilities.[10]

10. **J-1 Visa Waiver Program** allows graduates of foreign medical schools to obtain a waiver of the J-1 visa "home-residence" requirement, in return for providing primary care or general mental health care in Federally designated rural and urban communities that have shortages of primary care physicians or psychiatrists.[11]

Summary

Models of mental health care have predominantly been designed in urban locales in coordination with academic centers. The dissemination of these models to rural communities may be a mismatch in terms of resource allocation and culture. It is critical that rural mental health administrators and decision makers not only explore workforce development but the structure in which mental health services are embedded. Some mental health systems are successfully leveraging their resources by coordinating care with other service sectors, such as the schools and primary care, as well as natural systems of supports (e.g., faith-based and philanthropic organizations). The thoughtful linkage of service systems may increase service access to rural residents, while also acknowledging cultural norms leading persons to seek services outside of a traditional CMHC structure. Rural service delivery advances are challenging, but the available literature suggests that communities do have pragmatic options.

References

Amundson, B. (2001). "America's rural communities as crucibles for clinical reform: Establishing collaborative care teams in rural communities." Families, Systems & Health 19(1): 13- 23.

---

[10] http://www.bphc.hrsa.gov/CHC/CHCIntitiatives/fqhc_lookalike.asp

[11] http://www.globalhealth.gov/waiverannouncements.html

Badger, L., Robinson, H. et al. (1999). "Management of mental disorders in rural primary care: A proposal for integrated psychosocial services." Journal of Family Practice 48(10): 813-818.

Bird, D. Lambert, D., et al. (1998). "Rural models for integrating primary care and mental health services." Administration & Policy in Mental Health 25(3): 287-308.

Bray, J. H., Enright, M.F., et al. (1997). Collaboration with primary care physicians. Practicing psychology in rural settings: Hospital privileges and collaborative care. J. A. Morris. Washington, DC, American Psychological Association: 55-65.

Chandler, D., Meisel, J., et al. (1996). "Client outcomes in a three-year controlled study of an integrated service agency model." Psychiatric Services 47(12): 1337-1343.

Farrell, S. P., Blank, M., et al. (1999). "Predicting whether patients receive continuity of care after discharge from State hospitals: Policy implications." Archives of Psychiatric Nursing 13(6): 279-285.

Fekete, D.M., Bond, G.R., McDonel, E.C., Salyers, M., Chen, A., Miller, L. (1998). Rural assertive community treatment: A field experiment. Psychiatric Rehabilitation Journal, 21, 371- 379.

Gale, J. A. and Deprez, R.D., (2003). A public health approach to the challenges of rural mental health service integration. Rural behavioral health care: An interdisciplinary guide. B. H. Stamm. Washington, D.C., American Psychological Association: 95-108.

Gale J & Coburn A. *The characteristics and roles of Rural Health Clinics in the United States: A chartbook.* Portland: University of Southern Maine, Edmund S. Muskie School of Public Service, Institute for Health Policy, Maine Rural Health Research Center; 2003. Available at: http://muskie.usm.maine.edu/Publications/rural/RHChartboo k03.pdf.

Gamm, L., Tai-Seale, M. & Stone, S. (2002). White paper: Meeting the mental health needs of people living in rural areas. College Station, TX, Department of Health Policy and Management, School of Rural Public Health, Texas A&M University System Health Science Center.

Geller, J., Beeson, P., and Rodenhiser, R. , (1997). Frontier mental health strategies: Integrating, reaching out, building up and connecting. Letter to the Field No. 6. Frontier Mental Health Services Resource Network.

Hagopian A, Hart G. Rural Hospital Flexibility Program Tracking Project. Seattle: WWAMI Rural Health Research Center, University of Washington; 2002. Chapter 1: Introduction to the Rural Hospital

Flexibility Program Year 1 Report. Available at: http://www.rupri.org/rhfp track/year1/chapter1.html. Accessed May 7, 2003.

Hargrove, D. S. and Keller, P. A. (1997). Collaboration with community mental health centers. Practicing psychology in rural settings: Hospital privileges and collaborative care. J. A. Morris. Washington, D.C., American Psychological Association: 67-80.

Hartley, D. & Gale, J. (2003). Rural Health Care Safety Nets. In Weinick, Robin M. and John Billings, Eds. *Monitoring the Health Care Safety Net. Book III: Tools for Monitoring the Health Care Safety Net.* (AHRQ Pub. No. 03-0027). Rockville, MD: Agency for Healthcare Research and Quality.

Kane, C. F. and Ennis, J. M., (1996). "Health care reform and rural mental health: Severe mental illness." Community Mental Health Journal 32(5): 445-462.

Lachance, K. R., Deci, P. A., Santos, A. B. & Halewood, N. (1996). Rural assertive community treatment: Taking mental health services on the road. Innovative services for difficult to treat populations. Washington, D.C., American Psychiatric Press: 279-294.

Lachance, K.R., Santos, A.B. (1995). Modifying the PACT model: Preserving critical elements. Psychiatric Services, 46, 601-604.

Lambert, D. and Hartley, D., (1998). "Linking primary care and rural psychiatry: Where have we been and where are we going?" Psychiatric Services 49(7): 965-966.

Little, D. N., Hammond, C., et al. (1998). "Referrals for depression by primary care physicians: A pilot study." Journal of Family Practice 47(5): 375-377.

McCabe, S. and Macnee, C. L., (2002). "Weaving a new safety net of mental health care in rural America: a model of integrated practice." Issues in Mental Health Nursing. 23(3): 263-78.

McDonel, E. C., Bond, G. R., Salyers, M., et al., (1997). "Implementing assertive community treatment programs in rural settings." Administration and Policy in Mental Health 25(2): 153-173.

McGrew, J.H., Pescosolido, B. & Wright, E. (2003). Case managers' perspectives on critical ingredients of assertive community treatment and on its implementation. Psychiatric Services, 54(3), 370-376.

Mohatt, D. F. (2000). "Access to mental health services in frontier areas." Journal of The Washington Academy of Sciences 86(3): 35-48.

Motes, P. S., Melton, G., et al. (1999). "Ecologically oriented school-based mental health services: Implications for service system reform." Psychology in the Schools 36(5): 391-401.

Mulder, P. L., Linkey, H., et al. (2003). Needs assessment, identification and mobilization of community resources, and conflict management. Rural behavioral health care: An interdisciplinary guide. B. H. Stamm. Washington, D.C., American Psychological Association: 67-79.

Ricketts T, Slifkin R, Silberman P. *The Changing Market, Managed Care and the Future Viability of Safety Net Providers—Special Issues for Rural Providers*. Background Paper for the Institute of Medicine. Chapel Hill: Cecil G. Sheps Center for Health Services Research, University of North Carolina at Chapel Hill; 1998.

Rohland, B. M., Rohrer, J. E. et al., (1998). "Broker model of case management for persons with serious mental illness in rural areas." Administration & Policy in Mental Health 25(5): 549-553.

Santos, A.B., Deci, P.A., Lachance, K.R., et al. (1993). Providing assertive community treatment for severely mentally ill patients in a rural area. *Hospital and Community Psychiatry, 44*, 34-39.

Sears, S. F., Evans, G. D. , et al. (2003). Rural social service systems as behavioral health delivery systems. Rural behavioral health care: An interdisciplinary guide. B. H. Stamm. Washington, D.C., American Psychological Association: 109-120.

Shelton, D. A. and R. Frank (1995). "Rural mental health coverage under health care reform." Community Mental Health Journal 31(6): 539-552.

Van Hook, M. P. and Ford, M. E., (1998). "The linkage model for delivering mental health services in rural communities." Health & Social Work 23(1): 53-60.

Weist, M. D., Myers, C., et al. (2000). "Expanded school mental health services: Assessing needs related to school level and geography." Community Mental Health Journal 36(3): 259- 273.

5. WORKFORCE DEVELOPMENT

The Scope and Nature of Workforce Shortages in Rural America

Mental health workforce shortages have been a fact of life in rural America for decades (Flax, Wagenfeld, Ive & Weiss, 1979; Murray & Keller, 1991). For instance, consider these statistics identified from the President's *New Freedom Commission on Mental Health, Subcommittee on Rural Issues* report:

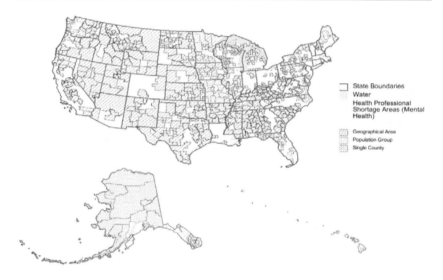

Map 1. Mental Health Professional Shortage Areas (generated at http://datawarehouse.hrsa.gov/).

- More than 85 percent of 1,669 Federally designated mental health professional shortage areas are rural (Bird, Dempsey & Hartley, 2001).
- Holzer and colleagues (2000) found that few psychiatrists, psychologists, or clinical social workers practice in rural counties and that the ratio of these providers to the population worsens as rurality increases.
- For the past 40 years, approximately 60 percent of rural America has been underserved by mental health professions.
- The National Advisory Committee on Rural Health (1993) noted that across the 3,075 counties in the United States, 55 percent had no practicing psychiatrists, psychologists, or social workers, and *all* of these counties were rural.
- These workforce shortages are even worse for specialty areas, such as children's mental health, older adult mental health and minority mental health.

The report goes on to describe factors that have impeded workforce development, which generally included an intricate mix of training, professional, organizational and regulatory issues. (For more details, see the report at http://www.mentalhealthcommission.gov/papers/ Rural.pdf).

Bird, Dempsey and Hartley (2001) offer other data that buttresses these statistics. For instance, the lack of mental health professionals is likely a key factor in explaining differences in access and use of mental health services in rural compared to urban areas. Additionally, it is difficult to translate methods for estimating workforce adequacy from health to mental health, as the mental health workforce is characterized by a considerable overlapping of roles. The authors suggest that baseline data on the reality of the mental health workforce in rural areas are needed in order to make adequate projections and/or comparisons. They encourage national and State mental health professional associations to participate in the collection, verification, and analysis of workforce data. State Medicaid agencies are also viewed as a potential resource for workforce data.

In a National Health Policy Forum (NHPF) Issue Brief, Koppelman (2004) describes the shortage of qualified providers to address children's mental disorders, possible causes, the relationship of managed care to practice patterns and difficulties deciding which providers are most qualified to deliver what care. In brief, she identifies issues similar to what has been discussed. For instance, the mental health workforce is described as "in flux," with practice boundaries between psychiatrists, psychologists, counselors and other mental health professionals becoming increasingly blurry to consumers and payers. Some of these professions are described as redefining their roles, which makes it difficult to determine how many more mental health professionals are needed to boost supply.

Furthermore, different mental health disciplines require different levels of training, have different areas of expertise and have different salaries (Koppelman, 2004). Indeed, money is noted to be a fundamental issue regarding the development of an adequate workforce. Education is expensive, health plans favor lower-paid providers and mental health professionals in the public system often get paid less.

The Western InterState Commission for Higher Education (WICHE) Mental Health Program analyzed data (from http://higheredinfo.org/) regarding population projections from 2000 to 2025 for its 15 member States (Alaska, Arizona, California, Colorado, Hawaii, Idaho, Montana, Nevada, North Dakota, New Mexico, Oregon, South Dakota, Utah, Washington and Wyoming). If these projections are accurate, only four States—Alaska, California, Hawaii and New Mexico—will have more people entering or in the workforce than leaving it.

Specifically, the 15-WICHE member States will average an 18 percent increase in persons age 18 to 64 (range of 1.4 percent in North Dakota to 37.8 percent in Hawaii) between 2000 and 2025. However, in the same time period, these States will average a 122 percent increase in those entering their retirement years (i.e., 65 years and older) (range of 72.6 percent in South Dakota to 159.7 percent in Utah).

While this is by no means an exhaustive list of issues that define the workforce shortage problem in rural America, one can get a good sense of its scope. Problems such as these will not be solved immediately, but work to address them is underway.

Policy Options & Goals for Rural Workforce Development

Three policy options regarding workforce development in rural America are offered in the *New Freedom Commission*, rural subcommittee report:

- "Policy Option 8: The Secretary of HHS is urged to convene a cross-agency work group to examine existing workforce enhancement programs and make recommendations for ensuring and enhancing their collaborative focus on rural mental health needs" (p. 10).
- "Policy Option 9: The Subcommittee encourages the Secretary of HHS to support an effort to articulate a rural mental health workforce strategy that includes a realistic use of and support of mid-level and alternative providers of mental health services" (p. 11).
- "Policy Option 10: The Subcommittee proposes that the Administrator of SAMHSA ensure the support of programs that specifically support the training, deployment and continuing education of rural mental health professionals. Such support might focus on strengthening the capacity and competency of the workforce to support an evidence-based practice care delivery system" (p. 11).

Furthermore, three specific goals in the final report to the President directly addressed workforce issues, especially for rural America. These included:

GOAL 3 Disparities in Mental Health Services Are Eliminated:

- 3.2 Improve access to quality care in rural and geographically remote areas.

GOAL 5 Excellent Mental Health Care Is Delivered and Research Is Accelerated:

- 5.3 Improve and expand the workforce providing evidence-based mental health services and supports.

GOAL 6 Technology Is Used to Access Mental Health Care and Information:

- 6.1 Use health technology and telehealth to improve access and coordination of mental health care, especially for Americans in remote areas or in underserved populations.

Additionally, consistent with the six goals of transforming the mental health system established by the President's *New Freedom Commission on Mental Health*, SAMHSA's Action Plan for Mental Health Systems Transformation includes as key activities in 2005 the creation and implementation of a National Strategic Workforce Development Plan.

Bird, Dempsey and Hartley (2001) make these recommendations:

1. The National Health Service Corps (NHSC) should allocate resources specifically reserved for mental health workforce development to State loan repayment programs;
2. Managed care and managed behavioral health organizations should experiment with ways of offering limited behavioral health credentials to primary care practitioners, especially in rural areas;
3. Credentialing standards should reflect the realities of rural service delivery by recognizing the important contributions of non-physical mental health professionals at all levels (Bachelors and Masters) and
4. CHCs, RHCs, and CMHCs should make judicious use of non-professional and paraprofessional mental health workers, especially for outreach and prevention activities.

Rural Mental Health Workforce Development Efforts

A number of organizations, agencies and entities have been undertaking workforce development efforts for the past several years. Among these are SAMHSA, HRSA, the National Center for Health Workforce Information and

Analysis (a part of HRSA's Bureau of Health Professions), the Annapolis Coalition on Behavioral Health Workforce Education, the Western InterState Commission for Higher Education Mental Health Program, the National Association for Rural Mental Health (NARMH), Edmund S. Muskie School of Public Service, the MacArthur Foundation, the Criminal Justice/Mental Health Consensus Project, the Council on Graduate Medical Education (COGME), the Quentin N. Burdick Rural Health Interdisciplinary Program, as well as the Child Healthcare Crisis Relief Act (H.R. 1359, 2003). Each of these organizations or legislative initiatives will be discussed in turn.

Substance Abuse and Mental Health Services Administration (SAMHSA): Some of the efforts of SAMHSA have been documented above. However, Bird, Dempsey and Hartley (2001) point out that the Center for Mental Health Services (CMHS) in SAMSHA currently administers most of the programs relevant to mental health workforce development and the mental health needs of underserved rural communities. For instance, in partnership with the Annapolis Coalition, SAMHSA has launched a new "Science to Service Agenda" initiative to promote best practices in mental health care (Koppelman, 2004). The initiative includes ongoing development of a national registry of effective programs and practices in mental health and substance abuse. So far, 150 programs are listed (see www.modelprograms.samhsa.gov). SAMHSA is also offering a range of grants to help public mental health systems implement evidence-based practice and develop the most effective ways to reduce service gaps.

Health Resources and Services Administration (HRSA): HRSA directs programs that improve the Nation's health by expanding access to comprehensive, quality health care for all Americans. HRSA works to train a health workforce that is both diverse and motivated to work in underserved communities by offering a number of funding mechanisms for health professions training. Two other major programs are the National Center for Health Workforce Information and Analysis and the National Health Services Corps (NHSC), which are described below.

National Center for Health Workforce Information and Analysis: Provides access to in-depth profiles regarding the supply, demand, distribution, education and use of health personnel. Estimated numbers of workers indicate the size of the State's health workforce. Per capita ratios facilitate comparisons with other States and the Nation. Each Profile has three sections: 1) a brief overview of residents' health status and health services that influence supply of and demand for health workers, 2) health care employment by place of work, including hospitals, nursing homes and other settings and 3) health care employment in more than 25 health professions and occupations, including mental health (see http://bhpr.hrsa.gov/healthworkforce/reports/profiles/).

National Health Service Corps (NHSC): Committed to improving the health of the Nation's underserved by uniting communities in need with caring health professionals supporting communities' efforts to build better systems of care, the NHSC provides comprehensive team-based health care that bridges geographic, financial, cultural and language barriers. The NHSC forms partnerships with communities, States, educational institutions and professional organizations; recruits caring, culturally competent clinicians for communities in need; provides opportunities and professional experiences to students through scholarship and loan repayment programs and a SEARCH (Student/Resident Experiences and Rotations in Community Health) program; establishes systems of care that remain long after an NHSC clinician departs, and shapes the way clinicians practice by building a community of dedicated health professionals who continue to work with the underserved even after their NHSC commitment has been fulfilled (see http://nhsc.bhpr.hrsa.gov/).

The Annapolis Coalition on Behavioral Health Workforce Education: The Coalition, which receives SAMHSA funding, was founded by the American College of Mental Health Administration, a multidisciplinary body, and the Academic Behavioral Health Consortium, a nonprofit group comprised of university departments of psychiatry. In 2003, the Coalition recommended to the President's *New Freedom Commission on Mental Health* that the Federal government use a number of strategies to improve the behavioral health workforce; including instituting policies in Federally funded health plans to promote appropriately prepared and supervised trainees. As noted earlier, they are also involved in SAMHSA's "Science to Service Agenda." They currently have a number of position papers regarding children's workforce issues, evidence-based teaching strategies, innovation in workforce education, behavioral health competencies (development & assessment) and best practices in workforce education (see http://www.annapoliscoalition.org/position_papers.php or http://www.annapoliscoalition.org/index.php).

The Western InterState Commission for Higher Education (WICHE) Mental Health Program: The Mental Health Program at WICHE was established in 1955 by the Western Regional Council of State Governments. It is governed by the Mental Health Oversight Council (MHOC), composed of the State mental health directors from the 15 WICHE States, plus special advisors and WICHE Commissioners. The mission of the program is twofold: 1) to assist States in improving systems of care for mental health consumers and their families and 2) to advance the preparation of a qualified mental health workforce in the West. The program collaborates with States to meet the challenges of changing environments through regional research and evaluation, policy analysis, program development, technical assistance and information sharing.

During 2004, the Mental Health Program worked with the University of Alaska (UA) system and the Alaska Division of Behavioral Health in a strategic planning effort to enhance collaboration between higher education and the public mental health system. This work evolved from existing efforts in Alaska, which were further focused by a WICHE Mental Health Program sponsored policy roundtable on rural mental health workforce issues held in Reno, Nevada in September 2003.

The Alaska work resulted in the creation of shared goals among the Division of Behavioral Health and University of Alaska system, as well as funding to achieve them. The goals fell into four categories (collaboration, education, funding and research & evaluation) and among them were:

1. Develop a behavioral health workforce vision and action plan;
2. Create collaborations to develop more rural-specific training and continuing education opportunities at all levels of competency;
3. Explore how UA should respond to the integration of mental health and substance abuse disciplines;
4. Support innovative approaches using distance education to expand access to continuing education that enables rural persons to obtain professional training;
5. Support the development of an articulated career pathway from paraprofessional through postgraduate training;
6. Offer financial incentives for graduates to return to or remain in Alaska to practice in rural and underserved areas;
7. Collect and analyze more data regarding articulation of coursework and training among UA behavioral health programs, as well as workforce needs;
8. Analyze factors that increase enrollments and declared majors, as well as factors that promote retention and degree completion.

WICHE is currently working on a project similar to Alaska's in Arizona.

In South Dakota and Wyoming, the Mental Health Program is actively engaged in training initiatives for community mental health staff to promote a shift to integrated care for children with serious emotional disturbances.

In Idaho, the WICHE Mental Health Program provided training to primary care providers on behavioral health care. Like in Alaska, the Mental Health Program is working with the Division of Mental Health to enhance collaboration between higher education and the public mental health system to ensure an adequate workforce.

National Association for Rural Mental Health (NARMH): The Center for Mental Health Services, Substance Abuse and Mental Health Services Administration (CMHS, SAMSHA) is currently collaborating with NARMH to review successful rural mental health outreach practices. It should be noted that some rural programs have developed innovative outreach efforts; however, more outreach approaches are still necessary. The most important finding that surfaced by the CMHS, SAMSHA and NARMH workgroup was the successful outreach efforts targeting the needs of consumers as defined by them (the consumers) and that the services are situated in the context of that community (Lambert et al., 2001).

Maine Rural Health Research Center (Edmund S. Muskie School of Public Service): Established in 1992, the Maine Rural Health Research Center (MRHC) draws on the multidisciplinary faculty and research resources and capacity of the Institute for Health Policy within the Edmund S. Muskie School of Public Service, University of Southern Maine. Rural health is one of the primary areas of research and policy analysis focus within the Institute for Health Policy. The Center builds upon the Institute's strong record of research, policy analysis and policy development that addresses critical problems in health care financing and delivery.

The MRHC's mission is to inform health care policymaking and the delivery of rural health services through high quality, policy relevant research, policy analysis and technical assistance on rural health issues of regional and National significance. The Center is committed to enhancing policymaking and improving the delivery and financing of rural health services by effectively linking its research to the policy development process through appropriate dissemination strategies. The Center builds upon a strong record of rural health services research that addresses critical problems in health care financing and delivery and which capitalizes on the health services research and health policy capacity and experience of the University of Southern Maine's Muskie School of Public Service.

Recent publications from MHRC regarding rural mental health workforce address such topics as the role of advanced practice psychiatric nurses (2004), CMHCs as rural safety nets (2002) and the impact of State licensure laws on workforce (2002) (see http://muskie.usm.maine.edu/ihp/ruralhealth/ papers.jsp for more; see also http://muskie.usm.maine.edu/ihp/ruralhealth/ for more information on MRHC's other activities).

MacArthur Foundation: The MacArthur Foundation is funding a major effort, the Network on Youth Mental Health, which is reviewing the evidence for therapies to treat the most common childhood disorders and testing methods of delivering evidence-based practices in community mental health centers. The initiative is also studying organizational and payment policies that discourage providers from practicing evidence-based care and will use this knowledge to develop ways to share evidence-based practices with a variety of clinics and providers (Koppelman, 2004).

Criminal Justice/Mental Health Consensus Project: As described at their Web site (http://www.consensusproject.org/about-theproject/history_methodology_ab), the Council of State Governments (CSG) developed the Criminal Justice/Mental Health Consensus Project in response to requests from State government officials for recommendations to improve the criminal justice system's response to people with mental illness. Among the reasons for the undertaking were tragedies involving people with mental illness that seemingly could have been prevented and the enormous strain on criminal justice and State budget resources resulting from the current approach to responding to people with mental illness.

CSG partnered with six organizations: 1) the Police Executive Research Forum (PERF), 2) the Pretrial Services Resource Center (PSRC), 3) the Association of State Correctional Administrators (ASCA), 4) the National Association of State Mental Health Program Directors (NASMHPD), 5) the Bazelon Center for Mental Health Law and 6) the Center for Behavioral Health, Justice and Public Policy. Together, staff from these organizations formed the *Consensus Project* Steering Committee, which two legislators (Rep. Mike Lawlor of Connecticut and Sen. Robert Thompson of Pennsylvania) co-chaired. The Steering Committee designed an 18-month initiative to build on the ideas developed during the first two working group meetings, to broaden the support base for these recommendations, and to identify efforts in jurisdictions across the country that could help inform the implementation of the recommendations.

Their recommendations include:

1. Plan to increase the supply of skilled and experienced mental health providers;
2. Promote the employment of current and former clients in the provision of mental health services;

3. Provide training that specifically addresses the consumer and family experience of mental illness and
4. Plan to increase the supply of skilled and experienced mental health providers in rural areas.

Quentin N. Burdick Rural Health Interdisciplinary Program: The goal of this program is to provide or improve access to health care in rural areas. Specifically, projects funded under this authority shall be designed to: 1) use new and innovative methods to train health care practitioners to provide services in rural areas; 2) demonstrate and evaluate innovative interdisciplinary methods and models designed to provide access to cost-effective comprehensive health care; 3) deliver health care services to individuals residing in rural areas, 4) enhance the amount of relevant research conducted concerning health care issues in rural areas and 5) increase the recruitment and retention of health care practitioners from rural areas and make rural practice a more attractive career choice for health care practitioners. The program provides about $5 to 6.5 million a year in support to demonstration programs that offer interdisciplinary learning experiences for clinicians in training and practice (see http://bhpr.hrsa.gov/interdisciplinary/rural.html for more information).

The Child Healthcare Crisis Relief Act (H.R. 1359, 2003): In March 2003, Rep. Patrick Kennedy (D-RI) introduced H.R. 1359, which would use educational incentives to lure more students into the children's mental health professions. The bill would extend Medicare graduate medical education funding to child psychiatry training programs and create a loan forgiveness program for child and adolescent psychiatrists. The bill would also offer scholarships and loan forgiveness to bolster the numbers of school psychologists and social workers, school counselors and psychiatric nurses (Koppelman, 2004). Taken together, these organizations, agencies and initiatives are making significant strides in addressing strategies to ensure an available and competent rural mental health workforce.

Summary

The troubling reality of mental health workforce shortages in rural America is well-documented and has persisted for decades. However, it is significant that the *New Freedom Commission, Subcommittee on Rural Issues* report has been one of the first to be released. Indeed, as of this writing, only four of 16 subcommittee reports have been released thus far. Rural America and issues facing rural residents are "back on the map." Moreover, a solid number of organizations, government agencies, advocacy groups and policy initiatives have taken up the call to ensure that workforce shortages will become not a fact of the present, but one of history.

References

Bird, D. C., Dempsey, P. & Hartley, D. (2001). *Addressing mental health workforce needs in underserved rural areas: Accomplishments and challenges.* Portland, ME: Maine Rural Health Research Center, Muskie Institute, University of Southern Maine.

Flax, J. W., Wagenfeld, M. O., Ive, R. E. & Weiss, R. J. (Eds.). (1979). *Mental health and rural America: An overview and annotated bibliography* (DHEW Publication No. 78-753rd ed.). Washington, DC: U.S. Government Printing Office.

Holzer, C.E. III, Goldsmith, H. F. & Ciarlo, J.A. (2000). The availability of health and mental health providers by population density. *Journal of the Washington Academy of Sciences, 86*(3), 25-33.

Koppelman, J. (2004). The provider system for children's mental health: Workforce capacity and effective treatment. NHPF Issue Brief No. 801, National Health Policy Forum, George Washington University. Washington, D.C.

Murray, J. D. & Keller, P.A. (1991). Psychology and rural America. *American Psychologist, 46*(3): 220-231.

National Advisory Committee on Rural Health. (1993). *Sixth Annual Report on RuralHhealth.* Rockville, MD: Office of Rural Health Policy, Health Resources and Services Administration, HHS.

New Freedom Commission on Mental Health. *Subcommittee of Rural Issues: Background Paper.* DHHS Pub. No. SMA04-3890. Rockville, MD: 2004.

6. WHERE TO GO FROM HERE: RURAL MENTAL HEALTH IN THE 21ST CENTURY

Information in previous sections presents two basic ideas. First, rural mental health in the 21st century faces significant challenges. Second, these challenges are being more widely recognized and addressed by organizations and agencies at local, State, regional and Federal levels.

The President's *New Freedom Commission on Mental Health* (2003) has provided a vision and framework for mental health care across the country. The Commission's six overarching goals are:

1. Americans understand that mental health is a critical part of overall health;
2. Mental health is consumer and family driven;
3. Disparities in mental health services are eliminated;
4. Early mental health screening, assessment and referral to services are common practice;
5. Excellent mental health care is delivered and research is accelerated; and,
6. Technology is used to access mental health care and information.

Specific to rural issues, three sub-goals are identified:

- Improve access to quality care in rural and geographically remote areas.
- Improve and expand the workforce providing evidence-based mental health services and supports.
- Use health technology and telehealth to improve access and coordination of mental health care, especially for Americans in remote areas or in underserved populations.

Looking to the future of rural mental health care, Sawyer and Beeson (1998), Stated that issues remain consistent and include (but are not limited to): 1) increasing needs and limiting resources; 2) geographic and cultural challenges to service delivery; 3) lack of available staff; 4) urban models applied to rural areas and 5) misunderstanding of rural communities by policy makers.

In creating a strategy to address these problems and improve care, Sawyer and Beeson (1998) propose a "Five Cs" approach: Consumers, Competence, Cost, Communicating and Connecting.

Consumer and family involvement is essential to ameliorating mental health services in rural communities. It is critical to identify consumer and family advocates who can articulate rural mental health needs to policy makers at all levels. Consumers should also be active participants in the planning of mental health services.

Second, it is important to understand that delivering care in rural areas requires a specific set of knowledge, skills and abilities in order to meet the unique needs of rural residents. In addition, best practices and evidence-based practice guidelines need to be identified and applied to the provision of mental health services in rural areas.

Third, rural mental health service providers must accurately estimate actual service delivery costs and operate a mental health system that is efficient and responsive to the target population.

Fourth, rural mental health providers who have successfully implemented innovative programs need to increase their communication about these programs with other providers, as well as policy makers.

Finally, rural mental health providers need to link with other organizations to create a viable and solid network of support. This will help to ensure service sustainability and will present a united front to potential funders. It will be important for rural mental health systems to be mindful of and proactive in increasing the visibility of rural mental health needs.

In a report by the Institute of Medicine (IOM), Wakefield (2004), as one of the authors, outlined a 5- pronged strategy to address unique quality challenges in rural communities, which overlaps with the model just described. In addition to enhancing human resource capacity, ensuring financial stability and integrating services, she recommends a prioritized approach to addressing health needs, establishing quality improvement mechanisms and building an information and communications technology infrastructure.

Taking these models together, one can see connections to the three primary issues facing rural mental health care described earlier: availability, accessibility and acceptability. Bearing these themes in mind, four primary areas of work in rural mental health arise: 1) Education and Training, especially as related to licensing; 2) Clinical Programs and Services; 3) Administration, particularly funding and 4) Research and Evaluation.

It is very difficult to determine which of these areas should take precedence, as they are intricately intertwined. Thus, it seems most appropriate to recommend strategies that, to the extent possible, include parallel, interconnected activities at each level. Short of such an approach, organizations or agencies taking on these tasks must decide for themselves which requires the most immediate or primary attention, as determined by available evidence.

Education and Training

Education and training efforts regarding rural mental health apply to two populations: clinicians and consumers.

Mental health clinicians in rural areas encounter a variety of cultural norms, values and ethics, as well as unique ethical dilemmas. However, at present, most clinicians working in rural areas learn about rural culture "on the job," and then only partially if they commute from more urban settings. The most logical place to acculturate clinicians in rural issues is academic institutions, especially universities in largely rural States. In particular, academic institutions offering specialized training in rural mental health, priority placement for projects with a rural emphasis and providing financial assistance to students either from rural areas or those who have a desire to work in rural communities could help meet workforce needs (Mulder et al., 2000).[12]

Situating some of these educational and training programs in rural communities cannot only help to acculturate students, but also provide them with a larger system of care context in which to understand their training and clinical experiences. Universities or colleges with rural-focused programs can also enter into partnerships with community organizations or agencies in rural areas that offer field training opportunities that include inter- or multidisciplinary experiences with an integrated continuum of services (e.g., collaborations among primary and preventive health care, mental health, substance abuse and social service agencies) (Mulder et al., 2000).

Additionally, all rural mental health academic and training programs should be conducted in a culturally competent manner that recognizes and provides academic and experiential training regarding indigenous and other ethnic groups (NRHA, 1999).

In addition to strengthening clinicians' rural and cultural competency, strategies are needed to increase the number of rural mental health providers. While there have been some attempts to recruit and retain mental health professionals to rural areas, more effective recruitment efforts and incentives must be provided to attract professionals to these mental health professional shortage areas. The National Health Service Corps offers incentives to students in the form of loan repayment in return for service in a professional shortage area. More programs with financial incentives are needed to motivate

---

[12] A listing of psychology training programs and internships with a rural emphasis can be found on the American Psychological Association Web site: http://www.apa.org/rural/.

mental health professionals to specialize in rural mental health. Academic institutions can play a role in outreaching to rural communities to attract applicants. This is particularly true for mid-level and paraprofessional mental health providers, who are likely to become the main group of providers of mental health care in rural areas.

Consumers of mental health services and their families, or persons with mental health problems not currently receiving services, need education about the nature of their difficulties and where to get help. As discussed in previous sections, rural residents tend to enter treatment later in the course of their disorders, usually in States of significant distress. On the one hand, many may not recognize symptoms or signs of mental health problems, or ascribe them to non-mental health causes. Those who do recognize a problem may be hesitant to pursue treatment for fear of stigma or ostracism, or because they are unsure about where and what treatment is available.

Effective educational and outreach campaigns designed for rural residents would go a long way in helping to connect care with those who need it. Organizations such as the National Alliance for the Mentally Ill (NAMI), the Federation of Families for Children's Mental Health (FFCMH), and numerous other State or local agencies (e.g., UPLIFT in Wyoming) have been instrumental in both educating and advocating for consumers and their families.

Although this section has focused on education for clinicians and consumers, it is very important to recognize the significant need for education campaigns regarding mental health and substance abuse problems for the general public. Indeed, as indicated at the beginning of this section, a large public education campaign is the number one goal of the *New Freedom Commission*.

Furthermore, the Center for Mental Health Services in the Substance Abuse and Mental Health Services Administration (CMHS, SAMSHA) collaborated with the National Association of Rural Mental Health (NARMH) to review successful rural mental health outreach practices. Although some rural programs have developed innovative outreach efforts, a wider variety of approaches are still necessary. The most important finding that surfaced by the CMHS, SAMSHA and NARMH work group was that successful outreach efforts target consumers' needs *as defined by consumers*, and that such efforts are situated in that community (Lambert et al., 2001).

The American Psychological Association (APA) has been instrumental in drawing increased attention to rural health issues by the formation of several advocacy groups including the Rural Task Force, the Committee on Rural

Health and the Rural Women's Work Group. These advocacy groups all incorporate similar goals, including disseminating information to members, legislative bodies, consumers, professionals and other relevant agencies (Mulder et al., 2000).

At the annual APA conference, the Rural Health Forum is a valuable place for mental health professionals to dialogue and strategize about the needs of rural communities. Additional efforts can be made with the publication of professional literature in traditional journals or on-line professional journals. In addition, APA has recognized the need for research on rural populations (Mulder et al., 2000).

A major legislative factor that bears on mental health professionals generally, especially in terms of provider mobility, is State licensure. At present, although most States have similar licensure criteria, there are still difficulties for mental health professionals moving from one State to another. As Jonason and colleagues (2003) indicate, local licensing laws have not embraced the reality that an increasing amount of business is conducted across jurisdictional lines, including mental health professions. Psychology, for example, has taken steps to facilitate mobility through InterState reciprocity (Kim & VandeCreek, 2003) with some level of success, but as yet there are no assurances that other States will recognize and grant equal status (Merrill, 2003).

Kim and VandeCreek (2003) describe efforts to facilitate mobility for psychologists. These include:

1. In February of 2001, the Committee for the Advancement of Professional Practice (CAPP) was given formal approval by the American Psychological Association (APA) Council of Representatives to continue with plans for the development of professional mobility mechanisms.
2. The Association of State and Provincial Psychology Boards (ASPPB) and State licensure boards have developed a reciprocity agreement. As of March 2003, 11 States and provinces were participating. Three States are in the process of implementing the reciprocity agreement.
3. ASPPB has also developed an endorsement mechanism to facilitate mobility: the Certificate of Professional Qualification in Psychology (CPQ). As of March 2003, 26 States and provinces had implemented the CPQ, and an additional 14 States and provinces are in the process of implementing it.

4. The National Register of Health Service Providers in Psychology credentials individuals who submit education and training information relevant to licensure. As of February 2003, 10 States and all 11 Canadian jurisdictions had approved the register's credential as a mobility mechanism.
5. The American Board of Professional Psychology (ABPP) awards certification to individuals who demonstrate competency in a specialty area of psychology, and five States accept an individual's certification by this board as a mobility mechanism, typically by waiving one or more licensing board requirements.

Licensure, mobility and reciprocity for healthcare disciplines are made more complex in the age of telemedicine or telehealth, which has been acknowledged by the Federal government. For example, Jonason and colleagues (2003) reported that the Telehealth Improvement Act of 1999 and the Comprehensive Telehealth Act of 1999 created a Joint Working Group charged with compiling data on the number of health care providers performing telehealth services across State lines and tracking efforts to develop uniform national sets of standards for telehealth licensure. The authors indicated that a provision of these legislative proposals is that if States are not making progress in facilitating telehealth services across State lines by eliminating unnecessary requirements and adopting reciprocal licensing arrangements for such services, then the Secretary of Health and Human Services should make recommendations concerning the scope and nature of Federal actions required to do so.

These issues also impact training. As Deleon, Crimmins, and Wolf (2003) observe, professional schools will likely develop innovative distance-learning (i.e., Web-based) oriented degrees or continuing education modules. Thus, these authors argue that "Telehealth compels us to conceive of boundaries in other than geographical terms" and psychology's elected leaders at the State and national association levels will have to address licensure mobility.

Delivering Education & Training

Whether one is targeting rural clinicians, consumers, or the general public, education and training can be difficult for all the reasons noted throughout this chapter (e.g., geographical distance, lack of funding and so forth). However, the use of technology and distance learning programs is beginning to show promise in breaking down these barriers. For example, clinical treatment via telemedicine has been growing for over a decade.

Frontier States, such as Alaska, use distance learning approaches to train Alaska Natives in remote areas.

The WICHE Mental Health Program, through funding from SAMHSA, has been offering a series of live grand rounds webcasts on clinical topics via the internet. In effect, the internet serves as an "E-Classroom" in which speakers and participants can interact in real-time to discuss issues. Presentations can also be stored for later viewing, which helps busy rural providers get needed information as it fits their schedules.

Clinical Programs & Services

One of the most significant trends in mental health generally, as well as, in rural areas is the emphasis on outcome-driven service delivery models. Within the context of connecting science to service, the *New Freedom Commission* identified the need to increase the use of evidence-based practices (EBPs). Evidence-based practice is "an approach to classifying health care outcome research according to the quality and quantity of empirical evidence supporting a particular intervention" (Anthony, Rogers & Farkas, 2003). It has also been defined by the Institute of Medicine as "the integration of best research evidence with clinical expertise and patient values." The mental health community strives to define practices and treatment interventions that have been demonstrated to be effective in clinical services research (Torrey et al., 2001).

At present, there is a significant time delay between scientific discovery and service delivery. The *Commission* recommends the use of EBPs via dissemination and demonstration projects, and developing a public-private partnership to guide this process. This recommendation is buttressed by the recent Institute of Medicine (IOM; 2005) report, which endorses using demonstration projects in rural communities, as such locations are smaller and have unique characteristics.[13] Methods for introducing EBPs into service delivery systems include educating clinicians and consumers about the short- and longterm benefits of EBPs, support and promotion by leadership and reimbursement policies to increase EBP use.

---

[13] The 2005 IOM report takes this recommendation from an earlier IOM report, titled Fostering Rapid Advances in Health Care: Learning from System Demonstrations.

The Commission also recommended that the Federal government create a partnership with private, interested funding, advocacy and professional organizations. Potential funding entities may be more willing to provide financial and other resources if evidence-based practices are explained and proposed. However, it is important to consider the need for clearer understanding regarding the degree to which EBPs generalize to different rural areas.

According to the Office of Rural Health Policy (1997), telepsychiatry is one of the five most common applications for telemedicine in rural hospitals. Technology has the potential to decrease the gap in services by increasing education, support and connectedness between the client and the provider. Telemedicine technology allows for two-way interactive physician/patient interviews to take place across long distances (Graham, 1996). The Internet can potentially provide a viable alternative to traditional office visits for rural residents with mental health issues (Ferrell & McKinnon, 2003).

Telemedicine can also be used for purposes other than therapy including case management, medication management, psychiatric consultations and psychiatric referrals (Rost et al., 2002). Evaluations of provider-patient encounters via interactive two-way video have generally demonstrated that the reliability of psychiatric assessment is comparable to that of face-to-face interviews (Baer et al., 1995; Baer et al., 1997; Baigent et al., 1997; Doniger et al., 1986; Rost et al., 2002; and Zarate et al., 1997).

A study by Graham (1996) found preliminary evidence that telehealth consultations between a psychiatrist and a client diagnosed with serious mental illness decreased the incidence of patient rehospitalization.

Administration

Administrators in mental health agencies are primarily concerned with two issues: 1) delivering high quality, cost-effective services and 2) securing and managing funding or reimbursement for those services.

Service Content and Structure

Delivering high quality, cost-effective care requires attention to service content and structure. Service content refers to the specific kinds of treatments available (e.g., individual or group therapy, residential programs), whereas service structure regards the formal administrative and clinical relationships of providers. As discussed in an earlier section of this section, evidence-based practices are becoming an increasingly important type of treatment. Such treatments are not only based on research indicating their effectiveness, but often involve the use of multiple providers (e.g., Assertive Community Treatment). In this regard, collaborative, inter- or multidisciplinary care is being promoted as a primary form of successful service structures.

A broad framework in which providers, researchers, rural community leaders and policy makers can understand collaborative care is the System of Care model (Dekraai, 2004; Stroul & Friedman, 1986). Although systems of care usually regard services for children and families, the core values and principles can be appropriately applied to adult services. The core values of a system of care are that it is:

1. Child-centered and family-focused (or, in the case of adults, client-centered), with the needs of the child and family (or client) dictating the types and mix of services provided;
2. Community-based, with the locus of services as well as decision-making responsibility resting at the community level and
3. Culturally competent, with agencies, programs and services that are responsive to and respective of the cultural, racial, ethnic, language and value differences of the populations they serve.

The principle components of a System of Care are:

1. Access to an extensive array of services that address physical, emotional, social and educational needs;
2. Individualized treatment that matches the unique needs of clients;
3. Services are provided in the least restrictive, most natural environment;
4. Families and/or main social support are participants in care;
5. Integrated services with linkages to other service agencies for planning, developing and coordinating services;
6. Case management to ensure coordination of services;
7. Early identification and intervention to increase the likelihood of positive outcomes;
8. Ensure smooth transition to other services;
9. Rights of clients should be protected and advocacy efforts should be promoted;
10. Culturally competent and
11. Community-based.

Implementing these principles will increase the likelihood of a seamless system of mental health care. Forming community partnerships and relationships should include funders, service providers, consumers and family members, as well as community and faith-based organizations (Dekraai, 2004). However, it is complex and time consuming to facilitate the creation of relationships between agencies that often have different priorities, policies and funding streams.

In terms of specific relationships among various provider groups, there is solid evidence that many rural residents in need of mental health services are initially seen by primary care physicians (PCPs) or other medical professionals (e.g., nurse practitioners, physician's assistants). If mental health professionals cannot be adequately recruited to rural areas, then PCPs will continue to provide the majority of mental health care. Thus, training that increases PCPs skills in identifying signs and symptoms of mental health and/or substance abuse problems is very important.

Increased collaboration between mental health providers and primary health providers would improve efficiency and effectiveness when providing mental health treatment or streamlining referral processes. To help promote collaboration between these provider groups, interdisciplinary training programs should be developed and supported (National Rural Health Association [NRHA], 1999). For example, several programs run through the Health Resources and Services Administration (HRSA) may provide avenues for interdisciplinary training, including the Quentin N. Burdick Rural Interdisciplinary Training Grant Program, Area Health Education Centers and Geriatric Education Centers.

Due to the high prevalence of substance use by people with serious mental illness, the NRHA (1999) suggested that programs provide simultaneous mental health and addiction treatment to rural residents with co-occurring disorders. The *New Freedom Commission, Subcommittee on Rural Issues* (2004) added that these services need to be linked to primary care settings, where most rural persons turn for assistance. Services can be more efficient if they are streamlined and integrated.

A curriculum for a community-based rural model of training has been published by the American Psychological Association (APA) (1995). Federal and State grants are needed to develop rural mental health services systems through such community-oriented training (NRHA, 1999). Although there are logistical issues in implementing collaborative training (e.g., different disciplines, funding and other resources), cross-training would ultimately foster collaborative relationships between these two groups.

Another potentially effective service structure is the use of telemedicine. Due to the geographical isolation of many rural communities, telehealth strategies may help address transportation and distance barriers faced by rural residents. If transportation services are offered by agencies, they consume part of the budget not incurred by urban services. While research has shown telemedicine's positive impact on access to mental health services (NFC-SRI, 2004), further research is necessary to demonstrate its effectiveness with rural mental health issues. The results of this research can then be used to advocate for increased funding and equipment for rural area service providers. Telehealth cannot only provide increased access for patients requiring care, but also for mental health professionals who may feel isolated in rural areas.

Despite the potential value of telemedicine technology, there are barriers to the successful integration of these advances from an administrative perspective. Graham (1996) detailed some of these obstacles, which include 1) initial and continuing operating costs of technology, 2) professional issues that require the field to reframe the doctor-patient relationship and 3) legal and confidentiality issues. Furthermore, census data indicate that Americans' access to usage of the internet varies greatly depending on socioeconomic level. Urban residents are more than two times as likely to have internet access as those in rural areas at the same lower income levels (Ferrell & McKinnon, 2003).

Funding

Mohatt, LaLumia and Yennie (2004) indicate that before the rural mental health system can be expected to improve, there needs to be an examination of the larger mental health system. In terms of current governance issues present in the United States' mental health system, they report that the major entities providing mental health care (e.g., State psychiatric hospitals, community-based general hospitals, community mental health centers) routinely lack any fiscal or management integration and often operate in virtual isolation from each other. The result is non-shared accountability for ensuring access to care, discontinuity of care, and/or poor use of limited fiscal and human resources. In other words, the system is "complex, confusing, and fragmented" (New Freedom Commission on Mental Health, 2003).

As a part of reform efforts, two strategies have been commonly employed to address the lack of access and integration in mental health systems: 1) developing a single funding envelope that integrates diverse funding streams and 2) establishing a single authority (i.e., organization) accountable for administration and management of public mental health care for a defined geographic area or population (Mohatt, Lalumia & Yennie, 2004).

Decisions affecting the provision of rural mental health care are likely to be made outside of rural communities. This trend requires mental health providers to be fiscally stable and connected to a strong network of resources (Sawyer & Beeson, 1998). Currently, Federal strategies for sustaining mental health infrastructure are non-existent (NFCSRI, 2004). While a myriad of enhanced financing options are available for rural health care (e.g., Critical Access Hospital Program, Rural Health Clinics Program), no such options to tailor rural financing strategies in mental health exist.

Rural mental health has a long history of being dependent on public sources of funding. However, there has been an increasing trend toward the semi-privatization of mental health services (e.g., transfer of Medicaid programs from government to managed care companies). There are several ramifications with the privatization of mental health services, including the inability of small employers to provide adequate benefit packages and the inability of some rural Americans to afford the cost of health care insurance.

Nevertheless, there are programs that have financial resources to support health care in rural areas. The Federal Office of Rural Health Policy (ORHP) coordinates a series of grants designed to increase access to and improve the quality of health care in rural areas (for further information, see http://ruralhealth.hrsa.gov/funding

Parity

Another major effort underway since the early 1990s is to achieve full parity in both private (individual and employer-based) and public (Medicare, Medicaid and other government-sponsored) insurance coverage for mental illnesses.[14] Involved in this effort are nationally organized groups, such as the National Alliance for the Mentally Ill (NAMI), Bazelon Center for Mental Health Law, the Mental Health Liaison Group and the Mental Health Association of America, to name just a few.

A fact sheet regarding parity is provided at the Mental Health Liaison Group website (http://www.mhlg.org/parity_4-03.pdf), which provides findings about the costs associated with lost productivity due to mental illness, whether or not mental health parity is affordable, as well as the rationale of and legislative efforts to achieve parity. In brief, the fact sheet indicates that

---

[14] (A brief history of these efforts can be found at http://www.nami.org/Content/Content Groups/Policy/WhereWeSta nd/Parity_in_Insurance_Coverage_-_WHERE_WE_STAND.htm.)

parity in coverage for mental illness can save money, does not result in a significant increase in cost and would end a type of discrimination.

The 1996 Domenici-Wellstone Mental Health Parity Act (MHPA), which prevents employer-sponsored health plans from imposing lifetime and annual dollar limits on mental health benefits that differ from those imposed on medical/surgical benefits, was a first national step toward insurance parity, but fell short of the final goal. For instance, findings from the U.S. General Accounting Office (2000) report titled *Compliance with the Mental Health Parity Act of 1996: Effects/Costs of Implementation* included:

1. Eighty-six percent of employers comply with the Federal parity requirements set forth in the MHPA of 1996. However, this does not apply to individuals outside of a group plan, plans with 50 or fewer employees, or plans whose claims costs have increased at least one percent due to compliance.
2. Despite a high percentage of compliance, employers continue to limit their mental health benefits. More specifically, 87 percent of those who comply end up restricting other mental health services in their health plans.
3. Initial concerns that the 1996 Act would increase claims costs by more than one percent seem to be unconfirmed. In fact, premium increases were estimated at 0.16 percent and 0.12 percent by Congressional Budget Office (CBO) and Coopers & Lybrand, respectively.
4. Several States have already enacted parity laws that exceed the Federal parity requirements. Premium cost increases for *full parity* are estimated to be between two percent and four percent, both nationally and for individual States.
5. Loopholes and limited scope of the MHPA of 1996 continue to impede overall access to mental health services.

Currently at the Federal level, Senators Pete Domenici (R-NM) and Edward Kennedy (D-MA) and Reps. Jim Ramstad (R-MN) and Patrick Kennedy (D-RI) introduced the Senator Paul Wellstone Mental Health Equitable Treatment Act of 2003. This would expand existing law by addressing limits on deductibles, co-insurance, co-payments, other cost sharing and limitations on the total amount that may be paid with respect to benefits under the plan or health insurance coverage. However, despite widespread support in Congress and by President Bush, the updated legislation has not yet passed.

Other Funding Opportunities for Rural

Hartley & Gale documented potential funding opportunities for rural communities (available online at http://www/ahrq.gov/data/safetynet/hartley.html), which include:

1. **The Rural Health Services Outreach Grant Program**: emphasizes the expansion of service delivery through networking strategies to encourage the development of new health care delivery systems in rural communities.
2. **The Network Development Grant Program**: designed to strengthen collaborative relationship between health care organizations by funding rural health networks that focus on strengthening their infrastructure by integrating clinical, administrative and financial systems.
3. **The Network Development Planning Grant Program**: provides one year of financial support to rural communities needing assistance in the development of an integrated health care network. The planning grants are to be used to develop a formal network with the purpose of improving the coordination of health services in rural communities and strengthening the rural health care system as a whole. Preference is given to applicants who serve medically underserved populations or in which at least 50 percent of the service area covered by the network is located in a health professional shortage area or medically underserved community.
4. **The Mississippi Delta Rural Development Initiative**: targets the Delta region, which covers 205 rural counties in Alabama, Arkansas, Illinois, Kentucky, Louisiana, Missouri, Mississippi and Tennessee. The program includes two components: a grant program to fund the creation of networks that improve access to primary care services and the development of a technical assistance program to help small rural hospitals improve their operations and financial performance.
5. **The Small Rural Hospital Improvement Grant Program**: provides funding to small rural hospitals for any one of the following activities: a) costs related to the implementation of Prospective Payment Systems; b) compliance with provisions of the Health Insurance

Portability and Accountability Act; or c) reducing medical errors and support quality improvement.

The ORHP also administers two additional grant programs created to support State involvement in meeting State and local rural health needs:

1. **The State Offices of Rural Health Grant Program**: has created offices of rural health in all 50 States. The mission of these offices is to help individual rural communities build health care delivery systems.
2. **The Rural Hospital Flexibility Grant Program (Flex Program)**: a Federal initiative that provides funding to State governments to strengthen rural health. This program: a) allows small hospitals the flexibility to reconfigure operations and be licensed as Critical Access Hospital (CAHs), b) offers cost-based reimbursement for Medicare acute inpatient and outpatient services, c) encourages the development of rural-centric health networks and d) offers grants to States to help implement a CAH program in the context of broader initiatives to strengthen the rural health care infrastructure.

Research & Evaluation

Current definitions of "rural" often fail to capture the relationship between rural characteristics and mental health service use (National Institute of Mental Health, Office of Rural Mental Health Research, 2003). Lewis (2003) indicated that the word "rural" suggests a cultural uniqueness that leads people to see "rurality" more as an abstract concept than a specific region. Others have emphasized that a rural area is not only a physical place but also a social place (Weisheit, Wells & Falcone, 1994). The concept of rural areas as social places requires the application of sensitive approaches to their cultural qualities (Lewis, 2003).

While there may not be one definition of "rural" that is acceptable to everyone, it is critical to, at a minimum, develop a set of definitions that are consistent and understandable when used in different contexts. The *New Freedom Commission on Mental Health, Subcommittee on Rural issues* (2004) Stated that a formalized process to define rural would be helpful in collecting richer data to use for planning rural initiatives (e.g., workforce development, recruitment, or program development). This would involve going beyond the simple population-based definitions that currently exist and would seek to operationalize other variables (e.g., available mental health services). This process would ultimately help to narrow the definition and offer more specificity when researching different rural communities.

Rural communities have many unique properties that need to be incorporated into and better captured by the research. Rural mental health research needs to be grounded in the rural context and experience. While traditional randomized clinical research allows for causal relationships of factors that influence change, qualitative methods (e.g., ethnographic, process analyses) can more fully demonstrate participant and community perceptions and experiences (Anthony, Rogers & Farkas, 2003). Qualitative methodology (e.g., correlational and quasi-experimental) can be used to guide the development of studies using more traditional research methods (Anthony et al., 2003). It is more important that the quantitative and qualitative research methods employed are complementary and not duplicative (Office of Behavioral and Social Sciences Research, 2001; Anthony et al., 2003).

One rural classification system that captures many of the aspects of rural, especially in relation to more urban areas, is the United States Department of Agriculture Economic Research Service (ERS) Rural-Urban Commuting Area (RUCA) codes. A full description of the RUCA codes can be found at http://www.ers.usda.gov/briefing/Rurality/RuralUrba nCommutingAreas/.

It is beyond the scope of this chapter to go into elaborate detail of the RUCA codes. However, in brief (and from the Web site), RUCA codes "are based on the same theoretical concepts used by the Office of Management and Budget (OMB) to define county-level metropolitan and micropolitan areas...[applying] similar criteria to measures of population density, urbanization, and daily commuting to identify urban cores and adjacent territory that is economically integrated with those cores." However, the RUCA codes use census tracts—the smallest geographic units—instead of counties as their building blocks to provide "a different and more detailed geographic pattern of settlement classification."

More specifically, the RUCA codes are composed of 10 primary and 30 secondary codes. The primary codes refer to either the primary or single largest commuting share and "offer a relatively straightforward and complete delineation of metropolitan and nonmetropolitan settlement based on the size and direction of primary commuting flows." The secondary codes identify areas where settlement classifications overlap, based on the size and direction of the secondary, or second largest, commuting flow.

Research Agendas and Questions

The NIMH's Office of Rural Mental Health Research (ORMHR) conducted a meeting in 2003 that sought to delineate a rural research agenda. The meeting included researchers, consumers and policy analysts interested in improving mental health services in rural areas. There was consensus that a common definition of "rural" is needed to use consistently in the research. However, as described in an earlier section, the Office of Management and Budget (OMB) has developed new definitions of metropolitan and non-metropolitan (or rural) areas (see Section 1 for more information).

It was also stressed that research in rural areas is often plagued by small sample sizes and insufficient power to confidently use the "community" as an explanatory variable. Community factors are often "nested" within the layers of a rural community and frequently exert powerful influence over the residents within that community.

ORMHR encouraged researchers to utilize the following methodologies in an attempt to better capture the characteristics and dynamics within a rural community: 1) multi-level studies that represent individuals within communities and communities within regions; 2) multivariate analysis, including structural equations and modeling and 3) methods for analyzing small samples (e.g., longitudinal data, hierarchical linear modeling) that estimate between-community and within-community characteristics (ORMHR, 2003). Six suggestions to improve the research that will eventually inform mental health service delivery in rural areas:

1. Encourage researchers to use conceptual and theoretical models in order to advance rural mental health research.
2. Conduct a meta-analysis of databases to inform the development of a typology for identifying rural communities at high risk for increased prevalence of mental illness and/or underutilization of mental health services.
3. Commission a "white paper" to examine frameworks and typologies for identifying rural communities at risk for disorder and/or service underutilization. These typologies could for example help to a) categorize epidemiological and services studies and b) prioritize research.
4. Encourage researchers to study the factors that comprise the typologies.

5. Conduct a four-day "Summer Institute" with senior-level rural mental health investigators and new or emerging investigators to encourage individuals to pursue a rural mental health research career.
6. Recruit senior- and junior-level rural mental health services researchers on the NIMH Services Research Initial Review Group (IRG). Encourage the Scientific Review Administrators to assemble ad hoc review teams with rural expertise.

The Evaluation Initiative at the National Assistance Center for Children's Mental Health was developed in response to a need for performance measurement, outcomes and system accountability for children's services. This program is housed at the Georgetown University Center for Child and Human Development. Although this initiative was created to address children's mental health services, it can be adapted to evaluate other mental health services. The following goals and tasks were modified to be used with other evaluation projects targeting different populations with various mental health needs.

1. Facilitate the capacity-building of States and local communities in their evaluation of mental health services;
2. Identify promising practices in the design and implementation of effective evaluation programs and integrated information systems and
3. Guarantee quality technical assistance services and products.

The Evaluation Initiative also detailed ongoing tasks in order to further the goals listed above:

1. Identify State and community evaluators;
2. Support evaluation efforts and develop integrated information systems;
3. Showcase promising practices in the design and implementation of evaluation programs and outcomes reporting;
4. Disseminate information regarding mental health services evaluation that are relevant and easily understood to stakeholders and
5. Assess the usefulness and impact of technical assistance activities. (http://gucchd.georgetown.edu/programs/ ta_center/topics/evidence_based_practices.html).

The rural mental health system could replicate some of these evaluation priorities. It would be useful for rural mental health professionals in partnership with Federal, State and local stakeholders to create standards and indicators of quality care to make the evaluation process more standardized. In addition, the Evaluation Initiative is exemplary in their efforts to be accountable to stakeholders. The ability to provide evidence on *how* and *why* services are effective or ineffective is critical to any evaluation project.

Particular research designs including epidemiology, morbidity, provider availability and provider access are more likely to yield useful information on rural residents. In addition, other methodologies including clinical community research (e.g., needs assessment, identification of community resources, program evaluation and efficacy of prevention-based services) may be beneficial in demonstrating the needs of specific communities. Lastly, it is essential to include community leaders and other community consumers as key informants to help ensure culturally sensitive and relevant research initiatives (Mulder et al., 2000).

Finally, Rost and colleagues (2002) identified seven areas for further research specific to the rural mental health agenda. Research suggestions were separated into two groups: 1) identifying and addressing rural-urban disparities in use, quality and outcomes of care and 2) continuing to improve use, quality and outcomes of care in rural areas. The research areas are presented in the form of questions.

Future Research to Identify and Address Rural-Urban Disparities in Use, Quality & Outcomes of Care

1. Compared to their urban residents, are rural residents of vulnerable or underserved populations (e.g., the impoverished, minority groups, the elderly, youth) less likely to seek care when they need it? If so, what modifiable factors associated with living in rural areas clarify this disparity?
2. Does living in a rural area increase the probability that an individual entering mental health treatment will not remain in treatment? If so, what interventions can be developed to achieve comparable rates of sustained engagement in treatment between rural residents with serious mental illness and urban residents struggling with similar mental health issues?
3. Do seriously mentally ill individuals living in rural areas receive a lower quality of care? If so, what are the relative contributions of the provider (e.g., provision of less evidenced-based care) and the patient

(e.g., failure to stay engaged in care) to these poor outcomes? What are some characteristics of the rural individual, the health plan or the service system that can be most cost-effectively modified to decrease disparities in outcome?

4. How do total and out-of-pocket expenditures for mental health care differ for rural and urban individuals with psychiatric disorders? How have these differences changed over time? Do differences in health benefits explain these differences? What policies can be initiated to equalize the cost-sharing burden for rural individuals with psychiatric disorders?

5. How does managed behavioral health care function in rural compared to urban areas? Does carving-out mental health benefits differentially impact entry in to treatment and/or quality of care in rural individuals with psychiatric disorders compared to urban residents? How do rural-urban differences in credentialing, selective contracting and risk sharing moderate the impact of managed behavioral health care?

Continuing to Improve Use, Quality & Outcomes of Care in Rural Areas

6. Can entry into treatment by rural individuals with psychiatric disorders be increased by direct marketing campaigns or by better utilizing the unique characteristics of the rural social network to increase the perceived need for and/or access to services?

7. Can quality of care and outcomes be enhanced by redesigning successful urban initiatives for rural primary and mental health care settings? What unique initiatives need to be developed to improve quality and outcomes for rural individuals with psychiatric disorders?

Summary

Rural mental health has been elevated to a higher priority status within the mental health community. In particular, Federal interest in rural mental health initiatives has helped to increase attention to the needs of rural communities. At the Federal level, the *New Freedom Commission on Mental Health, Subcommittee on Rural Issues* was one of only four subcommittee reports (out of 16) to be released, and overall goals of the Commission directly target rural issues. There are the Office of Mental Health Research at the National Institute of Mental Health (NIMH) and the Office of Rural Health Policy in the Health

Resources and Services Administration (HRSA). These programs have been responsible for creating research and service delivery opportunities. However, there is a lot of work to be done at multiple levels to create and sustain viable mental health systems in rural areas.

Four areas of future activity in rural mental health are education and training, clinical programs and services, administration, as well as research and evaluation. Education and training for clinicians and consumers in rural areas should regard evidence-based practices (EBPs), collaborative care and knowing when and how to access services. EBPs are continuing to be a focus of service delivery across mental health systems in the U.S., but the applicability of these treatments to rural still needs to be determined. The emergence of telehealth has made progress in linking rural mental health consumers with providers in urban areas, especially psychiatrists. The Internet is also becoming a vehicle for increased communication in rural areas. New developments in health care financing (e.g., managed care and for-profit health care corporations) are restructuring delivery systems. Specifically, the semi-privatization of public health insurance programs (e.g., Medicaid and Medicare) has created more incentives for corporate health care providers and insurance companies to enter rural markets.

A consistent theme emphasized in the literature is the importance of involving consumers in research and the planning of services. While this makes intuitive sense, it is common that consumers are left out of the planning processes for transforming mental health delivery systems. Rural communities and consumers should be allowed to speak authentically about their perspectives of their own needs. In order to advocate for the needs of rural communities to policy-makers, it is critical that solid research identifying the most effective services for rural residents is available. Outcome data based on current model programs will also be helpful in marketing the needs of rural communities.

References

Anthony, W., Rogers, E.S. & Farkas, M. (2003). Research on evidence-based practices: Future Directions in an Era of Recovery. *Community Mental Health Journal, 39(*2), 101-114.

Baer, L., Elford, D.R. & Cukor, P. (1997). Telepsychiatry at forty: What have we learned? *Harvard Review of Psychiatry, 5(*1), 7-17.

Baer, L., Cukor, P., Jenike, M.A., Leahy, L., O'Laughlen, J. & Coyle, J.T. (1995). Pilot studies of telemedicine for patients with obsessive-compulsive disorder *American Journal of Psychiatry, 152(*9), 1383-1385.

Baigent, M.F., Lloyd, C.J., Kavanagh, S.J., Ben-Tovim, D.I., Yellowlees, P.M., Kalucy, R.S. & Bond, M.J. (1997). Telepsychiatry: 'tele' yes, but what about the 'psychiatry'? *Journal of Telemedicine and Telecare, 3(*1), 3-5.

Dekraai, M. (2004, November). Building Child and Family Systems of Care in Rural Areas. Web-cast Presentation facilitated by the Western InterState Commission on Higher Education, Boulder, CO.

Deleon, P.H., Crimmins, D.B. & Wolf, A.W. (2003). Afterword—The 21st Century has Arrived. *Psychotherapy: Theory, Research, Practice, Training, 40,* 164–169.

Farrell, S.P. & McKinnon, C. (2003). Technology and rural mental health. *Archives of Psychiatric Nursing, 17(*1) Feb 2003, 20-26.

Graham, A.M. (1996). Telepsychiatry in Appalachia. *American Behavioral Scientist, 39(*5) Mar-Apr 1996, 602-615.

IOM Report: Quality Through Collaboration. (November, 2004). Presented by Mary Wakefield, Ph.D at the Office of Rural Health Policy Technical Assistance Meeting of the Rural Health Research Centers, Center for Rural Health.

Jonason, K. R., DeMers, S. T., Vaughn, T. J. & Reaves, R. P. (2003). Professional Mobility for Psychologists Is Rapidly Becoming a Reality. *Professional Psychology: Research and Practice, 34,* 468–473.

Kim, E. & VandeCreek, L. (2003). Facilitating Mobility for Psychologists: Comparisons With and Lessons From Other Health Care Professions. *Professional Psychology: Research and Practice, 34,* 480–488.

Lambert, D., Donahue, A., Mitchell, M. & Strauss, R. (2001). *Mental health outreach in rural area: Promising practices in rural areas.* Rockville, MD: Center for Mental Health Services, Substance Abuse and Mental Health Services Administration.

Lewis, S.H. (2003). *Unspoken crimes: Sexual assault in rural America.* National Sexual Violence Resource Center.

Merrill, T.S. (2003). Licensure Anachronisms: Is It Time for a Change? *Professional Psychology: Research and Practice, 34,* 459–462.

Mohatt, D.F., LaLumia, D., Yennie, H. (2004) Western InterState Commission on Higher Education – Mental Health Program, Boulder, CO; Washington State Behavioral Health Reform: An Overview of Governance and Financial Strategies

New Freedom Commission on Mental Health, *Subcommittee on Rural Issues: Background Paper.* DHHS Pub. No. SMA04-3890. Rockville, MD: 2004.

Office of Behavioral and Social Sciences Research. (2001). *Qualitative methods in health research: Opportunities and considerations in application and review* (NIH Publication No. 02-5046). Bethesda, MD: National Institutes of Health.

Office of Rural Mental Health Research. (2003). A rural mental health research agenda: Building on success by planning for the future. Boulder, CO, June 9-10, 2003. (Online). http://www.nimh.nih.gov/ormhr/

Sawyer, D. & Beeson, P. (1998). Rural Mental Health: Vision 2000 and Beyond. (Online) http://www.narmh.org/pages/future.html

Stroul, B. A. & Friedman, R.M. (1986). *A system of care for seriously emotionally disturbed children and youth.* Washington, D.C.: CASSP Technical Assistance Center, Georgetown University Child Development Center.

Torrey, W.C., Drake, R.E., Dixon, L., Burns, B.J., Flynn, L., Rush, A.J., Clark, R.E. & Klatzker, D. (2001). Implementing evidence-based practices for persons with severe mental illness. *Psychiatric Services, 52(*1), 45-50.

United States Department of Agriculature Economic Research Service (ERS). Rural-urban commuting area (RUCA) codes. http://www.ers.usda.gov /briefing/Rurality/RuralUrbanCommutingAreas/.

Wagenfeld, M.O., Murray, J.D., Mohatt, D.F. & DeBruyn, J.C. (Eds.). (1994). *Mental health and rural America: 1980-1993* (NIH Publication No. 94-3500). Washington, D.C.: U.S. Government Printing Office.

Wakefield, M. (2004). IOM Report: Quality Through Collaboration; ORHP Techinical Assistance Meeting of Rural Health Research Centers; Center for Rural Health. November 2, 2004. Powerpoint Presentation. Weisheit, R.A., Wells, E.L., Falcome, D.N. (1994). Community policing in small town and rural America. *Crime & Delinquency, (40)*4, 549-567.

Zarate, Jr., C.A., Weinstock, P., Cukor, C., Morabito, L., Leahy, Burns, C., and Baer, L. (1997). Applicability of telemedicine for assessing patients with schizophrenia: Acceptance and reliability. *Journal of Clinical Psychiatry, 58(*1), 22-25.

A USER'S GUIDE TO THE ANNOTATED BIBLIOGRAPHY

For readers wishing to stay abreast of developments in rural mental health, we recommend several journals. Some are specifically focused on rural mental health or human services, while others deal with rural health or rural life, with an occasional article on mental health. Some have devoted special issues or sections to rural mental health. Finally, as anyone who wades through the entire bibliography will note, other professional journals will, on occasion, publish an article on rural mental health. Without getting overly precise or making any claims to completeness, in roughly descending order of focus on rural mental health or related issues, they are as follows.

Journal of Rural Community Psychology
Human Services in the Rural Environment
The Journal of Rural Health
Rural Sociology
Journal of Health Care for the Poor and Underserved
American Journal of Community Psychology
American Psychologist
Journal of Community Psychology
Rural Sociologist
New Directions for Mental Health Services
Hospital and Community Psychiatry
Community Mental Health Journal
Journal of Public Health Policy

Of those listed, the *American Journal of Community Psychology, American Psychologist, New Directions for Mental Health Services,* and the *Journal of Rural Community Psychology* have had special issues or devoted sections to the problems of mental health and rural Americans.

References by Topics

To make this annotated bibliography more user friendly, we have arranged the references in terms of topics or key words that correspond roughly to the organization of the overview volumes. A reference can appear under more than one heading.

I. Aspects of Rural Life
A. Demography: 160, 168, 169, 276, 281, 282, 320, 335, 378, 381, 383, 392, 393, 395

B. Characteristics of Rural Life: 060, 071, 085, 091, 103, 104, 110, 120, 127, 132, 160, 161, 206, 244, 265, 272, 273, 275, 298, 320, 335, 336, 340, 358, 383, 392, 395, 403, 414

II. Epidemiology, Prevalence and Correlates of Disorder

A. Alcohol and Other Drugs: 001, 008, 012, 013, 025, 026, 028, 029, 033, 042, 044, 045, 046, 047, 049, 056, 062, 063, 068, 072, 078, 079, 083, 087, 089, 096, 097, 098, 101, 102, 106, 108, 118, 129, 139, 145, 151, 155, 156, 171, 179, 180, 181, 191, 192, 198, 199, 210, 227, 229, 240, 246, 262, 269, 279, 283, 286, 292, 293, 301, 304, 305, 306, 310, 323, 341, 349, 350, 351, 352, 353, 354, 355, 356, 369, 372, 382, 395, 401

B. Mental Disorder: 013, 016, 019, 020, 030, 044, 073, 128, 134, 135, 139, 144, 152, 171, 172, 173, 189, 191, 214, 221, 226, 244, 306, 310, 322, 368, 395

C. Special Populations/Topics

1. Adolescents and Children: 002, 006, 008, 012, 013, 026, 040, 049, 056, 058, 068, 074, 075, 076, 077, 078, 079, 081, 084, 087, 088, 089, 093, 096, 097, 098, 100, 102, 106, 108, 110, 114, 117, 138, 147, 148, 150, 151, 152, 155, 156, 159, 163, 164, 179, 180, 181, 187, 192, 197, 198, 199, 215, 216, 217, 220, 226, 227, 228, 240, 245, 250, 278, 279, 286, 287, 288, 292, 293, 295, 298, 307, 328, 341, 343, 344, 349, 350, 351, 352, 353, 354, 355, 356, 369, 374, 375, 391, 414

2. Severely Mentally Ill: 016, 017, 025, 039, 073, 082, 093, 115, 118, 130, 165, 174, 175, 183, 184, 190, 200, 208, 234, 262, 315, 317, 330, 362

3. Black/African Americans: 008, 013, 038, 039, 087, 088, 223, 384

4. Hispanic Americans: 004, 009, 062, 384, 387, 388

5. Native American/Alaskan Native: 323, 384, 408

6. Elderly: 024, 030, 051, 052, 053, 054, 064, 070, 092, 109, 137, 195, 196, 207, 222, 266, 274, 275, 302, 303, 311, 318, 335, 346

7. Women: 042, 044, 045, 046, 047, 057, 080, 093, 131, 154, 172, 185, 187, 212, 263, 326, 333, 399

8. Inmates/Prisoners: 185, 215, 216, 217, 364

9. Immigrants/Refugees: 107, 224, 225, 379

10. Men: 209

11. Veterans: 043, 219

12. Homeless: 270

13. Suicide: 176, 357

14. Religious/Spiritual: 060, 125, 164, 337, 390

III. Administrative Issues

A. Program Development: 011, 014, 055, 059, 117, 119, 162, 175, 236, 239, 245, 248, 254, 256, 257, 259, 260, 264, 280, 282, 291, 293, 294, 298, 320, 323, 325, 330, 332, 337, 338, 346, 349, 350, 351, 352, 353, 354, 355, 356, 362, 367, 372, 376, 395, 404, 405, 406, 409

B. Reviews and Overviews: 026, 031, 035, 105, 143, 236, 273, 276, 296, 298, 310, 321, 331, 383, 395, 396, 415

C. Needs Assessment: 005, 194, 272, 306, 331, 395, 410, 411

D. Health/Mental Health Linkage: 019, 034, 041, 048, 065, 066, 089, 113, 133, 203, 214, 230, 235, 258, 285, 298, 320, 367, 368, 385, 386, 395

E. Funding: 003, 015, 061, 065, 067, 093, 099, 146, 148, 162, 200, 202, 211, 213, 233, 237, 238, 241, 244, 249, 251, 252, 253, 255, 261, 271, 272, 280, 281, 302, 308, 313, 314, 315, 316, 317, 327, 331, 336, 338, 339, 340, 359, 361, 365, 367, 371, 372, 380, 400

IV. Issues and Models in Services Delivery: 018, 020, 021, 022, 037, 050, 059, 072, 075, 080, 100, 117, 123, 124, 126, 133, 136, 140, 142, 148,

157, 165, 170, 174, 179, 186, 198, 199, 201, 204, 205, 230, 232, 235, 249, 251, 252, 253, 254, 257, 267, 273, 276, 284, 290, 291, 295, 299, 300, 301, 306, 309, 310, 313, 314, 315, 316, 317, 320, 321, 322, 327, 331, 332, 334, 336, 337, 338, 340, 342, 346, 347, 348, 358, 360, 362, 367, 376, 377, 380, 385, 386, 390, 393, 394, 395, 396, 397, 398, 400, 402, 412

A. Alcohol and Other Drugs: 001, 008, 012, 013, 025, 026, 028, 029, 033, 036, 042, 044, 045, 046, 047, 049, 056, 062, 063, 068, 072, 078, 079, 083, 087, 088, 096, 097, 098, 101, 102, 106, 118, 129, 139, 145, 147, 148, 151, 152, 154, 156, 171, 179, 180, 181, 191, 192, 195, 198, 199, 210, 215, 227, 229, 245, 246, 248, 256, 262, 269, 279, 283, 286, 292, 293, 301, 304, 305, 306, 310, 323, 325, 349, 350, 351, 352, 353, 354, 355, 356, 360, 363, 364, 373, 389, 395, 398, 401, 413

B. Mental Disorder: 016, 019, 020, 030, 044, 045, 073, 128, 135, 139, 144, 152, 171, 172, 173, 189, 191, 214, 221, 226, 239, 245, 306, 310, 322, 368, 395

C. Special Populations/Topics

1. Adolescents and Children: 008, 012, 013, 026, 040, 049, 056, 058, 068, 074, 075, 076, 077, 078, 079, 081, 085, 087, 088, 089, 093, 097, 098, 099, 100, 102, 106, 110, 114, 119, 138, 151, 155, 156, 159, 163, 179, 180, 181, 187, 192, 197, 198, 199, 216, 217, 220, 226, 227, 228, 245, 248, 259, 260, 268, 278, 279, 286, 291, 292, 293, 298, 307, 325, 333, 338, 349, 350, 351, 352, 353, 354, 355, 356, 359, 363, 397, 413

2. Severely Mentally Ill: 016, 017, 019, 025, 039, 073, 082, 093, 115, 118, 130, 165, 174, 175, 183, 184, 190, 200, 208, 234, 236, 239, 313, 315, 316, 330, 362, 416

3. Black/African Americans: 008, 013, 038, 039, 087, 088, 223, 384

4. Hispanic Americans: 004, 009, 062, 223, 384, 387, 388

5. Native American/Alaskan Native: 223, 323, 384, 408

6. Elderly: 024, 030, 051, 052, 053, 054, 064, 070, 092, 109, 137, 195, 196, 207, 218, 222, 266, 274, 275, 302, 303, 311, 318, 335, 346, 347

7. Women: 042, 044, 045, 046, 047, 057, 080, 093, 131, 154, 172, 185, 188, 212, 263, 326, 333, 399

8. Inmates/Prisoners: 185, 215, 216, 217, 364

9. Immigrants/Refugees: 023, 107, 224, 225, 379

10. Veterans: 043, 121, 219, 319, 329

11. Homeless: 270

12. Suicide: 158, 176

13. Health/Mental Health Linkage: 019, 034, 041, 048, 065, 066, 089, 113, 133, 150, 203, 214, 230, 235, 258, 285, 299, 320, 367, 368, 385, 386

14. Telehealth/Tele-Mental Health: 020, 021, 022, 069, 090, 095, 110, 116, 142, 182, 193, 205, 247, 312, 345, 370, 377, 407, 416

V. Human Resources

A. Training: 063, 086, 096, 097, 167, 242, 243, 265, 276, 285, 327, 342, 393, 395, 400

B. Recruitment, Retention, Work Satisfaction: 111, 149, 166, 167, 178, 197, 242, 243, 276, 393, 395, 400

ANNOTATIONS

The annotations in this section include articles from the narrative sections of this chapter, as well as articles that were not included in those sections, yet are related to rural mental health in some way. The main reason for not including a given article was that it dealt with a highly specific aspect of rural mental health (e.g., a new but not frequently used or widely applicable treatment) that was not easily integrated into the sections. Additionally, while this chapter provides some specific information about general topics (e.g., epidemiology of mental health and substance disorders), it is not meant to be an all-encompassing work. It is mostly an overview of current literature, with some specificity regarding the most poignant topics. Finally, a very limited number of references from the sections (about five) were not included in this section due to being out of print or inaccessible via the Internet. Typically this was the case for works produced befpre 1985. In most cases, they were referenced in other, more recent, literature, but were included in the section to give appropriate credit to their authors.

001 Abbey, A., Pilgrim, C., Hendrickson, P. & Buresh, S. (2000). Evaluation of a family-based substance abuse prevention program targeted for the middle school years. *Journal of Drug Education*, 30(2), 213-228.

A family-based substance abuse prevention program which emphasizes family cohesion, school and peer attachment, self-esteem, and attitudes about adolescent use of alcohol and tobacco was evaluated. Baseline surveys were conducted with students and parents in four schools. Surveys were re-administered one year later. Analyses of covariance indicated that student participants, as compared to non-participants, had higher family cohesion, less family fighting, greater school attachment, higher self-esteem, and belief that alcohol should be consumed at an older age at the one year follow-up. Strategies for involving parents in prevention programs are discussed.

002 Adelsheim, S., Carillo, K. & Coletta, E. (2001). Developing school mental health in a rural State: The New Mexico School Mental Health Initiative. *Child & Adolescent Psychiatric Clinics of North America*, 10(1), 151-159.

This article discusses New Mexico's School Mental Health Initiative, a creative and innovative approach to developing the infrastructure to improve access to services as well as technical assistance to even the most isolated communities in this rural State. Topics covered include (1) development of the State-level school mental health infrastructure, (2) collaborative workgroups, (3) expanded school-based mental health services, (4) training for teachers and other school professionals, (5) school/community collaborative pilot sites, (6) collaboration with parents and higher education and (7) adequate underwriting for essential capacity building.

003 Agency for Healthcare Research and Quality (2000). *Medical Expenditure Panel Survey: MEPS HC-011, 1996. Preliminary Person Level Expenditure File.* [Electronic data file].

The 1996 Medical Expenditure Panel Survey Household Component (MEPS HC) data collection instrument is comprised of 44 separate sections that are divided according to specific topics. Each section contains a series of Computer Assisted Personal Interviewing (CAPI) computer screens with questions, interviewing instructions, and skip patterns based on the specific topics. During the household interview, the 1996 Showcards assist MEPS respondents by providing them with paper copy versions of definitions or response categories that pertain to specific questionnaire items throughout CAPI.

004 Aguilar-Gaxiola, S.A., Zelezny, L., Garcia, B., Edmondson, C., Alejo-Garcia, C. & Vega, W.A. (2002). Mental health care for Latinos: Translating research into action: Reducing disparities in mental health care for Mexican Americans. *Psychiatric Services*, 53(12), 1563-1568.

This article describes a case study in which epidemiologic research findings were translated for multiple stakeholders and applied to reduce disparities in mental health services for Mexican Americans in Fresno County, California. The aim of this evidence-based process was to educate the community and mobilize action, to translate research for multiple stakeholders to inform practitioners and policy makers about the need for improved mental health care for minorities, and affect regional policy changes to increase and improve the availability, accessibility and appropriateness of mental health care for Mexican Americans.

005 Ahr, P.R. & Halcomb, W.R. (1985). State mental health directors' priorities for mental health care. *Hospital and Community Psychology*, 36, 39-45.

This article provides useful information from the survey conducted in the 1980s by the National Association of State Mental Health Program Directors. The survey was sent via mail to all State mental health directors to determine a national priority for mental health care. The article summarizes the findings and rank orders the most important issues. The results hilights the top two priorities: providing services and supporting programs in the community for the chronically mentally ill.

006 Akers, R. L. (1977). *Deviant behavior: A social learning approach* (2nd ed.). Belmont, CA: Wadsworth Press.

This book describes deviant behavior in the context of social learning theory. Specifically, Akers believed individuals learned aggressive acts through operant conditioning. In this process, the aggression is acquired through direct conditioning and modeling others' actions. He believes that positive rewards and the avoidance of punishment reinforced aggression.

007 Akers, R. L. (1994). *Criminological Theories: Introduction and Evaluation*. Los Angeles: Roxbury Publishing.

Akers and Sellers review and evaluate the principal criminological theories on the basis of their empirical validity. For this fourth edition, they add separate chapters on biological and psychological theories, and expanded treatment of areas including peer groups, religious factors, behavioral genetics and evolutionary theory, and restorative justice. The book can be used as a text for courses in criminology, juvenile delinquency, deviance, and criminal behavior.

008 Albrecht, S.L., Amey, C. & Miller, M.K. (1996). Patterns of substance abuse among rural black adolescents. *Journal of Drug Issues*, 26, 751-781.

The authors used data from the most recently available Monitoring the Future survey to examine the role of race and residence in affecting substance abuse patterns among high school students. Overall, rural vs. urban residence differences were modest. Additionally, compared with Whites, Blacks were much less likely to report drug use. In the bivariate analysis, major correlates of use included gender, family structure, religious attendance, GPA, and availability of unearned income. In the multivariate analysis, race, family structure, religious attendance, GPA, and unearned income remained significant.

009 Alegria, M., Canino, G., Rios, R., Vera, M., Calderon, J. Rusch, D. & Ortega, A.N. (2002). Mental health care for Latinos: Inequalities in use of specialty mental health services among Latinos, African Americans, and non-Latino Whites. Psychiatric Services, 53(12), 1547-1555.

The authors investigated whether there are disparities in the rates of specialty mental health care for Latinos and African Americans compared with non-Latino Whites in the US. Data were analyzed from the 1990-1992 National Comorbidity Survey; with 8,098 English-speaking subjects (Ss) aged 15-54 years. Ss included 695 Latinos, 987 African Americans and 6,026 non-Latino Whites. Poor Latinos (family income of less than $15,000) had lower access to specialty care than poor non-Latino Whites. African Americans who were not classified as poor were less likely to receive specialty care than their White counterparts, even after adjustment for demographic characteristics, insurance status and psychiatric morbidity.

010 American Psychological Association (1995). *Caring for the rural community: An interdisciplinary curriculum.* Washington, D.C.: Rural Health Office

This curriculum offers suggestions for psychologists and other mental health professionals who are working in rural areas. While psychologists are often the most highly trained mental health providers in rural areas, their numbers are often small. This document was created to increase effectiveness and sensitivity when providing mental health services to rural residents.

011 Amundson, B. (2001). America's rural communities as crucibles for clinical reform: Establishing collaborative care teams in rural communities. *Families, Systems & Health*, 19(1): 13-23.

This paper describes the development of multidisciplinary health care teams ("Family Health Teams"; FHTs) in rural communities. The successful establishment of multidisciplinary teams through the participation of existing community provider organizations and agencies is described together with essential training and support systems for their establishment. A number of positive results are described and limiting factors are delineated. Providers and patients are supportive of the contribution of local FHTs to the coordination and management of patients with complex and multiple health problems.

012 Anderson, R. L. & Huffine, C. (2003). Child & adolescent psychiatry: Use of community-based services by rural adolescents with mental health and substance use disorders. *Psychiatric Services*, 54, 1339- 1341.

This column, by Dr. Anderson from the College of Public Health at the University of Iowa, deals with the conundrum of dual diagnosis among adolescents. The problems Dr. Anderson describes are all the more daunting because of the real-life issues of finding services in a rural setting. Her paper, which represents an overview of mental health, substance abuse, and public health, fits well with the column's theme of collaboration and building systems of care.

013 Angold, A., Erkanli, A., Farmer, E.M.Z, Fairbank, J.A., Burns, B.J., Keeler, G. & Costello, E.J. (2002). Psychiatric disorder, impairment, and service use in rural African American and White youth. *Archives of General Psychiatry*, 59(10), 893-904.

The authors examined the prevalence of DSM-IV psychiatric disorders and correlates of mental health service use in rural African American and white youth. Prevalence was similar in African American and white youth. The only ethnic difference was an excess of depressive disorders in white youth. White youth were more likely than African American youth to use specialty mental health services, but services provided by schools showed very little ethnic disparity. The effect of children's symptoms on their parents was the strongest correlate of specialty mental health care. In this rural sample, African American and white youth were equally likely to have psychiatric disorders, but African

Americans were less likely to use specialty mental health services. School services provided care to the largest number of youths of both ethnic groups.

014 Anthony, W., Rogers, E.S. & Farkas, M. (2003). Research on evidence-based practices: Future Directions in an Era of Recovery. *Community Mental Health Journal*, 39(2), 101-114.

Many mental health systems are trying to promote the adoption of what has come to be known as evidence-based practices while incorporating a recovery vision into the services they provide. Unfortunately, much of the existing, published research on evidence-based practices was conceived without an understanding of the recovery vision and/or implemented prior to the emergence of the recovery vision. As result, evidence-based practice research that has been published to date is deficient in speaking to a system being built on a recovery philosophy and mission; these deficiencies are detailed, and suggestions are advanced for new directions in evidence-based practice research.

015 Armstrong, S.C. & Took, K.J (1993). Psychiatric managed care at a rural MEDDAC. *Military Medicine*, 158(11), 717-721.

Mental health costs at General Leonard Wood Army Community Hospital (GLWACH) have risen every year. Gateway to Care, a plan of coordinated managed care conceived by Health Services Command, was initiated at GLWACH to give the commander and providers more flexibility to control costs and improve access to care. Five major changes were made under GLWACH's mental health coordinated care project. In the first full year of the project, CHAMPUS net costs were reduced while more comprehensive care was provided to beneficiaries. Cost reduction came primarily from dramatically increasing the size and scope of outpatient care to reduce inpatient admissions.

016 Ax, R.K., Fagan, T.J. & Holton, S.M.B. (2003). Individuals with serious mental illnesses in prison: Rural perspectives and issues. Stamm, B. Hudnall (Ed). *Rural behavioral health care: An interdisciplinary guide.* (pp. 203-215). Washington, D.C., US: American Psychological Association.

This article discusses issues specific to the treatment of persons with serious mental illness in rural prisons and jails. Telehealth technology has particular relevance to treatment in these facilities. Ideally, a range of community services would reduce the initial involvement of individuals with serious mental illness in the criminal justice system. If rehabilitation is once again to be a priority in American prisons, mental health professionals must become reinvolved in policymaking.

017 Bachman, S.S., Drainoni, M., Strickler, G., Dittmar, N.D. & Shon, S.P. (1996). Utilization of a State hospital by urban and rural local mental health authorities. *Administration & Policy in Mental Health*, 23(5), 439-454.

The authors gathered information about clients admitted to a State hospital in Texas from both a rural and an urban local mental health authority (LMHA) to determine if there are differences in the populations admitted to the hospital from these settings, and if the two authorities utilized the State hospital differently. Results suggest that despite several similarities, clients from the urban setting had different types of encounters with the State mental health hospital than did clients from the rural setting. Urban clients were younger, and were more likely to be persons of color, to have never married, and to have both admitting and ongoing forensic commitments. Results also suggest that LMHAs utilized the State hospital differently.

018 Backlar, P. (1996). The three Rs: Roles, Relationships, and Rules. *Community Mental Health Journal*, 32(5), 505-509.

This article discusses boundary issues in community mental health programs. The difficulty of defining boundaries in the therapeutic relationship is mentioned. The variations and changes in delivery and practice of mental health services are seen as one reason for the difficulty in defining boundaries. Relationship boundaries are presented and discussed as a unique problem for rural mental health providers.

019 Badger, L., Robinson, H. & Farley, T. (1999). Management of mental disorders in rural primary care: A proposal for integrated psychosocial services. *Journal of Family Practice*, 48(10), 813-818.

It is proposed that in the best interest of physicians and their patients, fully integrated psychosocial services in rural primary care settings would reduce the burden of time-consuming mental health care, conform to patient preference for immediate on-site care, reduce nonproductive medical care use, and eliminate duplication of effort by physicians and mental health professionals. The treatment model that is proposed would provide multiple arenas for psychosocial intervention—with the individual, the family, and the community—based on the patient's self-identified needs.

020 Baer, L., Cukor, P., Jenike, M.A., Leahy, L., O'Laughlen, J. & Coyle, J.T. (1995). Pilot studies of telemedicine for patients with obsessive-compulsive disorder. *American Journal of Psychiatry*, 152(9), 1383-1385.

The authors assessed the reliability of rating scales administered in person and over video to patients with obsessive-compulsive disorder. Rating scales for obsessive-compulsive, depressive, and anxiety symptoms were administered in person (N = 16) and by means of narrow-bandwidth video transmission over one digital telephone line (N = 10). Reliability was excellent in both conditions, and there was no degradation in reliability when the assessment was conducted over video.

021 Baer, L., Elford, D.R. & Cukor, P. (1997). Telepsychiatry at forty: What have we learned? *Harvard Review of Psychiatry*, 5(1), 7-17.

This article includes a literature review of articles describing video applications of telemedicine for psychiatry (i.e., "telepsychiatry"). Although the conclusions of all studies reviewed recommended the use of telepsychiatry, evidence currently available is insufficient to suggest its widespread implementation. The authors called for further studies in order to determine when and for what age groups and conditions telepsychiatry is an effective way to deliver psychiatric services, and whether it is cost-effective. The authors recommended that telepsychiatry be employed on a limited basis and be restricted to research settings and underserved communities (where it may be the only option) until further support is available.

022 Baigent, M.F., Lloyd, C.J., Kavanagh, S.J., Ben-Tovim, D.I., Yellowlees, P.M., Kalucy, R.S. & Bond, M.J. (1997). Telepsychiatry: 'tele' yes, but what about the 'psychiatry'? *Journal of Telemedicine and Telecare*, 3(1), 3-5.

The authors compared the interrater reliability between two psychiatrists interviewing 63 subjects in an observer/interviewer split configuration in a same-room and telepsychiatry settings to investigate what might be lost or gained during psychiatric evaluations that take place via telepsychiatry. The measures used were the BPRS and interviewer ratings from a semi-structured interview. Patients also rated their experience. There were some clear differences between the telepsychiatry and same-room evaluations. Despite these variations, diagnoses were as reliably made by telepsychiatry. Patient acceptance of telepsychiatry was high.

023 Baker R. (1992). Psychosocial consequences for tortured refugees seeking asylum and refugee status in Europe. In M. Basoglu (Ed.), *Torture and its*

consequences: Current treatment approaches (pp. 83–101). Cambridge: Cambridge University Press.

This chapter explores the "triple trauma paradigm of the tortured refugee." It focuses on the nature of refugee experience and its long-term psychosocial implications; the particular impact of torture on refugees; and the further trauma of the tortured refugee who seeks asylum and refugee status in Western Europe, and in particular the UK. It also discusses the present procedural and sociopolitical barriers facing refugees in Europe and identifies three repeating behavioral coping patterns. These are tentatively described as negative, adaptive and constructive forms of survival in the long term

024 Bane, S.D. & Bull, C. (2001). Innovative rural mental health service delivery for rural elders. *Journal of Applied Gerontology*, 20(2), 230-240.

This article describes rural mental-health service delivery models identified in a 1995 year-long search by the National Resource Center for Rural Elderly for innovative programs. The leadership role of a single individual, palatability to a rural elderly clientele, and flexibility are found to be shared characteristics of successful direct service models. Successful educationally oriented models are characterized by ongoing involvement of community leaders, development of specialized rurally specific curricula, and marketing that enabled programs to survive beyond their initial demonstration project funding. It is concluded that successful rural models of mental health care must be based on information that is germane to rural community life, specific training of mental health professionals to work in rural settings, engagement of rural elders as peer counselors in outreach, and strong linkages with existing services and programs.

025 Barry, K.L., Fleming, M.F., Greenley, J.R., Kropp, S.; et al. (1996). Characteristics of persons with severe mental illness and substance abuse in rural areas. *Psychiatric Services*, 47, 88-90.

The authors examined the prevalence of substance abuse problems (SBPs) among 1,551 clients with severe mental illness (ages 18-74) receiving care in community based mental health programs in rural areas, and developed a profile of characteristics to help case managers identify Ss at risk for SBP. High rates of current SBPs were found among the Ss. Those with a current SBP were younger than those with no such history and had more symptoms of anger, trouble with the law, and more suicidal threats than Ss in the other two groups.

026 Bazelon Center (2000). *Relinquishing Custody: the Tragic Result of Failure to Meet Children's Mental Health Needs*. http://www.bazelon.org

   This book describes the reality that many children in the United States are uninsured or underinsured for mental health care. In addition, some children who do have coverage often cannot access the care they need. When private or public insurance plans will not pay, many parents face a difficult dilemma: to get the mental health treatment their child needs, they must turn their son or daughter over to the child welfare or juvenile justice system. Frequently, the child is then put in institutional care far from home. Studies confirm that the practice of requiring custody relinquishment occurs in at least half of the States, affecting as many as 20 percent of families of children with serious emotional disturbance.

027 Becker, H.K., Agopian, M.W. & Yeh, S. (1992). Impact evaluation of Drug Abuse Resistance Education (DARE). *Journal of Drug Education*, 22, 283-291.

   This assessed the impact of the Drug Abuse Resistance Education (DARE) program and the impact of the lack of such a program in approximately 3,000 fifth graders in California. DARE did not significantly change the amount of drug use, which is minimal at the fifth-grade level. In general, Ss receiving DARE during the study period maintained existing levels of drug abuse and did not experiment with new illicit substances. DARE was unable to prevent a broad variety of substance use (e.g., cigarettes, alcohol, inhalants) by the Ss. It is concluded that administrative decision making must consider program effectiveness and curriculum time constraints.

028 Becker, L., Barga, V., Sandberg, M., Stanley, M. & Clegg, D. (1999a). *1999 county profile on risk and protection for substance abuse prevention planning in Ferry County*. Olympia, WA: Division of Alcohol and Substance Abuse, Research and Data Analysis, Department of Social and Health Services.

   This publication offers a comprehensive collection of county data related to substance use and abuse, and the risk factors that predict substance use among youth. Data are organized and presented within a risk and protective factor framework used across the State by substance abuse prevention planners. Data was collected from 1990-1997, some for 1998 for the August 1999 issue. All county data was summarized in the 2000 State report: "Profile on Risk and Protection for Substance Abuse Prevention Planning in Washington State." Available online: http://www1.dshs.wa.gov/rda/research/4/33/default.shtm

030 Bedford, S., Melzer, D., Dening, T. & Lawton, C. (1996). What becomes of people with dementia referred to community psychogeriatric teams? *International Journal of Geriatric Psychiatry*, 11(12), 1051-1056.

    This monitors a broad range of process and outcome indicators in joint health and social service community psychogeriatric teams in a six-month follow-up of new referrals to four teams in Cambridge, England. Results showed that rates of referral to urban teams were double of that of rural rates. The dementia group was significantly more dependent and received more informal and formal care, and, after six months, only 54 percent were alive and living outside institutional care, compared to 79 percent in the functionally ill group. Unmet needs were more common in the dementia group, and related principally to residential care and care respite.

031 Beeson, P.G., Britain, C., Howell, M.L., Kirwan, D. & Sawyer, D.A. (1998). Rural mental health at the millennium. In R.W. Manderscheid & M.J. Henderson (Eds.), *Mental Health United States 1998* (pp. 82-97). Rockville, MD: Center for Mental Health Services, SAMHSA, U.S. Department of Health and Human Services.

    This book summarizes statistical information related to health care reform, including managed care and policy considerations, lessons learned from behavioral managed care approaches, and the status of managed behavioral health care in America. It includes information on epidemiological data, mental health in Medicare and Medicaid programs, and mental health services in rural areas. This chapter reviews trends in rural mental health up to the point of publication.

032 Bergland, B. (1988). Rural mental health: Report of the National Action Commission on the Mental Health of Rural America. *Journal of Rural Community Psychology*, 9, 2-29.

    The problems that rural Americans have faced in the 1980s have taken serious emotional and psychological tolls. To understand this phenomenon better, the National Mental Health Association created the National Action Commission of the Mental Health of Rural Americans. The commission's activities have resulted in the 18 action recommendations discussed here.

033 Biglan, A., Duncan, T., Irvine, A.B., Ary, D., Smolkowski, K. & James, L. (1997). A drug abuse prevention strategy for rural America. In: Roberson, E.B.,Sloboda, Z., Boyd, G.M., Beatty, L, and Kozel, N.J., eds. *Rural Substance Abuse: State of Knowledge and Issues*. National Institute on Drug Abuse; U.S. Department of Health and Human Services; National Institutes of Health: NIH Publication No. 97-4177. Rockville, MD.

This chapter describes a range of issues involved in developing a drug abuse prevention strategy for rural America, including a contextual definition of "rural" and a number of risk or protective factors for youth and adolescents (e.g., association with deviant peers). They recommend a comprehensive approach that involves, schools, parents and community agencies. Use of media outlets is considered very helpful to getting prevention ideas and practices out.

034 Bird, D.C., Lambert, D., Hartley, D., Beeson, P.G. & Coburn, A.F. (1998). Rural models for integrating primary care and mental health services. *Administration & Policy in Mental Health*, 25(3), 287-308.

This identified and described models for integrating primary care and mental health services in rural communities. Data were obtained from telephone interviews with staff at rural primary care sites around the country. Findings were based on the responses of 53 primary care organizations in 22 States. Four integration models were identified: diversification, linkage, referral, and enhancement, which appeared to exist in combination, rather than as pure types. The proposed analytic framework outlines aspects of integration that are readily amenable to study.

035 Bird, D. C., Dempsey, P. & Hartley, D. (2001). *Addressing mental health workforce needs in underserved rural areas: Accomplishments and challenges.* Portland, ME: Maine Rural Health Research Center, Muskie Institute, University of Southern Maine.

This paper reviews efforts to address mental health workforce needs in underserved rural areas. In obtaining information, the authors relied on a review of the relevant literature, an analysis of Federal regulations and data, and interviews with experts on mental health workforce and rural mental health issues. Available online:
http://muskie.usm.maine.edu/Publications/rural/wp23.pd f

036 Blank, M.B., Chang, M.Y., Fox, J.C., Lawson, C.A. & Modlinski, J. (1996). Case manager follow-up to failed appointments and subsequent service utilization. *Community Mental Health Journal*, 32(1), 23-31.

This compares the relative effectiveness of follow-up techniques, including letters, phone calls, and home visits on subsequent service utilization. Follow-ups did result in better compliance with the next appointment and fewer emergency contacts. Letters were used most frequently (21.3 percent), followed by phone calls (18.7 percent), and then home visits (3.3 percent). Clients who received letters or phone calls were more likely to attend the subsequent appointment than those who received no follow-up. Although home visits were utilized the least, due to cost and time restrictions, those clients did not fail the next appointment and did not need later emergency services.

037 Blank, M.B., Fox, J.C., Hargrove, D.S. & Turner, J.T. (1995). Critical issues in reforming rural mental health service delivery. *Community Mental Health Journal*, 31(6), 511-524.

This discusses the reforming of mental health service delivery system (MHSD) in rural areas. It is argued that exclusive focus on health care financing reform fails to include obstacles to effective MHSD in rural areas, which should focus on issues of availability, accessibility, acceptability and accountability, as well as adequate diagnosis and treatment of mental disorders including costs of health care. Rural MHSD may be reformed by outreach treatment modalities and development of in-home services and existing rural organizations should be consulted.

038 Blank, M.B., Mahmood, M., Fox, J.C. & Guterbock, T. (2002). Alternative mental health services: The Role of the Black Church in the South. *American Journal of Public Health*, 92(10), 1668-1672.

This article examined the extent to which churches in the southern U.S. provide mental health and social services to congregations, and investigated any established linkages with formal systems of care. Results show that black churches reported providing many more services than did white churches, regardless of urban or rural location. Few links between churches and formal provider systems were found, regardless of location or racial composition.

039 Blank, M.B., Tetrick, F.L, Brinkley, D.F., Smith, H.O; et al. (1994). Racial matching and service utilization among seriously mentally ill consumers in the rural south. *Community Mental Health Journal*, 30(3), 271- 281.

This examined racial matching between case manager and client for 198 Caucasian and 479 African-American seriously mentally ill consumers served through a rural community mental health center. Client-case manager dyads were more likely to be of the same race than of different races. Same-race dyads tended to have greater service utilization as indicated by a greater number of made appointments over the study period. An interaction was found for failed appointments where African Americans in same-race dyads were more likely to fail appointments, while Caucasian consumers in same-race dyads were less likely to fail appointments.

040 Blankenship, B.L., Eells, G.T., Carlozzi, A.F., Perry, K. & Barnes, L.B. (1998). Adolescent client perceptions and reactions to reframe and symptom prescription techniques. *Journal of Mental Health Counseling*, 20(2), 172-182.

This article examined the extent to which the level of reactance of adolescent clients served as a mediating factor for counselor ratings and two paradoxical intervention techniques: reframe and symptom prescription. Ss were 86 adolescent clients (aged 13-20 years) in a rural mental health center. Multivariate analysis of variance (MANOVA) results revealed a significant interaction effect for level of reactance and intervention type. Results suggest that the level of reactance moderates perceptions of paradoxical interventions and also affects counselor ratings and treatment acceptability ratings.

041 Blount, Alexander (Ed) (1998). *Integrated primary care: The future of medical and mental health collaboration.*

Integrated primary care unifies medical and mental health care in a primary care setting. This book explains this practice as the most fully realized form of collaboration between medical and mental health providers and presents several different models for its practical application. Contributions to this book describe best practices in integrated care and spend as much effort showing how to successfully develop and implement these programs in different settings as they do arguing for their usefulness.

042 Booth, B.M. & McLaughlin, Y.S. (2000). Barriers to and need for alcohol services for women in rural populations. *Alcoholism: Clinical & Experimental Research*, 24(8), 1267-1275.

This reviews and summarizes the research on alcohol problems and issues related to alcohol services for rural women. The authors discuss the prevalence of alcohol problems, help-seeking behavior and barriers to help-seeking for rural women, and suggest directions for future research for rural women with alcohol problems. The authors also address key methodological issues in measuring rurality that must be considered when designing research on rural women.

043 Borowsky, S.J., Nelson, D.B., Nugent, S.M., Bradley, J.L., Hamann, P.R., Stolee, C.J. & Rubins, H.B. (2002). Characteristics of veterans using Veterans Affairs community-based outpatient clinics. *Journal of Health Care for the Poor & Underserved*, 13(3), 334-346.

This article examined factors that may be related to veterans' desire to transfer care from Veterans Affairs (VA)-based to community-based outpatient clinics. Results show that 54 percent of Ss requested community-based outpatient clinic care. Ss who were less satisfied with VA care were more likely to request a transfer to a community clinic, whereas health was not strongly associated with requests for community-based outpatient clinic care. Ss who had more VA clinic visits were less likely to request community-based outpatient clinic care. The likelihood of requesting also varied across VA facilities and by VA eligibility level.

044 Boyd, M.R. & Hauenstein, E.J. (1997). Psychiatric assessment and confirmation of dual disorders in rural substance abusing women. *Archives of Psychiatric Nursing*, 11, 74-81.

This article describes the difficulties encountered in screening and diagnosing dual disorders in 34 rural women (aged 20-52 years) with an alcohol or drug abuse disorder. All Ss were screened for depression and alcohol abuse using the Center for Epidemiologic Studies Depression Scale (CES-D) and the Michigan Alcohol Screening Test (MAST), respectively. The National Institute of Mental Health Diagnostic Interview Schedule (DIS), Version III was used to determine the presence of a psychiatric disorder. Based on the findings, it is concluded that incorporating the MAST and CES-D into routine health screening may identify women who need a more in-depth diagnostic interview for substance abuse and depression.

045 Boyd, M.R. (2000). Predicting substance abuse and comorbidity in rural women. *Archives of Psychiatric Nursing*, 14, 64-72.

The purpose of this study was to identify risk factors that would predict substance abuse and primary comorbid psychiatric disorders in rural women. Discriminant function analysis identified two factors, alcohol beliefs and threats of minor violence, which correctly identified substance abusing women from nonsubstance abusing women, and women with nonsubstance use psychiatric disorders from those with no psychiatric disorder. These two functions correctly classified 69 percent of women in the study.

046 Boyd, M.R. & Mackey, M.C. (2000). Alienation from self and others: The psychosocial problem of rural alcoholic women. *Archives of Psychiatric Nursing*, 14, 134-141.

This examined women's perspectives in becoming and being alcohol dependent. Using grounded theory techniques, 14 adult black and white women receiving treatment for alcohol addiction at rural substance abuse centers participated in an intensive interview. Data analysis focused on the identification of the basic psychosocial problem and the process of becoming alcohol dependent. The results are presented in two parts. This article focuses on the basic psychosocial problem faced by women in becoming alcohol dependent.

047 Boyd, M.R. & Mackey, M.C. (2000). Running away to nowhere: Rural women's experiences of becoming alcohol dependent. *Archives of Psychiatric Nursing*, 14(3), 142-149.

The purpose of this study was to describe women's perspectives in becoming and being alcohol dependent. Part 1, "Alienation From Self and Others," on page 134 in this issue of Archives, describes the study methods, the sample, and the basic psychosocial problem faced by rural, alcoholic women. Part 2, "Running Away to Nowhere," focuses on the basic psychosocial process that women used to resolve the pain caused by their "Alienation From Self and Others." The article concludes with suggestions for nursing intervention.

048 Bray, J.H., Enright, M.F., et al. (1997). *Collaboration with primary care physicians. Practicing psychology in rural settings: Hospital privileges and collaborative care.* J. A. Morris. Washington, D.C., American Psychological Association.

This book covers the history of psychology's advancement in hospital settings. Contributors also describe successful collaborative models with physicians and community mental health service providers and highlight the challenges and rewards of working in rural areas. This volume illustrates the greater quality of care that can be achieved when psychologists are made part of an interdisciplinary health care team-a model of care that will benefit both patient and hospital.

049 Britt, M.A. & Jachym, N.K. (1996). Cigarette and alcohol use among fourth and fifth graders: Results of a new survey. *Journal of Alcohol & Drug Education*, 43, 44-54.

This is a survey regarding factors affecting the use of cigarettes, tobacco and alcohol among fourth- and fifth-graders. Information was also collected from teachers regarding the students' participation in the Drug Abuse Resistance Education (DARE) program. While it was found that experimentation rates for cigarette use was low, use increased significantly from fourth to fifth grade. Use of alcohol was much higher than cigarettes, and it also increased significantly from fourth to fifth grade. Variables most strongly related to cigarette use were both peer use of cigarettes and peer pressure to smoke. Sibling use of cigarettes and a child's belief in the harmfulness of smoking were weakly related to cigarette use. Alcohol use was best predicted by peer use and peer pressure to drink. Exposure to the DARE program showed no significant relationship to either cigarette or alcohol use.

050 Brown, H.N. & Herrick, C.A. (2002). From the guest editors—Rural America: A call for nurses to address mental health issues. *Issues in Mental Health Nursing*, 23(3), 183-189.

This article introduces a special issue of Issues in Mental Health Nursing that examines the mental health needs of special populations residing in rural America. The authors believe that a new model for mental health care delivery must be developed that is sensitive to the cultural norms of the rural community, while addressing the needs of the local population.

051 Buckwalter, K. (1992). *Mental and social health of the rural elderly.* Paper presented at the Health and Aging in Rural America: A National Symposium, San Diego, CA.

This provides an overview of mental health services for older adults in America.

052 Buckwalter, K.C., Abraham, I.L., Smith, M. & Smullen, D.E. (1993). Nursing outreach to rural elderly people who are mentally ill. *Hospital & Community Psychiatry*, 44(9), 821-823.

This describes two nurse-led outreach models of care designed to provide services to rural elderly residents who are mentally ill. One program serves a relatively homogeneous elderly population in Iowa, and the other serves a more culturally diverse white and minority clientele in Virginia. Although the models differ in some important respects, both are multidisciplinary, emphasize geographical appropriateness of services, promote utilization of existing community resources, coordinate diverse services and offer supportive programs such as those for caregivers. Because the areas served are demographic, economic and epidemiologic microcosms of the rural Midwest and the rural Southeast, the programs are replicable models of rural geriatric mental health care.

053 Buckwalter, K., Smith, M. & Caston, C. (1994). Mental and social health of the rural elderly. In R. Coward, N. Bull, G. Kulkulka, and J. Gallager (Eds.), *Health services for rural elders.* New York: Springer Publishing Co.

This provides an overview of geriatric mental health services in rural America, including an examination of the need for services, obstacles to delivering those services, costs and service provider issues, regional and cultural variations, factors that influence mental health services to the rural elderly, and innovative programs that have successfully reached the rural elderly population. Research, policy, educational, and program development issues were also identified

054 Buckwalter, K. (1996). Interventions for family caregivers of patients with Alzheimer's disease in community-based settings: Items for consideration. *International Psychogeriatrics*, 8(Suppl 1), 121-122.

This article discusses the need for more rigorous evaluation research on existing services for Alzheimer's disease (AD) in rural areas. The needs, resources, and responses of rural caregivers, and the development, implementation, and evaluation of innovative services where they do not exist are of particular interest. Improved accessibility of diagnostic services in rural areas (e.g., mobile or traveling diagnostic clinics, coordinated by local health care professionals, with referral to local resources for follow-up) is needed.

055 Bull, C.N., Bane & S.D. (2001). Program development and innovation. *Journal of Applied Gerontology*, 20(2), 184-194.

This article argues that in the face of geographic isolation, economic deprivation, the lack of a well-defined human infrastructure, and limited economies of scale, innovation and flexibility must be the catchwords to ensure the adequate development of mental health services and programs in rural areas. The adaptation of urban models is possible, especially if rural cultural values are taken into account. The major components that should be part of a rural model of mental health service delivery are reviewed, focusing on the barriers of distance, individuals' privacy, the coordination and use of the present but often weak human infrastructure, and coordination between agencies and across political boundaries.

056 Burke, M.R. (2002). School-based substance abuse prevention: Political finger-pointing does not work. *Federal Probation*, 66, 66-71.

This describes the poor evaluation results of the Drug Abuse Resistance Education (D.A.R.E.) program, the most widely implemented youth drug prevention program in the United States, and recent speculation that adolescent drug use may again be on the rise, has focused much attention on substance abuse prevention programs administered in school settings. It is not uncommon to find school-based prevention in the spotlight, as schools have traditionally been the site of both alcohol and drug education and the collection of adolescent substance use data.

057 Bushy, A. (1993). Rural women: Lifestyles and health status. *Nursing clinics of North America*, 28(1), 187- 197.

This article presented a "snapshot" of the concerns and issues confronting America's rural women. The discussion highlighted demographic, economic, and sociocultural factors that impact the health status of women living in diverse rural environments. Recommendations were proposed to assist nurses to better address the health concerns of these women.

058 Bussing, R., Zima, B.T. & Belin, T.R. (1998). Differential access to care for children with ADHD in special education programs. *Psychiatric Services*, 49(9), 1226-1229.

This Article examined access to treatment in the general health, specialty mental health, and informal care sectors for children with attention-deficit hyperactivity disorder (ADHD). Special education of second to fourth grade students in a Florida school district were screened for ADHD. Children identified as high-risk and their parents completed diagnostic and services assessment interviews. Female gender, minority status and rural residence lowered the probability of ADHD service use in the general health sector. Use of services in the mental health and informal sectors was predicted by a child's need for services.

059 Campbell, C., Richie, S.D. & Hargrove, D.S. (2003). Poverty and rural mental health. In: Stamm, B. Hudnall (Ed). *Rural behavioral health care: An interdisciplinary guide.* (pp. 41-51). Washington, D.C.: American Psychological Association.

The purpose of this chapter is to explore the impact of poverty on the mental health of rural Americans and on the type and quality of mental health services that are available. The authors address prenatal care and care of children first, followed by care of adolescents and adults, and finally, the elderly. Several recommendations within a systems paradigm are offered: utilize and strengthen educational resources, increase people's options through vocational counseling, strengthen and increase community-based mental health resources, and tailor prevention and intervention activities to specific communities.

060 Campbell, C.D., Gordon, M.C. & Chandler, A.A. (2002). Wide open spaces: Meeting mental health needs in underserved rural areas. *Journal of Psychology & Christianity*, 21(4), 325-332.

The significant mental health needs and inadequate psychological services of rural communities are described. Many rural residents are highly religious and most espouse Christian beliefs. These residents are likely to turn to their pastors or primary care physicians for help with mental, emotional, and relational problems. It is recommended that Christian doctoral psychology programs collaborate with local clergy, physicians, and teachers to more adequately meet the mental health needs of rural residents.

061 Caplan, C. & Brangan, N. (November 2004). *Prescription Drug Spending and Coverage Among Rural Medicare Beneficiaries in 2003*. AARP Public Policy Institute: Washington, D.C. Available online: http://www.aarp.org/ppi.

This report by the AARP Public Policy Institute Data Digest identifies the projected out-of-pocket spending on prescription drugs by age 65+ Medicare beneficiaries living in rural areas in 2003. The report also highlights differences in income and prescription drug coverage among rural and urban beneficiaries.

062 Castro, F.G. & Gutierres, S. (1997). Drug and alcohol use among rural Mexican Americans. In: Roberson, E.B., Sloboda, Z., Boyd, G.M., Beatty, L, and Kozel, N.J., eds. *Rural Substance Abuse: State of Knowledge and Issues*. National Institute on Drug Abuse; U.S. Department of Health and Human Services; National Institutes of Health: NIH Publication No. 97-4177. Rockville, MD.

This chapter reviews literature related to the prevalence and incidence of substance abuse in the Mexican American population. Comparisons are made between those still living in Mexico, in either rural or urban areas, and those living in either location in the United States. It also discusses differences between adults and youth, males and females, and issues associated with substance abuse, such as cultural values and acculturation.

063 Cellucci, T. & Vik, P. (2001). Training for substance abuse treatment among psychologists in a rural State. *Professional Psychology - Research & Practice*, 32, 248-252.

Licensed psychologists in Idaho were surveyed about their training and provision of substance abuse services. Of 144 respondents (66 percent return rate), nearly all (89 percent) had contact with substance abusers, yet most rated their graduate training as inadequate preparation for practice. Rural psychologists reported seeing the highest percentage of substance abusers. Many psychologists limited their treatment to self-help group referral. Continuing education offers the most immediate solution and might be related to certification efforts. Pre-doctoral training of generalist psychologists, especially in rural areas, is advocated with an emphasis on integrated behavioral health care.

064 Chalifoux, Z., Neese, J., Buckwalter, K., Litwak, E. & Abraham, I. (1996). Mental health services for rural elderly: Innovative Service Strategies. *Community Mental Health Journal*, 32(5), 463-480.

This article reviews issues in planning and delivering mental health services to rural dwelling elderly. Several strategies for improving the development and delivery of geriatric mental health services to rural areas are discussed. These include 1) increasing the number and quality of rural mental health providers; 2) adapting or developing diagnostic techniques to improve case identification among rural elderly; 3) providing culturally sensitive mental health services; strengthening informal and formal care linkages in rural communities; 4) developing innovative service delivery models building upon the strengths of rural settings and 5) emphasizing fluidity as well as continuity in treatment models.

065 Chandler, D., Meisel, J., Hu, T.W., McGowen, M. & Madison, K. (1998). A capitated model for a cross-section of severely mentally ill clients: Hospitalization. *Community Mental Health Journal*, 34(1), 13-26.

This article examined hospitalization outcomes in a three-year random assignment controlled study of two capitated Integrated Service Agencies (ISAs) in California. Using the flexibility of capitated funding, the urban ISA reduced inpatient length of stay and days, but not admissions. Elements of the capitated ISA model worked together to produce clinically appropriate and less costly use of inpatient services. At the rural ISA, admissions, but not cost, were reduced substantially during the first to second years of the demonstration.

066 Chandler, D., Meisel J., et al. (1996). Client outcomes in a three-year controlled study of an integrated service agency model. *Psychiatric Services*, 47(12), 1337-1343.

In a three-year controlled study, two California integrated service agency (ISA) demonstration programs that combined structural and program reforms were tested to see if they produced improved outcomes for a cross-section of 439 clients with severe and persistent mental illness (schizophrenia and/or bipolar disorder). Compared with comparison Ss, ISA Ss had less hospital care, greater workforce participation, fewer group and institutional housing arrangements, less use of conservatorship, greater social support, more leisure activity, less family burden and greater client and family satisfaction. Ss in the urban ISA program, but not those Ss in the rural ISA program, did better than comparison Ss on measures of financial stability, personal wellbeing and friendship. 72.6 percent of urban ISA Ss participated in the work force during the three-year study period, compared with 14.6 percent of comparison Ss. The capitated costs for ISA Ss were much higher than the costs for services used by comparison Ss.

067 Chandler, D., Meisel, J., McGowen, M., Mintz, J., et al. (1996). Client outcomes in two model capitated integrated service agencies. *Psychiatric Services*, 47(2), 175-180.

This examined client outcomes for the first year of service at two integrated service agencies (ISAs) for severely mentally ill persons, to study the combined impact of assertive continuous treatment program, and consolidated funding and capitation. Participation of the demonstration Ss in the work force was higher than those in the CGs. No significant differences were found in hospitalization rates and costs, arrests, convictions, self-esteem, symptomatology, substance abuse, homelessness, or quality of life. Both ISA groups showed decreased use of hospital care and better treatment outcomes than CGs. Urban ISA Ss participated in more leisure and social activities than CG Ss.

068 Chassin, L., Pillow, D.R., Curran, P.J., Molina, B.S.G & Barrera, M., Jr. (1993). Relations of parental alcoholism to early adolescent substance use: A test of three mediation mechanisms. *Journal of Abnormal Psychology*, 102(1), 3-19.

This test assessed three hypothesized mediating mechanisms underlying the relation between parental alcoholism and adolescent substance use. Results suggested that parental alcoholism influenced adolescent substance use through stress and negative affect pathways, through decreased parental monitoring, and through increased temperamental emotionality. Both negative affect and impaired parental monitoring were associated with adolescents' membership in a peer network that supported drug use behavior. The data did not support a link between parental alcoholism and temperamental sociability.

069 Chen, D.T., Blank, M.B. & Worrall, B.B. (1999). Defending telepsychiatry: Comment. *Psychiatric Services*, 50(2), 266.

The comments by A. Werner and L. Anderson defend telepsychiatry use in rural environments, but disagree with some of the conclusions. Their objections fall into three categories: cost is considered alone without comparison analysis; new technologies are most expensive when first implemented, becoming more cost-effective over time and after full integration into a system; and cost alone should not determine the existence of a service.

070 Chumbler, N.R., Cody, M., Booth, B.M. & Beck, C.K. (2001). Rural-urban differences in service use for memory-related problems in older adults. *Journal of Behavioral Health Services & Research*, 28(2), 212-221.

The purpose of this study was to determine whether rural-urban differences exist in the probability of any service use of primary care physicians and mental health specialists in a full sample of 1,368 older adults (aged 60-91 years) and in a subset of 118 impaired respondents. In the full sample, rural respondents were 0.66 times as likely ($p = .06$) to have used primary care physicians for memory-related problems compared with urban respondents. In the subgroup, rural individuals were 0.26 times as likely ($p = .02$). In both groups, there were no rural-urban differences in the probability of mental health specialty use for memory-related problems.

071 Ciarlo, J.A., Wackwitz, J.H., Wagenfeld, M.O. & Mohatt, D.F. (1996). *Focusing on "frontier": Isolated rural America. Letter to the Field No. 2.* Boulder, CO: Frontier Mental Health Resource Network, WICHE Mental Health Program, http:/www.wiche/edu/mentalhealth

Frontier rural areas, distinguished primarily by low population density and great isolation, exist at the furthest end of the urban/rural continuum. Understanding and serving their mental health needs requires distinguishing them from the large number of rural communities closer to the urban end of the continuum. As most health and demographic data exist in the simplified binary classifications of metro/nonmetro and rural/urban, this task can be challenging.

072 Clark, J.J., Leukefeld, C. & Godlaski, T. (1999). Case management and behavioral contracting: Components of rural substance abuse treatment. *Journal of Substance Abuse Treatment,* 17(4), 293-304.

This article presents a model of case management with rural clients entering drug and alcohol treatment. As part of a larger treatment protocol called Structured Behavioral Outpatient Rural Therapy, behavioral contracting is combined with strengths perspective case management to help rural clients motivate themselves to engage and complete drug and alcohol treatment. This combined approach is designed to continually communicate and teach an "A-B-C" cognitive-behavioral approach to problem-solving and change.

073 Clayer, J; Bookless, C; Air, T; McFarlane, A. (1998). Psychiatric disorder and disability in a rural community. *Social Psychiatry & Psychiatric Epidemiology,* 33(6), 269-273.

This examined the relationship between psychiatric disorder and disability in a rural community and the use of formal and informal services in the management of such disabilities. It was found that of the 26 percent of the surveyed population who obtained a positive current psychiatric diagnosis, 48.3 percent had required assistance in managing at least one activity of daily living. The majority of those seeking assistance in managing these functional problems did so from family and friends rather than from formal agencies. Psychiatric disorder was found to lead to disability as frequently as did physical disorder, with almost 50 percent of those who had experienced mental health problems reporting that they were currently unable to carry out at least one activity of daily living.

074 Cohen, P. & Hesselbart, C.S. (1993). Demographic factors in the use of children's mental health services. *American Journal of Public Health*, 83(1), 49-52.

This ascertained demographic factors that distinguish youth with mental disorders who receive mental health services from youth who do not receive services. Mental health services were less used by youths ages 18-21 years, living in rural or semi-rural areas, and living in middle-income families. Ss from middle-income families had fewer consultations than did Ss from either poorer or wealthier families, but both the poorer and middle-income Ss received less treatment than did the wealthier Ss.

075 Conger, R.D., Conger, K.J., Elder, Jr., G.H., Lorenz, F., Simons, R. & Whitbeck, L. (1992). A family process model of economic hardship and adjustment of early adolescent boys. *Child Development*, 63, 526-541.

This found that objective economic conditions were related to parents' emotional status and behaviors through their perceptions of increased economic pressures. These pressures were associated with depression and demoralization for both parents, which were related to marital conflict and disruptions in skillful parenting. Disrupted parenting mediated the relations between the earlier steps in the stress process and ADA. The emotions and behaviors of both mothers and fathers were almost equally affected by financial difficulties, and disruptions in each parent's childrearing behaviors had adverse consequences for ADA.

076 Conger, R.D., Conger, K.J., Elder, Jr., G.H., Lorenz, F., Simons, R. & Whitbeck, L. (1993). Family economic stress and adjustment of early adolescent girls. *Developmental Psychology*, 29, 209-219.

This proposes a family process model that links economic stress in family life to prosocial and problematic adolescent adjustment. Economic pressures led to depression and demoralization for both parents, the result of which was greater marital conflict and disruptions in skillful parenting. The emotions and behaviors of both mothers and fathers were almost equally affected by financial difficulties, and disruptions in each parent's childrearing behaviors had adverse consequences for adolescent development. Parents' depressed mood and disrupted childrearing practices both directly affected girls' adjustment.

077 Conger, R.D., Ge, X., Elder, Jr., G.H., Lorenz, F.O. & Simons, R.L. (1994). Economic stress, coercive family process, and developmental problems of adolescents. *Child Development*, 65, 541-561.

This developed a model of family conflict and coercion that links economic stress in family life to adolescent symptoms of internalizing and externalizing emotions and behaviors. The theoretical model proposes that economic pressure experienced by parents would increase parental dysphoria and marital conflict as well as conflicts between parents and children over money. Results are consistent with the proposed model.

078 Conger, R.D. & Rueter, M.A. (1995). Siblings, parents, and peers: A longitudinal study of social influences in adolescent risk for alcohol use and abuse. In: Brody, G., ed. *Sibling Relationships: Their Causes and Consequences*. Norwood, NJ: Ablex Publishing.

This study describes how parents influence the development of adolescent drinking in a number of different ways. From a social learning perspective, parents are models for drinking behavior. Within this realm, they convey attitudes, model appropriate contexts for drinking and establish rules for the use or nonuse of alcohol by teenagers.

079 Conger, R.D. (1997). The social context of substance abuse: A developmental perspective. In: Roberson, E.B., Sloboda, Z., Boyd, G.M., Beatty, L, and Kozel, N.J., eds. *Rural Substance Abuse: State of Knowledge and Issues*. National Institute on Drug Abuse; U.S. Department of Health and Human Services; National Institutes of Health: NIH Publication No. 97-4177. Rockville, MD.

This chapter reviews literature related to the development of substance abuse, offering social-contextual approach. The author describes genetic and neurobiological precipitants, cognitive and emotional factors, as well as parenting and family practices that contribute to the development of substance use disorders and delinquency.

080 Constantine, M.G. (2001). Stress in rural farm women: Implications for the use of diverse mental health interventions. *Journal of Psychotherapy in Independent Practice*, 2(2), 15-22.

This article discusses the mental health needs of females living on rural farms, and the value of mental health interventions. Rural farm women may experience an inordinate amount of stress stemming from numerous sources in their lives, including role overload, a lack of acknowledgment for their contributions to the farm and home, and social isolation. Though informal help and support may be helpful, there may be at times a need for more deliberate or intensive intervention related to coping. Counseling techniques that focus on client empowerment, including cognitive-behavioral therapy, may be especially helpful.

081 Cook, A.D., Copans, S.A. & Schetky, D.H. (1998). Psychiatric treatment of children and adolescents in rural communities: Myths and realities. *Child & Adolescent Psychiatric Clinics of North America*, 7(3), 673-690.

Because of the relatively low number of child psychiatrists in rural settings, the child psychiatrist's presence in the community is vastly different from that of his or her urban colleagues. Although this setting has innumerable advantages for one's ability to understand the patient's ecology, it also can be an obstacle to the provision of appropriate treatment. Long distances, uneven resources, and rural culture can be special problems to overcome. The authors describe the challenges and pleasures of psychiatric practice in rural American communities, and reveal the reality of rural practice.

082 Cuffel, B.J. (1994). Violent and destructive behavior among the severely mentally ill in rural areas: Evidence from Arkansas' community mental health system. *Community Mental Health Journal*, 30(5), 495-504.

This article compared rates of violence among urban and rural admissions to the Arkansas State Hospital system to test the hypothesis that thresholds for admission to the hospital were greater in rural areas. Consistent with the hypothesis, rural patients showed increased likelihood of violent and destructive behavior prior to admission. The increased rate of violence was particularly evident in those using substances prior to admission, which suggests that community management of the violent, substance abusing patient may be particularly difficult for rural areas.

083 Cunningham, J.K. & Thielemier, M.A. (1995). *24 Trends and Regional Variations in Amphetamine-Related Emergency Admissions*: California, 1984-1993. Irvine, CA: Public Statistics Institute.

This describes data from epidemiological studies, which show that methamphetamine use has increased to the point that it is now a major national public health concern.

084 Cutrona, C.E., Halvorson, M.B.J & Russell, D.W. (1996). Mental health services for rural children, youth, and their families. In: Heflinger, C.A., Nixon, C.T. (Eds). *Families and the mental health system for children and adolescents: Policy, services, and research. Children's mental health services*, Vol. 2. (pp. 217-237).

This article reviews the difficulties that children and families in rural areas have had in accessing appropriate [mental health] services and provide examples of overcoming barriers.

085 Danbom, D. (1995). *Born in the country : A history of rural America.* Baltimore: Johns Hopkins University Press.

Born in the Country integrates agricultural, technological, and economic themes with new questions social historians have raised about the American experience from pre-Columbian times to the 20th century. Danbom also discusses the complex changes in the interrelationship between rural and urban America, as the character of rural living changed.

086 Davidson, R.A. (2002). Community-based education and problem-solving: The Community Health Scholars Program at the University of Florida. *Teaching & Learning in Medicine*, 14(3), 178-181.

This examined the community role of medical students' attitudes toward the Community Health Scholars program (CHSP). Results show that CHSP provided notable services to many communities. Over 80 percent of subjects (Ss) believed that CHSP was a good or excellent learning experience while over 90 percent believed that the program affected their career choice. All Ss believed that the program should be continued. It is concluded that CHSP successfully provides a service-learning experience for medical students while promoting solutions to problems in underserved communities.

087 Dawkins, M.P. (1996). The social context of substance use among African American youth: Rural, urban and suburban comparisons. *Journal of Alcohol & Drug Education*, 41, 68-85.

This study compared substance use perceptions and behavior of African American youth in metropolitan (urban and suburban) and nonmetropolitan (rural) settings. Based on an analysis of data from a subsample of 3,009 African American eighth graders who participated in the National Educational Longitudinal Study of 1988 and follow-ups in 1990 and 1992, the findings revealed that, overall, substance abuse is perceived as a relatively serious problem at school, and by the 12th grade most adolescents have tried alcohol and a substantial proportion have used marijuana. Early substance use and peer influence are major determinants of later substance use within each context. However, some important differences exist in the prediction of alcohol and marijuana use within each social context, suggesting a need to take into account the relative importance of selective socio-demographic, risk and protective factors for substance use within different social-environmental settings.

088 Dawkins, M.P. & Williams, M.M. (1997). Substance abuse in rural African American populations. In: Roberson, E.B., Sloboda, Z., Boyd, G.M., Beatty, L, and Kozel, N.J., eds. *Rural Substance Abuse: State of Knowledge and Issues*. National Institute on Drug Abuse; U.S. Department of Health and Human Services; National Institutes of Health: NIH Publication No. 97- 4177. Rockville, MD.

The authors describe literature related to substance abuse in rural African American populations, but note that research is relatively limited. Studies tend to regard alcohol abuse. Typically, research has involved ethnographic studies that look at the relation of alcohol use to culture, community services that compare blacks to whites on drinking behavior, attitudes, and problems, or findings from regional or national surveys. Future research recommendations are offered.

089 Dekraai, M. (2004, November). Building Child and Family Systems of Care in Rural Areas. Web-cast Presentation facilitated by the Western InterState Commission on Higher Education, Boulder, CO.

This web-cast presentation by Dr. Mark Dekraai discussed the following issues in the seminar: 1) components of a system of care, 2) developing strategies for intersystem collaboration, 3) conceptualizing family involvement, 4) evaluating evidence-based practices and 5) understanding financing options.

090 Deleon, P.H., Crimmins, D.B. & Wolf, A.W. (2003). Afterword—The 21st Century has Arrived. *Psychotherapy: Theory, Research, Practice, Training*, 40, 164–169.

This article describes how technology will continue to transform all aspects of professional psychology as a health care discipline in the 21st century. Educated consumers will expect empirically supported practice guidelines. Current and future practitioners will require training in the use of new technologies. Telehealth will further challenge the constraints of State-bound licensing laws by requiring legislation to provide mobility to professional licensure. The central role of the Federal government in facilitating these changes is reviewed.

091 DeLeon, P.H., Wakefield, M. & Hagglund, K.J. (2003). The behavioral health care needs of rural communities. In: Stamm, B.H. (Ed). *Rural behavioral health care: An interdisciplinary guide*. (pp. 23-31). Washington, D.C.: American Psychological Association.

The authors first review some of the policy and history of rural health care. The chapter then addresses the underlying issues surrounding current provision of quality health care to residents of the rural U.S. The authors suggest that common ground between the involved parties—including nonphysician practitioners, physicians, and consumers—must be reached before demands of public policy regarding the scope of practice issues and determinations of clinical competency can be made.

092 Dellasega, C. (1991). Meeting the mental health needs of elderly clients. *Journal of Psychosocial Nursing*, 29(2): 10-14.

This study found that lack of referrals and failure of the aged to seek services partially accounted for underuse. Legislative changes mandating that aged persons be screened for and receive appropriate mental health services will increase the demand for qualified providers. Nursing's approach to care of the older adult, which focuses on both physiological and psychological needs, can facilitate the delivery of comprehensive effective mental health interventions in and out of the institutional setting.

093 Dimmitt, J. & Davila, Y. (1995). Group psychotherapy for abused women: A survivor group prototype. *Applied Nursing Research*, 8, 3-8.

Theoretical and research-based clinical psychiatric nursing interventions are prerequisites for the advancement of the psychiatric mental health nursing practice. Based on these prerequisites, the authors implemented a group psychotherapy intervention for battered women using Campbell's adaptation (1986) of Litton's survivor-group prototype (1976). This group prototype was chosen because it specifically recognizes the strengths of survivors of violent experiences. Major process and content themes were identified through analysis of group psychotherapy sessions, substantiating the efficacy of this group prototype as a basis for intervention with women abuse.

094 Dollard, N., Evans, M.E., Lubrecht, J. & Schaeffer, D. (1994). The use of flexible service dollars in rural community-based programs for children with serious emotional disturbance and their families. *Journal of Emotional & Behavioral Disorders*, 2(2), 117-125.

This article examined the actual uses of flexible service dollars (FSDs) in two highly individualized service-provision efforts in the rural settings in North Idaho and up State New York. The elements that contributed to successful use of FSDs in these States were: 1) the ready availability of FSDs with which to individualize services, 2) the dissemination of flexible funds at the local intensive-treatment team level and 3) fiscal accountability at the local team level. A call for additional research on outcomes associated with individualized care was made.

095 Doniger, M., Tempier, R., Lalinec-Michaud, M. & Meunier, D. (1986). Telepsychiatry: Psychiatric consultation through two-way television. A controlled study. *Canadian Journal of Psychiatry*, 31(1) 32-34.

This study obtained ratings of a psychiatric consultation from 50 patients interviewed via closed-circuit TV (telepsychiatry) and 35 patients seen in face-to-face interviews. Although ratings by patients, consultees, and consultants all tended to be higher in face-to-face interviews, the magnitude of the difference was relatively small. Results support the broader application of interactive TV in psychiatric consultation, particularly as a complement to live consultations in isolated areas.

096 Donnermeyer, J.F. & Wurschmidt, T.N. (1997). Educators' perceptions of the D.A.R.E. program. *Journal of Drug Education*, 27, 259-276.

The authors examined the perceptions of educators about the Drug Abuse Resistance Education (DARE) program, based on the results of a Statewide survey among 286 fifth and sixth grade teachers and principals. Educators gave their highest ratings to teacher/officer interaction, the role playing exercises, and the graduation ceremony. Ratings of overall program quality and the impact of the program on students were both high.

097 Donnermeyer, J.F. (2000). Parents' perceptions of a school-based prevention education program. *Journal of Drug Education*, 30, 325-342.

This article is an analysis of 720 parents' views of the Drug Abuse Resistance Education (DARE) program based on a Statewide survey of adults from rural, suburban, and urban communities who had a child participate in the program within the past year. Parent involvement and knowledge of DARE. was high. Generally, parents were very positive about DARE, especially when they viewed the DARE. officer as an effective educator.

098 D'Onofrio, C.N. (1997). The prevention of alcohol use by rural youth. In: Roberson, E.B., Sloboda, Z., Boyd, G.M., Beatty, L, and Kozel, N.J., eds. *Rural Substance Abuse: State of Knowledge and Issues*. National Institute on Drug Abuse; U.S. Department of Health and Human Services; National Institutes of Health: NIH Publication No. 97-4177. Rockville, MD.

The author reviews literature and presents available data regarding the use of alcohol by youth in urban and rural areas (although it is noted that this data is lacking). The etiological context of youth drinking, as well as its consequences are described. Ultimately, a variety of prevention programs, program design and policy issues are described.

099 Dorwart, R.A. (1990). Managed Mental Health Care: Myths and Realities in the 1990s. *Hospital & Community Psychiatry*, 41, 1087-1091.

The author discusses the origins, actors, and major issues involved in managed health care in terms of prevailing myths and future realities. He calls for more and better research to answer important clinical and policy questions about managed care and for improved communication between mental health professionals and managed care organizations.

100 Drake, R.E., Essock, S.M., Shaner, A., Carey, K.B., Minkoff, K., Kola, L., Lynde, D., Osher, F. C., Clark, R. E., & Rickards, L. (2001). Implementing dual diagnosis services for clients with severe mental illness. *Psychiatric Services*, 52, 469-476.

Effective dual diagnosis programs combine mental health and substance abuse interventions that are tailored for the complex needs of clients with comorbid disorders. The authors describe the critical components of effective programs, including a comprehensive, longterm, staged approach to recovery; assertive outreach; motivational interventions; provision of help to clients in acquiring skills and support to manage the illnesses and to pursue functional goals; and cultural sensitivity and competence. Many State mental health systems are implementing dual diagnosis services but high-quality services are rare. The authors provide an overview of the numerous barriers to implementation and describe implementation strategies to overcome the barriers. Current approaches to implementing dual diagnosis programs involve organizational and financing changes at the policy level, clarity of program mission with structural changes to support dual diagnosis services, training and supervision for clinicians, and dissemination of accurate information to consumers and families to support understanding, demand, and advocacy.

101 Drug Abuse Warning Network (1997). *Number of Methamphetamine and Amphetamine-Related Episodes: 1988-1995*. Substance Abuse and Mental Health Services Administration,

This provides national data on the number of methamphetamine and amphetamine-related episodes from 1988 to 1995.

102 Dukes, R.L., Ullman, J.B & Stein, J.A. (1996). Three-year follow-up of drug abuse resistance education (D.A.R.E.). *Evaluation Review*, 20, 49-66.

The review assessed the long-term effectiveness of Drug Abuse Resistance Education (D.A.R.E) by contrasting 497 ninth-grade students from 21 elementary schools who received the D.A.R.E program in the sixth grade with 352 others from 17 elementary schools who did not receive the program. A follow-up survey assessed central D.A.R.E concepts such as self-esteem, resistance to peer pressure, delay of experimentation with drugs, and drug use. Employing latent variables to represent the concepts, no significant differences were found between D.A.R.E participants and controls.

103 Dyer, J. (1997). *Harvest of rage: Why Oklahoma City is only the beginning.* Boulder, CO: Westview Press.

In this book, Joel Dyer discusses the link between the farm crisis of the 1980s and the increase of the antigovernment movement of the 1990s. Small farmers have witnessed fewer markets, decreasing prices, and the rise of multinational food companies. With the increase in multinational food companies, many small farmers were forced out of business during the 1980s. The author discusses some of the repercussions of these changes including increased number of suicides, murders, racist views and conspiracy theories.

104 Eberhardt, M.S., Ingram, D.D & Makuc, D.M. (2001). *Urban and rural health chartbook: Health United States 2001.* Hyattsville, MD: National Center for Health Statistics.

This report documents differences in a wide-ranging set of health characteristics for people residing in communities from the most rural to the most urban. The report also presents detailed analysis of population characteristics, health risk factors, health status indicators, and health care access measures for residents of counties grouped by five urbanization levels. It also examines patterns by region of the country. Full report available online: http://www.cdc.gov/nchs/data/hus/hus01.pdf

105 Economic Research Service (ERS); United States Department of Agriculture (2005). http://www.ers.usda.gov/

The ERS website features: 1) five research emphasis areas that reflect the agency's strategic goals; more than 80 briefing rooms offering in-depth synthesis of the economic issues that frame the research; 22-key topic areas populated with data, publications, and other products; 4) access to around 9,000 data sets; 5) hundreds of publications and 6) a section with job listings and other services.

106 Edwards, R.W. (1997). Drug and alcohol use among youth in rural communities. In: Roberson, E.B., Sloboda, Z., Boyd, G.M., Beatty, L, and Kozel, N.J., eds. *Rural Substance Abuse: State of Knowledge and Issues.* National Institute on Drug Abuse; U.S. Department of Health and Human Services; National Institutes of Health: NIH Publication No. 97-4177. Rockville, MD.

The author describes findings from available literature (at that time) regarding drug and alcohol use among youth in rural communities, including the context in which it occurs, gender differences, prevalence, and community variability.

107 Effland, A. B. W. & Butler, M. A. (1997). Fewer immigrants settle in nonmetro areas and most fare less well than metro immigrants. *Rural Conditions and Trends,* 8(2), 60-65.

This issue of *Rural Conditions and Trends* provides a review of annual data regarding the socioeconomic well-being of rural areas in the United States. The article States that fewer immigrants live in nonmetro areas than in metro areas. The article also notes that Mexico is the largest source of immigration to the nonmetro United States. The authors also discuss how immigrants in nonmetro areas compare to immigrants in metro areas (e.g., unemployment rates, poverty rates).

108 Elliot, D.S., Huizinga, D. & Menard, S. (1989). *Multiple Problem Youth: Delinquency, Substance Use, and Mental Health Problems.* New York: SpringerVerlag.

This book relies on data from the National Youth Survey to examine underlying causes and treatment strategies for youth struggling with substance use, mental health issues, and delinquency.

109 Ellor, J.R. & Kurz, D.J. (1982). Misuse and abuse of prescription and nonprescription drugs by the elderly. *Nursing Clinics of North America,* 17, 319–330.

This describes issues of prescription and nonprescription drug misuse or abuse by the elderly, including how home remedies, nutritional supplements, vitamins, and alcohol can potentially interact with prescribed medications as well as with each other.

110 Ermer, D.J. (1999). Experience with a rural telepsychiatry clinic for children and adolescents. *Psychiatric Services,* 50(2), 260-261

Access to child and adolescent psychiatric services in many rural areas is limited by lack of physicians and long travel times. A child and adolescent telepsychiatry clinic that is part of the University of Kansas Medical Center's telemedicine program addresses this problem by linking the medical center with a county mental health center in rural Pittsburgh, Kansas. The clinic receives ten to 18 visits a week and has been able to serve severely disturbed children and children in crisis. The quality of clinical interactions in the telepsychiatry clinic appears comparable to that in face-to-face meetings.

111 ERS/USDA (1995). *Understanding Rural America.* Agricultural Information Bulletin No. 710. Washington, D.C.: Economic Research Service, U.S. Department of Agriculture.

The diversity of rural America and the changes it has undergone in the last half century have resulted in a wide variety of economic conditions and needs. This full-color report documents changes in rural employment, population, and well-being for six categories of rural counties: those that depend on farming, manufacturing, and services, and those that have high concentrations of retirees, Federal lands, and poverty.

112 Eveland, A.P., Dever, G.E.A., Schafer, E., Sprinkel, C., Davis, S. & Rumpf, M. (1998). Analysis of health service areas: Another piece of the psychiatric workforce puzzle. *Psychiatric Services*, 49(7), 956-960.

This examines the application of two benchmark standards for the number of psychiatrists needed per 100,000 population—the standard developed by the Graduate Medical Education National Advisory Committee and the Average Requirement Benchmark— to the supply of psychiatrists in Georgia in 1996 by county and by health service regions, which are geographical units based on health care utilization patterns of Medicare and Medicaid recipients. Areas with a surplus or deficit of psychiatrists are identified. The findings provide contextual evidence of a surplus of psychiatric physicians in the most populous areas of the State, given a substantial presence of health maintenance organizations.

113 Farley, T. (1998). Integrated primary care in rural areas. Blount, A. (Ed). *Integrated primary care: The future of medical and mental health collaboration.*

The author describes how he went about setting up an integrated mental and medical health care practice in a rural Texas town. He makes the case for the importance of integrated care in rural settings. At the same time, he gives an account of the difficulties and challenges involved in setting up such a practice. Specific issues addressed include: differences between rural and urban communities; setting up integrated care in rural areas; and the small Texas town in which this practice was established.

114 Farmer, E.M.Z, Burns, B.J., Angold, A. & Costello, E.J. (1997). Impact of children's mental health problems on families: Relationships with service use. *Journal of Emotional & Behavioral Disorders*, 5(4), 230-238.

Impact on the family resulting from children's emotional and behavioral problems, with particular attention to relationships between such family impact and use of mental health services, is explored in this article. Data come from the Great Smoky Mountains Study, an epidemiologic, longitudinal study of children's mental health problems and service use in a rural region of the southeastern US. Youths who first used services when they were 10-15 years of age showed significantly higher rates and levels of family impact than similar youths who did not enter services. Such impacts were most notable in the areas of parental well-being (e.g., depression, worries) and parents' sense of competence to handle the child's problems. Youths in this age range who used services but were not new to the system showed somewhat higher rates of family impact than youths who were new to the system, particularly in the area of parental use of mental health services.

115 Farrell, S.P., Blank, M., Koch, J.R., Munjas, B. & Clement, D.G. (1999). Predicting whether patients receive continuity of care after discharge from State hospitals: Policy implications. *Archives of Psychiatric Nursing*, 13(6), 279-285.

This reports the results of a comprehensive study of predictors of predisposing, enabling and need factors influencing or impeding continuity of care for individuals discharged from State hospitals and re-entering communities. Results show that a person discharged from a State hospital to a rural Community Mental Health Center (CMHC) is twice as likely to have continuity of care when compared to a person discharged to a CMHC classified as urban. Other results show that the predisposing factors age risk and race were significant predictors of receiving continuity of care. Of the need factors associated with continuity of care, length of stay in hospital, substance abuse and diagnosis were significant predictors.

116 Farrell, S.P. & McKinnon, C. (2003). Technology and Rural Mental Health. *Archives of Psychiatric Nursing*, 17(1) Feb 2003, 20-26.

The authors describe how technology has the potential to decrease the gap in services and improve education, support, and connectedness between the client and the provider. As an alternative to traditional face-to-face contact for those in rural and geographically dispersed areas, the Internet potentially can bridge the disparities in health care access for rural mental health services.

117 Fekete, D.M., Bond, G.R., McDonel, E.C., Salyers, M., Chen, A., Miller, L. (1998). Rural assertive community treatment: A field experiment.

The authors assessed the effectiveness of Assertive Community Treatment (ACT) compared to traditional mental health services for individuals with severe mental illness in four rural communities. Two-year findings were mildly encouraging. Experimental differences on staff rating of quality of life, level of functioning, and symptoms favored ACT clients. There were no experimental differences in hospital use. ACT clients exhibited less residential stability than control clients. Problems implementing the model and suggestions for adapting it for rural areas are discussed.

118 Fischer, E.P., Owen, Jr., R.R. & Cuffel, B.J. (1996). Substance abuse, community services use, and symptoms severity of urban and rural residents with schizophrenia. *Psychiatric Services*, 47(9), 980-984.

The authors examined relations between substance abuse, use of community-based services (CBSs), and symptom severity among 139 rural and urban residents with schizophrenia in the six months after discharge from short-term inpatient care. On average, BPRS scores indicated symptom improvement between baseline and follow-up, but symptoms worsened for 27 percent of Ss. Multivariate analysis, adjusted for baseline symptom severity, indicated poorer outcomes for rural residents, substance abusers, and Ss who did not use CBSs. The greater likelihood of symptom worsening among rural residents was attributed to their less frequent use of CBSs.

119 Flaherty, L.T., Weist, M.D. & Warner, B.S. (1996). School-based mental health services in the United States: History, current models and needs. *Community Mental Health Journal*, 32, 341-352.

This reviews the background of school-based mental health services, compares various models of service delivery, and highlights issues important to the future development and advancement of these services.

120 Flax, J.W., Wagenfeld, M.O., Ive, R.E. & Weiss, R.J. (Eds.). (1979). *Mental health and rural America: An overview and annotated bibliography* (DHEW Publication No. 78-753rd ed.). Washington, DC: U.S. Government Printing Office.

This provides a comprehensive, two-part resource on rural mental health: first, a narrative state-of-the-art overview of the field and, second, an annotated bibliography of the literature.

121 Fontana, A., Rosenheck, R., Spencer, H., Gray, S. & lla, D. (1999). *The long journey home VII: Treatment of posttraumatic stress disorder in the Department of Veterans Affairs: Fiscal year 1998 service delivery and performance*. West Haven, CT: U.S. Department of Veterans Affairs Northeast Program Evaluation Center.

This report examines the services and outcomes of those services to veterans who received treatment at specialized inpatient and residential posttraumatic stress disorder programs at Departments of Veterans Affairs in fiscal year 1998.

122 Fortney, J.C., Owen, R. & Clothier, J. (1999). Impact of travel distance on the disposition of patients presenting for emergency psychiatric care. *Journal of Behavioral Health Services & Research*, 26(1), 104-108.

For veterans presenting for emergency psychiatric care, this research tested the hypothesis that patients with poor geographic accessibility to ambulatory mental health services would be more likely to be hospitalized. Results indicate that distant patients (> 60 miles) were 4.8 times more likely to be admitted for acute psychiatric treatment than were proximal patients (< 60 miles), controlling for clinical and demographic case-mix factors. This finding suggests that the Department of Veterans Affairs might be less effective in its effort to substitute intensive outpatient care in place of expensive inpatient treatment for rural veterans with emergent mental health problems.

123 Fortney, J., Rost, K. & Zhang, M. (1998). A joint choice model of the decision to seek depression treatment and choice of provider sector. *Medical Care*, 36(3), 307-320.

Using a community-based sample of currently depressed subjects, this research modeled the joint decision to seek depression treatment and choice of provider sector (primary care or specialty mental health). The objective was to identify those subject-specific casemix factors and those provider sector-specific access measures that significantly impacted this joint decision. In the six months after baseline, 73.3 percent of the sample did not seek depression treatment, 18.9 percent sought care from a primary care provider, and 7.8 percent sought care from a mental health specialist. The expected maximum utility of sector choice significantly affects the decision to seek treatment. Provider sector-specific access measures (e.g., insurance coverage and availability) significantly impacted sector choice and, thus, the decision to seek treatment. Subject-specific casemix factors (e.g., age, gender, employment status, depression severity and psychiatric comorbidity) significantly affected the decision to seek treatment. Sector-specific access measures significantly impact both provider sector choice and the decision to seek treatment.

124 Fortney, J., Rost, K. & Warren, J. (2000). Comparing alternative methods of measuring geographic access to health services. *Health Services and Outcomes Research Methodology*, 1(2), 173-184.

This research compared alternative measures of geographic access to health care providers using different levels of spatial aggregation (county, zip code and street) and different methods of calculating the cost of space (Euclidean distance, road distance and travel time). Results demonstrated that the most commonly used county-based measures of geographic access (e.g., MSA designation and providers per capita) explained three percent–10 percent of the variation in accessibility and 34 percent–70 percent of the variation in availability. Results indicate that Geographic Information Systems can be used to accurately measure geographic access to health services in a cost effective manner.

125 Foskett, J.H. (1999). Soul searching within the service. *Mental Health, Religion & Culture,* 2(1), 11-17.

This author explores a process of consultation about the religious and spiritual needs and resources of people suffering from severe mental health problems in a rural community and how these are matched with the religious and mental health services within that community. The process of consultation led to the planning and initiating of the service which involved local religious groups and service users and staff. The first year of the project's work is reviewed.

126 Fox, J.C., Blank, M.B., Kane, C.F. & Hargrove, D.S. (1994). Balance theory as a model for coordinating delivery of rural mental health services. *Applied & Preventive Psychology,* 3(2), 121-129.

The authors propose a model for the linkage of formal and informal caregivers for mental health service provision to seriously mentally ill consumers in rural areas. The model is based on the balance theory of coordination (BTC) developed by E. Litwak and H. Meyer (1966) and applies to service delivery systems in the rural areas. The BTC offers a viable perspective to guide service system development and evaluation. By testing the applicability of such a model to rural case management services, it may be possible to ascertain the factors necessary to provide optimal care to seriously mentally ill persons who live in rural areas.

127 Fox, J., Merwin, E. & Blank, M. (1995). Defacto mental health services in the rural south. *Journal of Health Care for the Poor and Underserved,* 6(4), 434- 468.

This describes the availability, accessibility, and use of mental health services in the rural South and the applicability of the de facto model to rural areas. The de facto system combines specialty mental health services with general medical services such as primary care and nursing home care, ministers and counselors, self-help groups, families, and friends. The critical need for data necessary to inform changes in health care relative to rural mental health service delivery is emphasized.

128 Fox, J., Blank, M., Berman, J. & Rovnyak, V.G. (1999). Mental disorders and help seeking in a rural impoverished population. *International Journal of Psychiatry in Medicine*, 29(2), 181-195

This study examined the impact of an in-home screening and educational intervention on help seeking among rural impoverished individuals with untreated mental disorders. Almost one-third (32.4 percent) of these respondents screened positive for at least one disorder. Eighty-four subjects who screened positive and received the educational intervention reported in follow up that they had discussed the interview with a friend or family member, but only eleven (13.1 percent) received encouragement to seek treatment. The predominant reason endorsed for not seeking help was "felt there was no need," even among respondents who were informed that they had a disorder.

129 Freese, T.E., Obert, J., Dickow, A., Cohen, J. & Lord, R.H. (2000). Methamphetamine abuse: Issues for special populations. *Journal of Psychoactive Drugs*, 32, 177-182.

The Center for Substance Abuse Treatment (CSAT) established a multisite Methamphetamine Treatment Program (MTP) that compares the Matrix model treatment program for methamphetamine (MA) to the treatments as usual at seven community-based clinics in California, Montana and Hawaii. Specifically, this article examines cultural, geographic and situational barriers to accessing and completing treatment and presents strategies that have been used to overcome these barriers.

130 Fried, B.J., Johnson, M.C., Starrett, B.E., Calloway, M.O. & Morrissey, J.P. (1998). An empirical assessment of rural community support networks for individuals with severe mental disorders. *Community Mental Health Journal*, 34(1), 39-56.

This describes a strategy for studying system coordination in rural communities and presents results from a pilot study of community support networks for individuals with severe mental disorders in seven rural counties in North Carolina. Exchanges of information were the most common type of interaction among organizations in each network. Client referrals occurred less frequently, and sharing of resources was an even rarer phenomenon.

131 Gale, B.J. (1993). Psychosocial health needs of older women: Urban versus rural comparisons. *Archives of Psychiatric Nursing*, 7(2), 99-105.

The author used a stress-coping framework to study the psychosocial health needs in 55 urban and 55 rural elderly women. Urban women reported higher levels of stress and greater use of community services.

Forty-two percent of the total group of women reported that they had either used psychotropic drugs or felt a need for them and, yet only two percent had ever used outpatient mental health services.

132 Gale J & Coburn A. (2003). *The characteristics and roles of Rural Health Clinics in the United States: A chartbook.* Portland: University of Southern Maine, Edmund S. Muskie School of Public Service, Institute for Health Policy, Maine Rural Health Research Center. Available at: http://muskie.usm.maine.edu/Publications/rural/ RHChartbook03.pdf.

This report used information from the Center for Medicare and Medicaid Services Online, Survey, Certification, and Reporting (OSCAR) database to further understand the attributes and roles of Rural Health Clinics in the United States. Rural Health Clinics were created as a result of the Rural Health Clinic Services Act, passed by Congress in 1977.

133 Gale, J.A. & Deprez, R.D. (2003). A public health approach to the challenges of rural mental health service integration. In: B.H. Stamm (Ed.). *Rural behavioral health care: An interdisciplinary guide.* Washington, D.C., American Psychological Association.

The authors suggest a public health model perspective to inform the discussion of delivering mental health services in rural areas. Within the context of the public health model, they take a broad view of mental health services that includes both a mental health orientation and a mental illness orientation. They describe the de facto rural mental health system, discuss the populations served by the existing systems and their service needs, identify access issues and barriers for these populations, and provide a series of tools with which stakeholders can begin to analyze their local delivery system.

134 Gamm, L., Tai-Seale, M. & Stone, S. (2002). *White paper: Meeting the mental health needs of people living in rural areas.* College Station, TX, Department of Health Policy and Management, School of Rural Public Health, Texas A&M University System Health Science Center.

This paper focused on presenting the prevalence, barriers, and other trends in rural mental health. The paper also offers some solutions to increase access and availability of mental health services for rural residents.

135 Gamm, L.G., Stone, S. & Pittman, S. (2003). Mental Health and Mental Disorders – A Rural Challenge. Rural Healthy People 2010: A companion document to Healthy People 2010. Volume 1. College Station, TX: The Texas A&M University System Health Science Center, School of Rural Public Health, Southwest Rural Health Research Center.

This summary addresses the Healthy People 2010 mental health and mental illness goals to improve mental health and ensure access to appropriate, quality mental health services emphasizing access to treatment by mental health providers in rural areas. This overall goal encompasses three of the 467 specific Healthy People 2010 objectives. These include: 1) primary care screening and assessment, 2) treatment for children with mental health problems, 3) treatment for adults with mental disorders.

136 Geller, J., Beeson, P. & Rodenhiser, R. (1997). Frontier mental health strategies: Integrating, reaching out, building up and connecting. Letter to the Field No. 6. Frontier Mental Health Services Resource Network.

This paper explores the strengths, weaknesses and utilization of four global strategies that are in place today to serve the mental health needs of frontier populations. However, a comprehensive approach to meeting the mental health needs of persons living in frontier areas should consider programs that employ all of these strategies.

137 Gilmour, H., Gibson, F. & Campbell, J. (2003). People with dementia in a rural community: Issues of prevalence and community care policy. *Dementia*, 2(2), 245-263.

This local study, a follow-up to one carried out 10 years earlier, focuses on prevalence rates and living circumstances of 435 people with dementia residing in a rural county in Northern Ireland. The cross-disciplinary, collaborative nature of the research process and the impact of community care policy and variation in place of residence over a decade are discussed. The advantages to be gained by carrying out similar pieces of local research are highlighted.

138 Godley, S.H., Fiedler, E.M. & Funk, R.R. (1998). Consumer satisfaction of parents and their children with child/adolescent mental health services. *Evaluation & Program Planning*, 21(1), 31-45.

This assessed the satisfaction of parents/guardians and their children who received services at 22 community mental health agencies using standardized measures and procedures. Statewide analyses indicate that youths' satisfaction was significantly less than that of their parents. According to segmentation analyses, the best predictor of parents' satisfaction was their rating of the severity of their child's problem. The best predictor of youths' satisfaction was the type of school attended, though problem severity and agency location (e.g., suburban, urban, or rural) also figured prominently in the prediction model.

139 Godley, S.H., Finch, M., Dougan, L., McDonnell, M., McDermeit & M., Carey, A. (2000). Case management for dually diagnosed individuals involved in the criminal justice system. *Journal of Substance Abuse Treatment*, 18, 137-148.

    A case-management model for individuals with substance abuse and mental health disorders who are involved in the criminal justice system is described, based on the experience of a rural demonstration project. Detailed descriptions of case-management activities and the philosophy underlying this model of case management are provided. Six-month follow-up data revealed significantly fewer legal problems and apparent symptom relief for participants in the project. Participants reported improvement in most life areas measured compared to the year before, and were generally satisfied with the case-management services. Barriers observed in implementing these types of services and issues for replication are outlined and discussed.

140 Goldsmith, H.F., Wagenfeld, M.O., Manderscheid, R.W. & Stiles, D. (1997). Specialty mental health services in metropolitan and nonmetropolitan areas: 1983 and 1990. *Administration & Policy in Mental Health*, 24(6), 475-488.

    This provides longitudinal information about the changes between 1983 and 1990 in the availability and quantity or volume of specialty mental health services (overnight or inpatient) in counties with different levels of metropolitanization and urbanization. The results indicate that during the study period, metropolitan counties experienced increasing availability and volume of specialty mental health services, while nonmetropolitan counties did not. Over 95 percent of the most urbanized metropolitan counties were likely to have overnight and inpatients services in 1990, while 25 percent of the least urbanized counties had them.

141 Gottfredson, M.R. & Hirschi, T. (1990). *A General Theory of Crime*. Stanford, CA: Stanford University Press.

    This is the Third edition of this book that expands upon on previous editions with coverage of newly emerged theories of crime and includes empirical updates. The book provides policy implications of crime and offers practical applications of theoretical information.

142 Graham, A.M. (1996). Telepsychiatry in Appalachia. *American Behavioral Scientist*, 39(5), 602-615.

    The author examined the use of digital technology to provide health care services to underserved communities. The APPAL-LINK telepsychiatry project is described beginning with its inception as a response to a critical shortage of psychiatric manpower in the public mental health system. The methods used in the project and a preliminary six-month assessment of chronically mentally ill patients, providers, and community satisfaction are described. The article concludes with a discussion of the obstacles to the wider implementation of telepsychiatry/telemedicine projects in rural areas.

143 Grob, G.N. (1994). Government and mental health policy: A structural analysis. *Milbank Quarterly*, 72(3), 471-500.

The author analyzes how intergovernmental relations shape and transform social policy and mental health. From informal, rural care in the early days of the U.S., to public asylums between the 1820s and World War II, to community-based care and deinstitutionalism in the last few decades, the role of the Federal government has slowly increased.

144 Group for the Advancement of Psychiatry, Committee on Therapeutic Care, Dallas, TX, US. (1995). Mental health in remote rural developing areas: Concepts and cases. Book Series Title GAP report, No. 139.

This book uses examples from [remote] rural villages in Alaska and other developing areas of the world. It illustrates the social and environmental influences that shape health and mental health care. It includes cases and discussions that focus on the role of the public psychiatrist, who, in these settings, often has limited ability to pick and choose which problems to deal with and who also has multiple options for conceptualizing a problem and taking action. Approaches described in the book include extensive use of community education to encourage local people to maintain healthy lifestyles.

145 Guyll, M., Spoth, R.L., Chao, W., Wickrama, K. & Russell, D. (2004). Family-focused preventive interventions: Evaluating parental risk moderation of substance use trajectories. *Journal of Family Psychology*, 18, 293-301.

Four years of longitudinal data from 373 families participating in a randomized intervention–control clinical trial were used to examine whether intervention effects on adolescent alcohol and tobacco use trajectories were moderated by family risk, as defined by parental social emotional maladjustment. Analyses confirmed that both the Preparing for the Drug Free Years program and the Iowa Strengthening Families Program favorably influenced alcohol use index trajectories across the time frame of the study; only the latter program, however, evidenced positive effects on a tobacco use index. Concerning the primary research question, analyses provided no support for family risk moderation of any intervention effect.

146 Hagopian, A. & Hart, G. (2002). *Rural Hospital Flexibility Program Tracking Project.* Seattle: WWAMI Rural Health Research Center, University of Washington; 2002. Chapter 1: Introduction to the Rural Hospital Flexibility Program Year 1 Report. Available at: http://www.rupri.org/rhfp-track/year1/chapter1.html. Accessed May 7, 2003.

This chapter provides information on the creation and goals of the Rural Hospital Flexibility Program Tracking Project in its first year. The project seeks to maximize the effectiveness of the Rural Hospital Flexibility Program by tracking and reporting implementation successes and barriers.

147 Hansen, W.B. (1996). Pilot test results comparing the All Star program with seventh grade D.A.R.E.: Program integrity and mediating variable analysis. *Substance Use & Misuse*, 31, 1359-1377.

The author reports on pilot test findings of All Stars, a program developed to address each of the four mediators of high-risk behaviors: 1) personal commitment to avoid participating in high-risk behaviors, 2) ideals incongruent with high-risk behaviors, 3) bonding with prosocial institutions and 4) conventional beliefs about social norms regarding high-risk behaviors. Ninety-six seventh graders who completed the All Stars program were compared to students who received the seventh grade D.A.R.E. booster program. Results showed that students who received the All Stars program had significantly better outcomes on each mediator. All Stars students also gave superior ratings to the program and their involvement in it.

148 Hansen, W.B. & McNeal Jr., R.B. (1997). How D.A.R.E. works: An examination of program effects on mediating variables. *Health Education & Behavior*, 24, 165-176.

This examines 12 postulated mediators of substance use prevention programs to determine the degree to which Drug Abuse Resistance Education (D.A.R.E.) has an effect on those mediators and the degree to which those effects account for behavioral outcomes of the program. Results indicate that the primary effect of D.A.R.E. is a change in commitment not to use substances. This change significantly mediates behavioral effects. However, the magnitude of D.A.R.E.'s effect on the mediator is relatively small. Other mediators that offer strong potential paths for intervention effectiveness are not affected by the program. These results suggest that in order to achieve prevention effectiveness, the curriculum used in the D.A.R.E. program needs to be replaced with one that targets and meaningfully changes appropriate mediating variables.

149 Hargrove, D.S. & Breazeale, R.L. (1993). Psychologists and rural services: Addressing a new agenda. *Professional Psychology-Research & Practice*, 24(3), 319-324.

Rural people in the 1990s are struggling with serious individual and community problems that threaten their very survival. The growth of professional psychology into a viable health, mental health, and social service profession places it in a position to be of assistance to rural communities. To do this, however, adequate training models must be developed to equip psychologists to apply their trade in rural areas. A strategy and model for training practicing psychologists is presented.

150 Hargrove, D. S. & Keller, P.A. (1997). Collaboration with community mental health centers. Practicing psychology in rural settings: Hospital privileges and collaborative care. J.A. Morris. Washington, D.C., American Psychological Association.

The book covers the history of psychology's advancement in hospital settings. This chapter, by Hargrove and Keller, offers suggestions on how mental health professionals in hospitals can collaborate more effectively with community mental health centers in rural areas.

151 Harmon, M.A. (1993). Reducing the risk of drug involvement among early adolescents: An evaluation of Drug Abuse Resistance Education (DARE). *Evaluation Review*, 17, 221-239.

This evaluation examined the effectiveness of the 17-week DARE program in Charleston County, South Carolina, by comparing 341 fifth-grade DARE students to 367 non-DARE students. Significant differences were found in the predicted direction for alcohol use in the last year, belief in prosocial norms, association with drug-using peers, positive peer association, attitudes against substance use, and assertiveness. No differences were found on cigarette, tobacco, or marijuana use in the last year; frequency of any drug use in the past month; attitudes about police; coping strategies; attachment and commitment to school; rebellious behavior; and self-esteem.

152 Hartley, D., Bird, D. & Dempsey, P. (1999). Mental health and substance abuse. In Ricketts, T. (Ed.). *Rural Health in the United States*. New York: Oxford University Press.

This book provides a broad look at the health status and health care resources of the rural areas in the United States. The authors of this section specifically address behavioral health issues common to rural areas in the United States.

153 Hartley, D. & Gale, J. (2003). Rural Health Care Safety Nets. In Weinick, Robin M. and John Billings, Eds. *Monitoring the Health Care Safety Net. Book III: Tools for Monitoring the Health Care Safety Net.* (AHRQ Pub. No. 03-0027). Rockville, MD: Agency for Healthcare Research and Quality.

This book offers strategies and concrete tools for assessing local health care safety nets. The chapter by Hartley and Gale on Rural Health Care Safety Nets provides a description of rural safety net providers, programs, and populations, details eligibility criteria to be considered a rural safety net provider, and presents special issues for rural safety net providers.

154 Hauenstein, E.J. & Boyd, M.R. (1994). Depressive symptoms in young women of the Piedmont: Prevalence in rural women. *Women and Health,* 21(2/3), 105-123.

The authors determined the extent to which 181 rural adult women users of a community health center experienced depressive symptoms and examined the relationships among common risk factors for depression, perceptions of physical and emotional health, and reports of depressive symptoms. Young, unemployed, and poorly educated Ss reported more depressive symptoms than did older Ss with greater resources. Unemployed black Ss were more likely to report depressive symptoms than were Caucasian or employed Ss with children. Perceptions of both poor physical and mental health were associated with reports of depressive symptoms.

155 Hawkins, J.D., Catalano, R.F. & Miller, J.Y. (1992). Risk and protective factors for alcohol and other drug problems in adolescence and early adulthood: Implications for substance abuse prevention. *Psychological Bulletin,* 112, 64-105.

This suggests that the most promising route to effective strategies for the prevention of adolescent alcohol and other drug problems is through a risk-focused approach. This approach requires the identification of risk factors for drug abuse, identification of methods by which risk factors have been effectively addressed, and application of these methods to appropriate high-risk and general population samples in controlled studies. The authors review risk and protective factors for drug abuse, assess a number of approaches for drug abuse prevention potential with high-risk groups, and make recommendations for research and practice.

156 Hays, R. D. & Ellickson, P. L. (1996). Associations between drug use and deviant behavior in teenagers. *Addictive Behaviors*, 21, 291–302.

These authors collected data from 701 female and 662 male grade-10 students (mean age 15.76 years) in 30 high schools. Confirmatory factor analyses of Ss' self-reports of drug use and deviant behavior (DB) revealed three correlated higher-order dimensions of behavior: alcohol use and sociability, rebelliousness and DB, including drug use other than alcohol. Eight lower- order factors included cannabis and cigarette use, hard drug use, and school problems. Males were significantly more likely than females to report using PCP, glue or inhalants, and hashish; to be rebellious, engage in DB and to ride around for fun. Females reported a greater number of absences, more frequent truancy, and higher levels of smoking than males.

157 Heckman, T.G., Kalichman, S.C., Roffman, R.R., Sikkema, K.J., Heckman, B.D., Somlai, A.M. & Walker, J. (1999). A telephone-delivered coping improvement intervention for persons living with HIV/AIDS in rural areas. *Social Work with Groups*, 21(4), 49-62.

The current article describes a telephone-delivered, coping improvement group intervention for HIV-infected rural residents based on a widely accepted cognitive-behavioral model of coping. An eight-session coping intervention is outlined and recommendations intended to increase the intervention's efficacy are provided. As the prevalence of rural AIDS escalates, mental health interventions that address the emotional and psychological needs of HIV-infected rural residents are increasingly needed.

158 Heckman, T., Miller, J., Kochman, A., Kalichman, S.C.; Carlson, B. & Silverthorn, M. (2002). Thoughts of suicide among HIV-infected rural persons enrolled in a telephone-delivered mental health intervention. *Annals of Behavioral Medicine*, 24(2), 141-148.

This study characterized rates and predictors of suicidal thoughts among HIV-infected persons living in rural communities of eight U.S. States. At baseline, participants reported on thoughts of suicide, psychological symptomatology, life-stressor burden, ways of coping, coping self-efficacy, social support and barriers to health care and social services. Thirty-eight percent of HIV-infected rural persons had engaged in thoughts of suicide during the past week.

159 Heflinger, C.A. & Nixon, C.T. (Eds.) (1996). *Families and the mental health system for children and adolescents: Policy, services, and research.* Book Series Title Children's mental health services, Vol. 2.

The contributors to this volume examine a myriad of policy, research, and practice issues related to families of children with serious emotional disorders. Throughout this book, the contributors take into account the complexity and diversity of families today and the consequent impact on service delivery at the societal and policy levels.

160 Hewitt, M. (1989). *Defining "Rural" Areas: Impact on Health Care Policy and Research*. Staff paper, Office of Technology Assessment. Washington D.C. Supt. of Docs. U.S. Gov. Print. Office.

The problems of health care in rural areas have long occupied a special niche in policies designed to advance the Nation's health. Mounting concerns related to rural residents' access to health care prompted the Senate Rural Health Caucus to request that OTA conduct an assessment of these and related issues. This Staff Paper was prepared in connection with that assessment.

161 Hill, C.E. & Fraser, G.J. (1995). Local knowledge and rural mental health reform. *Community Mental Health Journal*, 31(6), 553-568.

This discusses the role of local knowledge and practice, health seeking behavior, beliefs, and values of rural people in the development of integrated and holistic mental health (MH) policy. MH problems cannot be separated from the economic and political situation of rural communities and their cultural contexts, as there is a causal relationship between SES and mental stress. Similarly, societal racism and color consciousness affect their mental status. Rural MH care reform must include cultural competency training for providers to increase their awareness of the cultural differences of their professional and personal context, and that of the people they serve.

162 Hill, G., Howard, A., Weaver, D.L. & Stamm, B.H. (2003). Health planning for rural and frontier mental and behavioral health care. In: Stamm, B.H. (Ed). *Rural behavioral health care: An interdisciplinary guide*. Washington, DC, U.S.: American Psychological Association.

In this chapter, the authors present information for health planning and funding for rural and frontier mental and behavioral health care in the U.S. The first section encompasses identifying and selecting target areas and robust models for designing service delivery systems that incorporate the formal and informal health resources and allow for the incorporation of new health needs or resources. The second portion of the chapter provides information about locating and securing funds for building and sustaining health systems.

163 Hirschi, T. (1969). *Causes of Delinquency.* Berkeley, CA: University of California Press.

This book compares three major theories of delinquency using a large sample of adolescents. The author found that Social Control Theory, the traditional theory of sociological processes, was superior to other more modern theories.

164 Hodge, D.R., Cardenas, P. & Montoya, H. (2001). Substance use: Spirituality and religious participation as protective factors among rural youths. *Social Work Research,* 25, 153-162.

These authors explored the relationship between substance use and spirituality and religious participation with a multicultural sample of rural youths in the American Southwest. Data show that although increased participation in religious activities predicted greater probability of never using alcohol, increased spirituality predicted greater probability of never using marijuana and hard drugs. This article concludes with a discussion of the implications of these findings for prevention programs, social work education, and research.

165 Hollingsworth, E.J. (1997). Services for clients of community support programs in rural Wisconsin. *Journal of Mental Health Administration,* 24(1), 55-63.

The author identified services of rural community support programs (CSPs) for people with severe mental illness most used by clients and the amounts of services used. Most CSP clients use case management, community support, medication checks, counseling and medication counseling services. Much smaller percentages use other outpatient, residential, vocational and inpatient services. Significant amounts of only two services, case management and community support, are reported.

166 Hollingsworth, E.J., Pitts, M.K. & McKee, D. (1993). Staffing patterns in rural community support programs. *Hospital & Community Psychiatry,* 44(11), 1076-1081.

The authors surveyed 12 community support programs in small cities and rural areas of Wisconsin to determine staff size and characteristics, staff-to-client ratios, and the relative use of paraprofessional (PP) staff and professional staff, excluding psychiatrists. The programs surveyed had an average of 5.6 full-time-equivalent caregiving staff and an average caregiving-toclient ratio of one to 13. Caregiving staff were predominantly female, had been in the mental health field a mean of 8.8 years and received an average salary of $20,732. Although program directors indicated that about one-fifth of staff left in the previous year, they reported little difficulty recruiting staff. Thirty-eight percent of all caregivers were PPs; in several programs more than half of the caregivers were PPs.

167 Hollister, W., Edgerton, J., and Hunter, R. (1985). *Alternative services in community mental health: programs and processes.* Chapel Hill, North Carolina. University of North Carolina.

This book examined the relative effectiveness of nonprofessional mental health providers (e.g., traditional healers). The authors suggest that more paraprofessionals who are competent to deliver specific services in rural communities should undergo basic training in mental health.

168 Holzer, C.E., Goldsmith, H.F. & Ciarlo, J.A. (1998). Chapter 16: Effects of rural-urban county type on the availability of health and mental health care providers. *Mental Health, United States.* DHHS Pub. No. (SMA)99-3285. Washington, DC: Superintendent of Documents, U.S. Government Printing Office.

This chapter provides statistical data by county comparing the number of health and mental health care providers in rural versus urban areas of the United States.

169 Holzer, C.E. III, Goldsmith, H.F. & Ciarlo, J.A. (2000). The availability of health and mental health providers by population density. *Journal of the Washington Academy of Sciences*, 86(3), 25-33.

This paper explores the local availability of mental health service providers in different rural areas. Emphasis is placed upon the services available to frontier and isolated rural areas.

170 Hovestadt, A.J., Fenell, D.L. & Canfield, B.S. (2002). Characteristics of effective providers of marital and family therapy in rural mental health settings. *Journal of Marital & Family Therapy*, 28(2), 225-231.

Characteristics of effective providers of marital and family therapy (MFT) in rural mental health settings were investigated. The findings yielded six major rank-ordered characteristics of effective MFT providers in rural mental health settings, with effective skills in MFT ranked first. Rural community understanding, appreciation and participation ranked second. Specific competencies contributing to each major characteristic were also identified and are discussed. Recommendations for use of this information are provided

171 Howland, R.H. (1995). The treatment of persons with dual diagnoses in a rural community. *Psychiatric Quarterly*, 66, 33-49.

This describes the characteristics of a rural community mental health system, which illustrate the difficulties in treating persons with dual diagnoses of psychiatric illness and substance abuse in rural communities. These problems include a fragmented system of services, centralized services in a large geographic area, overly restrictive regulations, conceptual differences in treatment approaches, confidentiality and stigma in a rural culture and the academic and professional isolation of mental health workers, leading to high turnover and a shortage of staff having sufficient training and experience to work with persons with dual diagnoses.

172 Hoyt, D.R., Conger, R.D., Valde, J.G. & Weihs, K. (1997). Psychological distress and help seeking in rural America. *American Journal of Community Psychology*, 25(4), 449-470.

Using data from a panel study of 1,487 adults, a model predicting changes in depressive symptoms was specified and tested. Results show effects by size of place for men but not for women. Men living in rural villages of under 2,500 or in small towns of 2,500 to 9,999 people had significantly greater increases in depressive symptoms than men living in the country or in larger towns or cities. Size of place was also related to level of stigma toward mental health care. Persons living in the most rural environments were more likely to hold stigmatized attitudes toward mental health care and these views were strongly predictive of willingness to seek care. The combination of increased risk and less willingness to seek assistance places men living in small towns and villages in particular jeopardy for continuing problems involving depressed mood.

173 Human, J. & Wasem, C. (1991). Rural mental health in America. *American Psychologist*, 46, 3, 232-239.

Mental health services are in short supply in rural America. This article describes both the mental health service needs in rural areas and the barriers to improving the availability, accessibility and acceptability of rural mental health services. Federal programs in rural mental health care in the Departments of Health and Human Services, Agriculture and Education are described, as well as selected congressional initiatives. The role of the Federal Office of Rural Health Policy is emphasized, and policy recommendations for improving rural mental health care delivery are presented.

174 Husted, J., Wentler, S.A. & Bursell, A. (1994). The effectiveness of community support programs for persistently mentally ill in rural areas. *Community Mental Health Journal*, 30(6), 595-600.

The authors examined the effectiveness of a community support program (CSP), as implemented in five contracting rural western

Minnesota counties, by comparing the number of days hospitalized for an equal amount of time before and after participation in the program. Total number of days hospitalized for all Ss before CSP was 2,526 (mean 57.409) compared to 640 days after CSP (mean 14.545). Females spent fewer days hospitalized than males; the CSP was slightly less effective with schizophrenic Ss.

175 Husted, J., Wentler, S., Allen, G. & Longhenry, D. (2000). The effectiveness of community support programs in rural Minnesota: A ten-year longitudinal study. *Psychiatric Rehabilitation Journal*, 24(1), 69-72.

This paper studies the rates of rehospitalization as well as the average length of stay in a ten-year period of 59 individuals (mean age 49.7 years) with serious and persistent mental disorders. All individuals in this study participated in a community support program (CSP) and come from rural Western Minnesota. Findings indicate no lessening of the effectiveness of CSP over the ten-year period as measured by both rate of rehospitalization and length of treatment. The study gives further evidence for the importance of milieu in treatment of people with serious and persistent mental disorders, with the more sparsely populated areas having a lower rate of rehospitalization.

176 Institute of Medicine (2002). *Reducing Suicide: A National Imperative*. Goldsmith, S.K., Pellmar, T.C., Kleinman, A.M. & Bunney, W.E. (Eds). Washington, DC: National Alchemy Press.

The Committee on Pathophysiology and Prevention of Adolescent and Adult Suicide s report, *Reducing Suicide: A National Imperative*, explores the epidemiology, risk factors, and interventions for suicide and suicide attempts. The committee provides recommendations to improve the detection, diagnosis, treatment, and prevention of suicidality in primary care.

177 Institute of Medicine (2005). *Quality Through Collaboration: The Future of Rural Health*. The Committee on the Future of Rural Health Care; Board on Health Care Services. The National Academies Press: Washington, D.C.

This report presents next steps for the rural health care community. It focuses on the potential for the National Rural Health Association (NRHA) and its membership to transform the IOM report from recommendations to living reality. The IOM report presents rural healthcare stakeholders with an opportunity to improve and attract resources previously unavailable to rural communities.

178 Ivey, S.L., Scheffler, R. & Zazzali, J.L. (1998). Supply dynamics of the mental health workforce: Implications for health policy. *Milbank Quarterly*, 76, 25-58.

The data on the supply of several specialists— psychiatrists, clinical psychologists, and clinical social workers—indicate that the distribution of mental health professionals varies widely by State. The composition, supply, and distribution of workers in this field also affect the care of vulnerable populations. Broader policy questions, including the lack of parity between mental and physical health insurance coverage and barriers to entry by nonphysician professions, may limit the cost-effective expansion of this diverse and dynamic workforce.

179 Johnson, K., Bryant, D., Strader, T., Bucholtz, G., Berbarum, M., Collins, D. & Noe, T. (1996). Reducing alcohol and other drug use by strengthening community, family, and youth resiliency: An evaluation of the Creating Lasting Connections Program. *Journal of Adolescent Research*, 11, 36-67.

This evaluation examines the Creating Lasting Connections (CLC) program, a five-year demonstration project for delaying and reducing alcohol and drug use among high-risk 12-14 year olds, and reports the findings from its implementation in multiple church communities. Data collected before CLC initiation, after parent and youth training, and after the follow-up case management reveals that CLC successfully engaged church communities in substance abuse activities, and produced positive direct effects on family and youth resiliency. It had moderating effects on onset and frequency of alcohol and drug use.

180 Johnston, L.D., O'Malley, P.M. & Backman, J.G. (1996). *National survey results on drug use from the Monitoring the Future study, 1975–1995. Vol. I: Secondary school students.* (NIH Pub. No. 97-4139). Rockville, MD: National Institute on Drug Abuse.

This report provides the yearly results from the Monitoring the Future Survey in 1995 compared with results from 1975. This report focused on drug use by secondary school students.

181 Johnston, L., O'Malley, P. & Bachman, J. (2000). *Monitoring the future: National survey results on drug use, 1975–1999: Vol. 1. Secondary school students* (NIH Publication No. 00-4802). Washington, DC: U.S. Department of Health and Human Services.

This report focused on drug use by secondary school students. This report provides the yearly results from the Monitoring the Future Survey in 1999 compared with results from 1975.

182 Jonason, K.R., DeMers, S.T., Vaughn, T.J. & Reaves, R.P. (2003). Professional Mobility for Psychologists Is Rapidly Becoming a Reality. *Professional Psychology: Research and Practice, 34*, 468–473.

This article describes how professional mobility for psychologists has been a problem since States first passed psychology licensing laws because of relatively small but crucial variations in licensing requirements. Although the profession of psychology and the association of psychology regulatory bodies in the United States and Canada (i.e., the Association of State and Provincial Psychology Boards [ASPPB]) have recognized this problem for decades, little progress was made in resolving it. Recently, the ASPPB launched two different approaches to facilitating professional mobility: one to forge agreements between regulatory bodies to accept each other's licensees, and another to certify or endorse individual psychologists who meet ASPPB standards for licensure and therefore, can be recommended to licensing boards for relicensure. The specific requirements of each of these programs and their success in addressing the professional mobility problem are described.

183 Kane, C. F. & J. M. Ennis (1996). Health care reform and rural mental health: Severe mental illness. *Community Mental Health Journal*, 32(5), 445-462.

This addresses the service needs of rural severely mentally ill and strengths of rural communities. Health care reform policy development at present appears to neglect the seriously mentally ill in general and rural services specifically. Integration of the health and mental health service system, assertive community treatment, utilization of lay and informal caregivers and rural adult homes are possible strategies for meeting the needs of the seriously mentally ill. The advantages and drawbacks of such efforts are considered.

184 Kane, C., Blank, M. & Hundley, P. (1999). Care provision and community adjustment of rural consumers with serious mental illness. *Archives of Psychiatric Nursing*, 13(1), 19-29.

The authors examined the predictors of successful community living in a sample of 40 rural 26-74-year-old non-hospitalized consumers (32 females, eight males) with severe and persistent mental illness, proposed by a simple model of rural community adjustment (RCAM). Analyses suggest that CA is primarily predicted by life stress and informal care-provider attitudes. Life stress was predicted by symptoms, poor living skills and formal help provision. Quality-of-life satisfaction was predicted primarily by consumer status characteristics. This test of the RCAM shows that consumer status characteristics are most predictive of CA.

185 Kane, M. & DiBartolo, M. (2002). Complex physical and mental health needs of rural incarcerated women. *Issues in Mental Health Nursing*, 23(3), 209-229.

A descriptive design was used in a convenience sample of 30 incarcerated female offenders (ages 20-50 year) in a rural detention center to investigate the complex health care needs of this population and formulate appropriate community-based nursing interventions. 63 percent of the women reported drug problems and 80 percent reported alcohol problems, while 84 percent reported physical or sexual abuse. Scores on the Global Severity Index of the Brief Symptom Inventory showed that 70 percent of the women were in the clinical range for mental health problems.

186 Karim, G. (1997). In living context: An interdisciplinary approach to rethinking rural prevention. In: Roberson, E.B., Sloboda, Z., Boyd, G.M., Beatty, L, and Kozel, N.J., eds. *Rural Substance Abuse: State of Knowledge and Issues*. National Institute on Drug Abuse; U.S. Department of Health and Human Services; National Institutes of Health: NIH Publication No. 97-4177. Rockville, MD.

This chapter argues that knowledge of local context and latest teaching and learning models is crucial in successfully disseminating national school-based drug and alcohol prevention programs for youth in rural areas. Successful programs achieve their intended goals, such as delaying the onset of substance use. The author attempts to help prevention programs improve their effectiveness.

187 Kelleher, K.J., Taylor, J.L. & Rickert, V.I. (1992). Mental health services for rural children and adolescents. *Clinical Psychology Review*, 12, 841-852.

Rural children and adolescents have rates of mental disorders comparable to metropolitan youth, but face additional barriers to effective delivery of mental health care that are unique to rural areas. Rural communities and providers have responded by changing the structure and organization of mental health services for youth, relying more often on Federal and State dollars, and focusing on noncategorical and preventive services. Rural communities have also relied more heavily on alternative types of providers for mental health services for children and adolescents while increasing efforts to retain current providers. The effectiveness of the adaptations used by rural mental health organizations is largely unknown, although most children and adolescents with mental disorders in rural areas do not receive adequate mental health services.

188 Kenkel, M.B. (2003). Rural women: Strategies and resources for meting their behavioral health needs. In: Stamm, B.H. (Ed). *Rural behavioral health care: An interdisciplinary guide.* (pp. 181-192). Washington, DC, U.S.: American Psychological Association. xiv, 250pp.

The purpose of this chapter is to substitute a more realistic portrayal of rural women for the stereotype. Asking questions about rural women's behavioral health is an important first step in bringing attention to their needs. The behavioral health needs of rural women addressed in this chapter include mental health issues, access to and use of mental health treatment, women with HIV and AIDS, occupational health, violence and minority women.

189 Kessler, R.C., McGonagle, K.A., Zhao, S., et al. (1994). Lifetime and 12-month prevalence of DSM-III-R psychiatric disorders in the United States: Results from the national comorbidity survey. *Archives of General Psychiatry,* 51(1), 8-19.

This study presents estimates of lifetime and 12- month prevalence of 14 DSM-III-R psychiatric disorders from the National Comorbidity Survey, Nearly 50 percent of respondents reported at least one lifetime disorder, and close to 30 percent reported at least one 12-month disorder. The most common disorders were major depressive episode, alcohol dependence, social phobia, and simple phobia. More than half of all lifetime disorders occurred in the 14 percent of the population who had a history of three or more comorbid disorders. Less than 40 percent of those with a lifetime disorder had ever received professional treatment, and less than 20 percent of those with a recent disorder had been in treatment during the past 12 months. Consistent with previous risk factor research, it was found that women had elevated rates of affective disorders and anxiety disorders, that men had elevated rates of substance use disorders and antisocial personality disorder, and that most disorders declined with age and with higher socioeconomic status.

190 Kessler, R.C., Berglund, P.A., Zhao, S., Leaf, P.J., Kouzis, A.C., Bruce, M.L., Friedman, R.M., Grosser, R.C., Kennedy, C., Narrow, W.E., Kuehnel, T.G., Laska, E.M., Manderscheid, R.W., Rosenheck, R.A., Santoni, T.W. & Schneier, M. (1996). The 12-month prevalence and correlates of serious mental illness (SMI). In R. W. Manderscheid & M. A. Sonnenschein (Eds.), *Mental health United States, 1996* (DHHS

Publication No. SMA 96-3098, pp. 59–70). Washington, DC: Superintendent of Documents, U.S. Government Printing Office.

This study presents estimates of lifetime and 12- month prevalence of 14 DSM-III-R psychiatric disorders from the National Comorbidity Survey. The majority of people with psychiatric disorders fail to obtain professional treatment. Even among people with a lifetime history of three or more comorbid disorders, the proportion who ever obtain specialty sector mental health treatment is less than 50 percent. These results argue for the importance of more outreach and more research on barriers to professional help-seeking.

191 Kessler, R.C., McGonagle, K.A., Zhao, S., Nelson, C.B., Hughes, M., Eschleman, S., et al. (1994). Lifetime and 12-month prevalence of DSM-III-R psychiatric disorders in the United States: Results from the national comorbidity survey. *Archives Of General Psychiatry*, 51, 8-19.

This presents data on the lifetime and 12-month prevalence of 14 Diagnostic and Statistical Manual of Mental Disorders-III-Revised (DSM-III-R) psychiatric disorders assessed in the National Comorbidity Survey (NCS). The diagnostic interview used by the NCS is a modified version of the Composite International Diagnostic Interview (CIDI), based on the Diagnostic Interview Schedule. The most common psychiatric disorders were major depression and alcohol dependence. The vast majority of lifetime disorders (79 percent) were comorbid disorders.

192 Killeen, T. & Brady, K.T. (2000). Parental stress and child behavioral outcomes following substance abuse residential treatment: Follow-up at 6 and 12 months. *Journal of Substance Abuse Treatment*, 19, 23-29.

In this article, outcome data from a study of a residential substance abuse treatment program for women and young children in rural South Carolina are presented. Results showed that women who completed treatment had better scores on addiction severity and parental stress, and their children had improved behavioral and emotional functioning at six and 12 months after discharge from the program. These results suggest that residential treatment has benefits for mothers and their children.

193 Kim, E. & VandeCreek, L. (2003). Facilitating Mobility for Psychologists: Comparisons With and Lessons From Other Health Care Professions. *Professional Psychology: Research and Practice*, 34, 480–488.

This article describes how psychology and other health care professions are giving increasing attention to facilitating the movement of practitioners across jurisdictions. One of the greatest deterrents to mobility is the variability in licensing requirements among States and provinces. The authors review the status of mobility systems for licensed members of the professions of psychology, optometry, dentistry, medicine, nursing and pharmacy. Each profession has, at a minimum, addressed the issue of mobility and licensure. With the exception of medicine, each profession currently has in place a version of licensure by endorsement and/or by reciprocity, although the professions differ in breadth of use and user-friendliness. Implications for enhancing mobility for psychologists are discussed.

194 Kimmel, W.A. (1992). *Rural mental health policy issues for research: A pilot exploration.* Rockville, MD: National Institute of Mental Health, Office of Rural Mental Health Research.

The author describes results from a survey of State mental health directors. It was found that there was few State mental health staff with fulltime responsibility for rural issues and that State mental health agencies were rarely asked to address rural issues in a direct and sustained way.

195 King, C.J., Van Hasselt, V.B., Segal, D.L. & Hersen, M. (1994). Diagnosis and assessment of substance abuse in older adults: Current strategies and issues. *Addictive Behaviors,* 19, 41–55.

This reviews and critically evaluates diagnostic and assessment strategies that have been employed with older adults who abuse alcohol and other drugs. It is concluded that the existing Diagnostic and Statistical Manual of Mental Disorders-III-Revised (DSM-III-R) diagnostic criteria are inadequate and that diagnostic variables specific to the elderly need to be identified so that objective, operationalized diagnostic criteria can be elucidated. In terms of assessment, three major concerns are evident: 1) existing instruments must be validated with older clinical populations, 2) elder-specific alcohol and substance abuse measures must be constructed and appropriately validated and 3) discriminant analytic studies are needed to identify correlates and risk factors salient to substance abuse by the elderly.

196 Knight, B.G., Rickards, L., Rabins, P., Buckwalter, K. & Smith, M. (1995). Community-based services for older adults: A role for psychologists? In: Knight, B.G., Teri, L. (Eds.); et al. *Mental health services for older adults: Implications for training and practice in geropsychology.* (pp. 21-29).

Several community-based mental health programs for older adults are described. Model programs include several common components: active case-finding, home visits, use of interdisciplinary teams and collaboration with other service agencies in the community.

197 Koppelman, J. (2004). *The provider system for children's mental health: Workforce capacity and effective treatment.* NHPF Issue Brief No. 801, National Health Policy Forum, George Washington University. Washington, D.C.

This issue brief examines two issues that are important to meeting children's unmet needs for mental health care: 1) ensuring that the provider availability is sufficient, and 2) the care delivered is effective. It reviews the lack of qualified providers to address children's mental disorders, and discusses the role of managed care in this issue. This brief also discusses the importance of evidence-based care in children's mental health, whether evidence-based practices are being utilized, and the effect of using evidence-based practices on the composition of the mental health provider field.

198 Kosterman, R., Hawkins, J.D., Spoth, R., Haggerty, K.P. & Zhu, K. (1997). Effects of a preventive parent-training intervention on observed family interactions: Proximal outcomes from preparing for the drug free years. *Journal of Community Psychology*, 25, 337-352.

This article reports the results of an experimental test of the effects of Preparing for the Drug Free Years (PDFY) on targeted parental behaviors. Consistent with hypotheses, the PDFY intervention was found to be effective in promoting proactive communication from parent to child and in improving the quality of parent-child relationships. PDFY also reduced mothers' negative interactions with their children in the study.

199 Kosterman, R., Hawkins, J.D., Haggerty, K.P., Spoth, R. & Redmond, C. (2001). Preparing for the drug free years: Session-specific effects of a universal parent-training intervention with rural families. *Journal of Drug Education*, 31, 47-68.

This study tested the effects on parenting practices of specific sessions of a parent-training intervention. Two hundred andnine rural families were randomly assigned to an intervention or a wait-list control condition. Post-test scores revealed that parents (mean age 38.9 years for mothers and 41.0 years for fathers) in the intervention condition reported significant improvements in parenting behaviors targeted by specific intervention sessions when compared with controls. Effects were most pronounced among mothers. No significant effects were found for nontargeted parenting behaviors, and targeted behaviors were most improved among parents attending relevant program sessions.

200 Lachance, K.R., Deci, P.A., Santos, A.B. & Halewood, N. (1996). Rural assertive community treatment: Taking mental health services on the road. Innovative services for difficult to treat populations. Washington, DC, American Psychiatric Press: 279-294.

The idea of taking mental health services to the clients is not new. Mental health professionals have long recognized a need for outreach to rural areas. What is not known is the value of such services in terms of their cost-effectiveness. In this chapter we describe a pilot study and introduce a controlled clinical trial designed to address this question. The program named Rural Outreach, Advocacy, and Direct Services (ROADS) was developed by the Charleston/Dorchester Community Mental Health Center in South Carolina in 1988 to target 18-65 year-old individuals with chronic psychotic disorders who are high users of centralized inpatient facilities.

201 Lachance, K.R., Santos, A.B. (1995). Modifying the PACT model: Preserving critical elements. *Psychiatric Services*, 46, 601-604.

The author discusses issues in modifying the Program for Assertive Community Treatment (PACT) model, especially for use in rural areas, focusing on six basic elements: multiservice teams, 24-hour service availability, small caseloads that do not vary in composition, ongoing and continuous services, assertive outreach, and in vivo rehabilitation. Adapted programs in South Carolina that have retained these elements and achieved desired outcomes with smaller teams operating on modified schedules are described.

202 Lambert, D. & Agger, M. (1995). Access of rural Medicaid beneficiaries to mental health services. *Health Care Financing Review*, 17(7), 133-145.

This article examines geographic differences in the use of mental health services among Aid to Families with Dependent Children (AFDC)-eligible Medicaid beneficiaries in Maine. Findings indicate that rural AFDC beneficiaries have significantly lower utilization of mental health services than urban beneficiaries. Specialty mental health providers account for the majority of ambulatory visits for both rural and urban beneficiaries. However, rural beneficiaries rely more on primary-care providers than do urban beneficiaries. Differences in use are largely explained by variations in the supply of specialty mental health providers. This finding supports the long-held assumption that lower supply is a barrier to access to mental health services in rural areas.

203 Lambert, D. & Hartley, D., (1998). Linking primary care and rural psychiatry: Where have we been and where are we going? *Psychiatric Services*, 49(7), 965- 966.

The authors describe a national survey that identified 53 successfully linked programs, ranging from small local efforts to sophisticated multicounty networks. Findings indicated that lessons from successful integrations are not easily reduced to a how-to list. Organizations cooperate with each other when it is in their interests to do so. Motivation to integrate cannot be mandated, nor is the availability of funding alone sufficient to provide motivation. The authors discuss ways that managed care may facilitate or hinder the link between rural primary care and rural psychiatry.

204 Lambert, D., Donahue, A., Mitchell, M. & Strauss, R. (2001). *Mental health outreach in rural area: Promising practices in rural areas.* Rockville, MD: Center for Mental Health Services, Substance Abuse and Mental Health Services Administration.

This article discusses various strategies for planning mental health outreach services in rural areas. The authors cite current practices that have been more effective in reaching rural residents regarding mental health issues.

205 LaMendola, W.F., Mohatt, D.F. & McGee, C. (2002). *Telemental health: Delivery models and performance measurement.* Boulder, CO: WICHE Mental Health Program.

This paper analyzed the use of telecommunication in the delivery of health services by: 1) reviewing archival data and literature; 2) administering a key-informant survey to grantees attending a Health Resources and Services Administration Office for the Advancement of Telehealth (HRSA/OAT) meeting in January 2002 and 3) conducting telephone surveys of persons in telemental health throughout the United States who did not attend this meeting. The analysis sought to identify and understand the various models for service delivery via tele-mental health technologies, as well as methods of evaluating the performance of these systems.

206 Larson, M.L., Beeson, P.G. & Mohatt, D.F. (1993). *Taking rural into account: A report of the National Public Hearing on Rural Mental Health.* St. Cloud, MN: National Association for Rural Mental Health and the Federal Center for Mental Health Services.

This report describes various issues regarding rural mental health care, including the fact that for rural Americans with mental health emergent needs, law enforcement is often their emergency responder and transport out of the community for care is the emergency response. Many rural providers are not rural natives, are trained in urban-centered models and programs, and travel to rural practice from metropolitan areas on an itinerant basis, creating a rural knowledge gap. Public mental health policies and programs are routinely based on urban models and experiences and are scaled down to fit the rural environment.

207 Lawrence, S.A. & McCulloch, B.J. (2001). Rural mental health and elders: Historical inequities. *Journal of Applied Gerontology*, 20(2), 144-169.

This article provides a historical review of the pathways this care has taken, with particular focus on the persistent inequities older and rural adults experience with regard to mental health care. The care of people with mental illness has taken different forms as social, political, and economic environments have changed. The persistent social construction of myths about aging in rural areas and ageist biases necessitate greater advocacy if more equitable care is to be provided.

208 Lehman, A.F., Steinwachs, D.M., Dixon, L.B., Postrado, L., Scott, J.E., Fahey, M., Fischer, P., Hoch, J., Kasper, J.A., Lyles, A., Shore, A. & Skinner, E.A. (1998). Patterns of usual care for schizophrenia: Initial results from the Schizophrenia Patient Outcomes Research Team (PORT) Client Survey. *Schizophrenia Bulletin*, 24(1), 11-20.

To examine the conformance of current patterns of usual care for persons with schizophrenia to the Schizophrenia Patient Outcomes Research Team (PORT) Treatment Recommendations, the PORT surveyed a stratified random sample of 719 adults diagnosed with schizophrenia in two States. The types of treatment settings surveyed included acute inpatient programs and continuing outpatient programs in urban and rural locales. The rates at which patients' treatment conformed to the recommendations were modest at best, generally below 50 percent. Conformance rates were higher for pharmacological than for psychosocial treatments and in rural areas than in urban ones. Rates of treatment recommendation conformance for minority patients were lower than those for Caucasians, and patterns of care varied between the two States.

209 Levant, R.F. & Habben, C. (2003). The new psychology of men: Application to rural men. In: Stamm, B.H. (Ed). *Rural behavioral health care: An interdisciplinary guide*. Washington, D.C.: American Psychological Association.

This provides an introduction to the new psychology of men, covering the gender role strain paradigm, masculinity ideology, and types of male gender role strain—discrepancy strain, dysfunction strain, and trauma strain. The chapter continues with an application of this new work to rural men and ends with a series of recommendations for behavioral health care work with rural men.

210 Leukefeld, C.G., Godlaski, T., Clark, J., Brown, C. & Hays, L. (2002). Structured stories: Reinforcing social skills in rural substance abuse treatment. *Health & Social Work*, 27, 213-217.

The authors discuss how structured stories can be a part of a therapy for rural substance abusers. Stories are part of culture, and there seems to be something special about them that helps with understanding. Stories are interpretive: therapists can help clients understand the relationship between a behavioral choice and the feelings or thoughts about that choice and the consequences of alternative choices. The case of using a structured story about employer-employee interaction allowed a client and the group to better understand negative thinking.

211 Levitt, L., Holve, E., Wang, J. (2001). *Employer Health Benefits 2001 Annual Survey*. Menlo Park: Henry J. Kaiser Family Foundation.

This annual survey of employers provides detailed insights into trends in employer-based health coverage, including changes in premiums, employee contributions, cost-sharing policies and other relevant information. The Kaiser Family Foundation and the Health Research and Educational Trust jointly conduct the survey.

212 Lewis, S.H. (2003). *Unspoken crimes: Sexual assault in rural America*. National Sexual Violence Resource Center.

This booklet examines sexual assault from a rural perspective. Its goal is to present service providers with a better sense of the unique characteristics that are so often a part of rural regions. It considers the issue of prevalence of rural sexual assault by examining National data as well as information from several States. In general, it suggests that rural sexual assault may be more prevalent than indicated by national data, and that in order to provide effective services in rural areas we must adopt a culturally sensitive approach.

213 Libby, A.M. (1997). Contracting between public and private providers: A survey of mental health services in California. *Administration & Policy in Mental Health*, 24(4), 323-338.

This paper reported on a public authority's decision to "make" or "buy" mental health services. The questionnaire measured the extent of contracting and the importance of factors that are hypothesized to affect the relative costs of contracting. The percent of contracting by programs ranged from zero to 100, averaging 41 percent. Sixty-two percent of rural programs perceived little or no competition for public mental health contracts, and contracted significantly less than urban programs. The extent of contracting was related to economic and public organizational factors.

214 Little, D.N., Hammond, C., Kollisch, D., Stern, B. & Dietrich, A.J. (1998). Referrals for depression by primary care physicians. A pilot study. *Journal of Family Practice*, 47, 375-377.

This study investigated referrals from PCPs to MHPs in a rural research network. Analysis of the initial referral process showed that the referring physicians felt a greater sense of urgency for the referrals for depression. Written evidence of the referral in the patient's chart at the three-month survey was more common for non-mental health disorders. This pilot study demonstrates that there are communication barriers between PCPs and their mental health colleagues.

215 Lo, C.C. & Stephens, R.C. (2002). Arrestees' perceived needs for substance-specific treatment: Exploring urban-rural differences. *American Journal of Drug & Alcohol Abuse*, 28, 623-642.

An interview study among a group of arrestees in seven county jails was conducted in the State of Ohio between June 1999 and September 2001, examining the prevalence of alcohol and drug dependence within the group and assessing the need for substance-abuse treatment. The results show that some of the factors assessed do exert differential effects on rural and urban arrestees' perceived needs for substance-specific treatment. Future treatment policy within the criminal justice system should perhaps take into account inmates' individual characteristics and the rural or urban location of the jail initiating their processing.

216 Loeber, R. & LeBlanc, M. (1990). Toward a developmental criminology. In: Tonry, J. and Morris, N., eds. *Crime and Justice*. Vol. 12. Chicago: University of Chicago Press.

This describes how the study of criminality will benefit from a developmental perspective that employs analyses of within-subject changes. A variety of documentation indicates that developmental sequences can be identified for conduct problems, substance use, and delinquency. Examining developmental processes as youngsters grow older, such as increases in physical strength and motor skills, the emergence of personality traits, sexual maturation, and greater opportunities for crime commission, provides important contextual information for studies of offending. Developmental theories have direct implications for the prevention of offending and treatment of offenders.

217 Loeber, R. & Stouthhamer-Loeber, M. (1986). Family factors as correlates and predictors of juvenile conduct problems and delinquency. In: Tonry, J. and Morris, N., eds. *Crime and Justice*. Vol. 7. Chicago: University of Chicago Press.

A meta-analysis was performed of concurrent and longitudinal studies on the relation of family factors to juvenile conduct problems and delinquency. Analyses of longitudinal data indicate that socialization variables, such as lack of parental supervision, parental rejection, and parent-child involvement, are among the most powerful predictors of juvenile conduct problems and delinquency. Medium-strength predictors include background variables such as parents' marital relations and parental criminality. Weaker predictors are lack of parental discipline, parental health, and parental absence. The effect of these factors seems to be about the same for boys and for girls.

218 Lubben, J.E., Weiler, P.G., Chi, L. & De Jong, F. (1988). Health promotion for the rural elderly. *Journal of Rural Health, 4*(3), 85-96.

This article describes issues in rural and gerontology on health promotion strategies for the rural elderly.

219 Lyons, J.A. (2003). Veterans Health Administration: Reducing barriers to access. In: Stamm, B.H. (Ed). *Rural behavioral health care: An interdisciplinary guide*. Washington, D.C.: American Psychological Association.

In this chapter, the author discusses the complexities of providing health care to rural veterans. In the initial sections, the U.S. veteran population and veterans' health care system are described. Then reforms designed to manage costs and increase access for a broader range of veterans are discussed, particularly in rural areas. The next section focuses on provision for posttraumatic stress disorder, a disorder for which many veterans require specialized treatment. The chapter closes with conclusions and recommendations, and emphasis is place on the importance of family services.

220 Lytton, H. (1990). Child and parent effects in boys' conduct disorder: A reinterpretation. *Developmental Psychology*, 26, 683-697.

The importance of parent and child influences on the development of conduct disorder (CD) in boys is evaluated. Evidence from this research and from research on parental influences, reviewed in detail elsewhere, is interpreted as demonstrating the primacy of the child's own contribution to CD within a reciprocal parent-child interactive system, thus corroborating control systems theory (R. Q. Bell, 1977). Demonstrated parental influences are interpreted as actions that are elicited by or that exacerbate the child's tendencies and that may represent genetic continuities. The heuristic utility and consequences of this model are outlined.

221 MacFarlane, M.M. (2001). Systemic treatment of obsessive-compulsive disorder in a rural community mental health center: An integrative approach. In: MacFarlane, M.M. (Ed). *Family therapy and mental health: Innovations in theory and practice.* (pp. 155- 183). Binghamton, NY, US: Haworth Clinical Practice Press.

This chapter describes the treatment available to sufferers of OCD at the Ross Memorial Hospital in rural southern Ontario, which offers Community Counseling Services (CCS). In treating OCD, staff at CCS draw on an integrative biopsychosocial model that incorporates elements of cognitive behavioral therapy within the framework of a broader contextual systemic approach.

222 Maiden, R.J. & Peterson, S.A. (2002). Use of mental health services by the rural aged: Longitudinal study. *Journal of Geriatric Psychiatry & Neurology*, 15(1), 1- 6.

This study examined historic shifts in the use of mental health services in a rural population. In 1987, the authors administered a survey to 358 randomly selected rural individuals investigating their willingness to use mental health services. In 1994, the authors resurveyed 110 individuals (mean age 75 year) from their original sample. As predicted, they found that there was a shift in the participants' willingness to use mental health services, increasing from five percent to 18 percent. This increased use, although improved, still fell somewhat below the actual need for mental health services, which had remained constant (about 25 percent). Interestingly, there was no greater reliance on psychotropic medication in lieu of psychotherapy (about 10 percent).

223 Markstrom, C.A., Stamm, B.H., Stamm, H.E., Berthold, S.M. & Running Wolf, P. (2003). Ethnicity and rural status in behavioral health care. In Stamm, B.H. (Ed). *Rural behavioral health care: An interdisciplinary guide.* Washington, D.C.: American Psychological Association.

In the first section of this chapter, the authors address general factors that aggravate and serve as barriers to adequate behavioral health care for minorities in rural areas. The next section describes the characteristics of four ethnic groups in the U.S.: African Americans, Latinos and Latinas,

American Indians and Alaska Natives, and Asians. The authors also provide information on working with refugees, because many ethnic groups are part of the greater refugee community. In the final sections, specific suggestions for working with ethnic groups in rural areas are provided.

224 Marsella, A.J., Bornemann, T., Ekblad, S. & Orley, J. (Eds.) (1994). *Amidst peril and pain: The mental health and well-being of the world's refugees.* Washington, DC: American Psychological Association.

This multidisciplinary volume offers mental health professionals, scientists and policy administrators a conceptual, factual and clinical resource for understanding and addressing the challenges posed by the growing problem of international refugees and displaced persons. Included are actual accounts of the experiences of refugees and how they dealt with adversity. The book also provides information on demographics, history, epidemiology, policy formation, mental health services, training and specific regional concerns. It is intended for psychologists, psychiatrists, social workers, medical doctors and policy makers involved in the mental health and well-being of the world's refugees.

225 Martin, P. (1997). Immigration and the changing face of rural America. In *Increasing understanding of public problems and policies* (pp. 201-212). Oak Brook, IL: Farm Foundation.

The author explores immigration patterns, the attractions for immigrants, and the impacts of immigrants in rural America. The article contains insights on the following: an overview of immigration patterns and the current status of immigration integration policy; an examination of the economics of the major industries that attract immigrants to the area; a series of industry/community studies that explore patterns of immigration and integration, and reactions to immigrants.

226 Martin, S.L., Kupersmidt, J.B. & Harter, K.S.M. (1996). Children of farm laborers: Utilization of services for mental health problems. *Community Mental Health Journal,* 32(4), 327-340.

The authors examined use of various types of services for children's mental health problems among 112 agricultural farm worker families. Sixty-four percent of Ss met criterion for one or more psychiatric diagnoses. Although having a psychiatric diagnosis increased the odds of seeing a health professional for these problems five-fold over Ss who did not have a psychiatric diagnosis, fewer than half of the Ss with a psychiatric diagnosis saw a health professional for their mental health problems. Physicians were the most commonly consulted health care professionals. Families also consulted with school professionals, religious leaders and non-professionals concerning their children's mental health.

227 Mason, W.A., Kosterman, R., Hawkins, J.D., Haggerty, K.P., Spoth, R.L. (2003). Reducing adolescents' growth in substance use and delinquency: Randomized trial effects of a parent-training prevention intervention. *Prevention Science*, 4, 203-212.

The relationship between growth in adolescent substance use and delinquency was examined in a longitudinal, randomized controlled study of the Preparing for the Drug Free Years Program (PDFY). Results showed that adolescents assigned to the PDFY intervention condition had a slower rate of linear increase over time in both substance use and delinquency compared with adolescents assigned to the control condition. Moreover, pre-test level of delinquency was a reliable, positive predictor of growth in substance use, whereas pretest level of substance use did not predict growth in delinquency.

228 Mathews-Cowey, S. (2000). Too much responsibility, too little help: Family carers and the rural mental health care system. *Journal of Family Studies*, 6(2), 267-271.

This paper addresses key issues raised by family caretakers of a relative with a mental disorder about the availability of rural mental health services. The results highlight that mental health care services in rural communities are not providing adequate support for the family, with the consequence that too much responsibility for such care is placed on the family.

229 McAuliffe, W.E., LaBrie, R., Woodworth, R., Zhang, C. & Dunn, R.P. (2003). State substance abuse treatment gaps. *American Journal on Addictions*, 12(2), 101-121.

This study estimated the adequacy of State substance abuse treatment rates relative to treatment needs. States varied substantially in per capita alcohol and drug treatment needs, although the two did not correlate with each other. While the need indexes correlated significantly with State treatment rates, the adequacy of State treatment rates varied greatly. States with the largest treatment gaps were in the South, Southwest, and northern plains and mountain regions. The failure of the Block Grant formula to reflect the needs of rural States with high-risk minority populations may contribute to disparities in access to services.

230 McCabe, S. & Macnee, C.L. (2002). Weaving a new safety net of mental health care in rural America: a model of integrated practice. *Issues in Mental Health Nursing*, 23(3), 263-78.

This article focuses on the current State of psychiatric-mental health care in the context of these realities and discusses the impact of the current trend of mental illness being treated by non-mental health professionals. The article concludes by proposing a model of advanced practice nursing that the authors believe will increase both access and efficacy of treatment for the mentally ill living in rural America. This Integrated Model presents a new model regarding how to provide integrated health care to meet the needs of rural mentally ill.

231 McCain, V.M. & Day, H.D. (1999). Values held by office-based and home-based therapists in northern New England. *Counseling & Values*, 43(2), 116-128.

As a first study of the values of rural mental health professionals, the Survey of Personal Values and the Survey of Interpersonal Values were completed by 51 office-based psychotherapists and 87 home-based therapists from rural areas in three northern New England States. Discriminate function analyses using the two sets of values as predictors of therapist group did not support the hypothesis that the home-based therapists would more highly value Independence and Goal Orientation than the office-based therapists; in fact, the therapists in the two settings were remarkably similar in their values. The rural therapists, as one group, more frequently endorsed the personal values of Achievement and Decisiveness and the interpersonal values of Independence, Benevolence, and Support.

232 McDonel, E.C., Bond, G.R., Salyers, M., Fekete, D., Chen, J.H., et al. (1997). Implementing assertive community treatment programs in rural settings. *Administration & Policy in Mental Health*, 25(2), 153- 173.

The authors present a controlled evaluation of a rural adaptation of the assertive community treatment (ACT) model for clients with serious and persistent mental illness (SPMI). Four community mental health settings adopted an ACT model, while a fifth site blended ACT principles with those of the Rhinelander model, another approach to case management for persons with SPMI. A broad array of client and system outcomes were evaluated at six, 12, and 24 months into the intervention. Twelve-month findings alerted potential problems in implementing the treatment model in study year one; the implementation was qualitatively evaluated and weaknesses were addressed at the beginning of the second treatment year.

Small, positive findings at 24 months suggested that the mid-study course correction may have had an impact.

233 McDonnell, K. & Fronstin, P. (1999). *EBRI health benefits data book* (1st ed.). Washington, DC: Employee Benefit Research Institute.

The EBRI Health Benefits Databook is a statistical reference work on private- and public-sector health benefit programs. Organized into five sections, this resource presents data from multiple authoritative sources in table and chart form, supplemented with concise explanations. Appendixes provide technical, legislative and source information on health benefits, a glossary of terms and a complete index.

234 McFarland, B.H., Brunette, M., Steketee, K., Faulkner, L.R., et al. (1993). Long-term follow-up of rural involuntary clients. *Journal of Mental Health Administration,* 20(1), 46-57.

A cohort of 72 persons who had entered a rural Oregon county's involuntary treatment system in 1979 through 1982 was followed for six years. While schizophrenia was the most frequent diagnosis, other conditions were represented including adjustment disorders, organic mental disorders, and substance abuse. Fifty-five percent of persons with organic mental disorders died as did 12 percent of the individuals with schizophrenia. During the follow-up period, only 39 percent of the initial cohort received treatment from a community mental health program, whereas 28 percent were newly admitted (involuntarily) to a State mental hospital.

235 McGinty, K., McCammon S.L. & Koeppen, V.P. (2001). The complexities of implementing a wraparound approach to service provision: A view from the field. In: Dosser Jr., D.A., Handron, D. (Eds.), et al.. *Child mental health: Exploring systems of care in the new millennium.* New York, NY,: Haworth Press, Inc.

The authors offer the perspective of several service providers on the benefits and barriers encountered in implementing the wrap-around model within the context of a Federally funded project to enhance a local system of care. The Pitt Edgecombe Nash-Public Academic Liaison project was instituted in three rural counties in eastern North Carolina. While implementing the wraparound model, benefits and barriers were encountered at all levels of intervention. The authors suggest that quality-monitoring efforts should include the task of assessing implementation on an ongoing basis with an emphasis on analysis of the barriers and benefits encountered and subsequent midstream corrections to improve the wrap-around model for each individual community.

236 McGrew, J.H., Pescosolido, B. & Wright, E. (2003). Case managers' perspectives on critical ingredients of assertive community treatment and on its implementation. *Psychiatric Services*, 54(3), 370-376.

This identified case managers' perspectives on the critical ingredients, therapeutic mechanisms of action, and gaps in implementation of the critical ingredients of assertive community treatment. Results show that at least 50 percent of the teams rated 24 of the 27 critical ingredients as "very important." Having a full-time nurse on the team was rated as the most important ingredient, and medication management was rated as the most beneficial clinical activity. The ratings of teams from urban and rural settings were highly correlated. Critical elements that the teams reported as being the most underimplemented included the presence of a full-time substance abuse specialist, a psychiatrist's involvement on the team, team involvement with hospital discharge and working with a client support system.

237 Medicare Payment Advisory Committee. Report to the Congress: *Medicare in rural America*. Washington, DC: Medicare Payment Advisory Committee; 2001. Available at: http://www.medpac.gov/publications/congressional_reports/Jun01%20 Entire%20report.pdf. Accessed May 7, 2003.

Analyses confirm that some rural communities face adverse economic conditions that may limit providers' abilities to furnish needed services. Nevertheless, Medicare beneficiaries in rural areas receive similar amounts of health services, on average, as do urban beneficiaries. Although similar use rates do not guarantee that rural and urban beneficiaries receive equally appropriate and effective care, this finding suggests that major new Medicare policy interventions may not be needed to preserve rural beneficiaries' access to high-quality care.

238 MedPAC. (2000). Report to the Congress: *Selected Medicare Issues*, June 2000. Washington, DC: Medicare Payment Advisory Commission (MedPAC).

This report analyzes a number of issues in which Medicare policies affect and are affected by other actors in the health care system. It examines prescription drug coverage for Medicare beneficiaries, the need to assess options to expand coverage and the impact of these options on other Federal programs, private coverage, and pharmaceutical research and development. This report also addresses several aspects of Medicare payment policy. It recommends updates to payments for hospital inpatient services and ways to improve the accuracy of payments for inpatient care and payments to teaching hospitals. The report also contains recommendations on the new prospective payment system for hospital outpatient services.

239 Meisler, N. & Williams, O. (1998). Replicating effective supported employment models for adults with psychiatric disabilities. *Psychiatric Services*, 49(11), 1419-1421.

The authors discuss the obstacles to implementing two model programs of supported employment (the Program for Assertive Community Treatment and Individual Placement and Support) for seriously mentally ill consumers in a rural mental health center in South Carolina. They describe how the individuals responsible for adopting these model programs had to make many compromises, leading to a common feature of successful adoption of innovations—"reinvention" of the model program to fit the unique constraints, resources, limitations and staffing available in the host setting.

240 Melby, J.N., Conger, R.D., Conger, K.J. & Lorenz, F.O. (1993). Effects of parental behavior on tobacco use by young adolescent males. *Journal of Marriage and Family*, 55, 439-454.

The authors evaluate a social-developmental model of early adolescent tobacco involvement. They use data from a sample of 204 seventh grade boys (12-14 years old), their parents, and siblings (9 - 17 years old). The study examines the influence of parental childrearing strategies (harsh/inconsistent and nurturant/involved) and reported parent, sibling, and peer tobacco use on tobacco involvement by early adolescents. Results support three of the four proposed models. Even after controlling for the effects of parental and sibling tobacco use, positive relationships are reported between harsh/inconsistent parenting and adolescent tobacco use, and negative relationships between nurturant/involved parenting behaviors and adolescent tobacco use. Of particular interest, parenting behaviors have both direct and indirect effects on adolescent tobacco use through the adolescents' associations with tobacco-using peers.

241 Merrill, T.S. (2003), Licensure Anachronisms: Is It Time for a Change? *Professional Psychology: Research and Practice, 34*, 459–462.

The author describes his experience when applying for licensure in three States as a way of identifying barriers encountered by psychologists during this process. Suggestions are made to improve the process so that licensing board activity might be more in line with its designated function, which is the protection of the consumer.

242 Merwin, E.I., Goldsmith, H.F. & Manderscheid, R.W. (1995). Human resource issues in rural mental health services. *Community Mental Health Journal*, 31(6), 525-537.

This discusses the human resource (HR) issues related to the provision of mental health care in rural areas. Rural areas utilize more non-specialty providers in the provision of mental health care. There are rural and urban differences in HR allocation in terms of diversity of rural areas, the availability of specialists, roles of mental health professionals, training strategies and processes of care. Training strategies of professionals in rural areas must include continuing education programs, service research, forming coalitions, multidisciplinary training and an expansion of roles beyond traditional boundaries in order to form public-academic relationships. Urban trained professionals should be retrained to develop skills for rural communities. Process of care should also take the rural setting into consideration.

243 Merwin, E., Hinton, I., Dembling, B. & Stern, S. (2003). Shortages of rural mental health professionals. *Archives of Psychiatric Nursing*, 17(1), 42-51.

This study presents a conceptual model of the supply and demand for mental health professionals. It uses national data to profile differences in the supply of mental health professionals in different types of rural and urban areas. It contrasts the availability of general health and mental health professionals. It examines shortage areas identified in 2000 and their related community characteristics. The authors State that to improve rural mental health service delivery it will be necessary to implement system changes to promote the increased availability, competency, and support of rural health professionals.

244 Meyer, H. (1990). Rural America: Surmounting the obstacles to mental health care. *Minnesota Medicine*, 73, 24-31.

The author describes obstacles to mental health care for rural Americans, including the stigma associated with treatment, and clashes between treatment and traditional rural values such as independence and privacy. The economic downturn in the 1980s left farmers and other rural residents with fewer resources to afford them adequate health insurance coverage, out-of-pocket expenses for such care, decreased employment opportunities in rural communities and raised stress levels among residents.

245 Miano, G., Forest, A. & Gumaer, J. (1997). A collaborative program to assist at-risk youth. Professional *School Counseling*, 1, 16-20.

The authors describe a university and school collaborative project that provided a full range of counseling services to a secondary school population and the larger community of a rural locality to meet the needs of the growing population of at-risk students. Both day and evening counseling programs were implemented to begin to address issues such as failure in school work, substance abuse, incarceration of a close family member, and death of a significant person in a student's life—the typical presenting problems for counseling. Results from a survey of eight of the county's high school, middle school, and elementary school counselors show that the drop-out rate has decreased steadily over the years, from 7.09 percent of the school population in the 1989-1990 academic year to 3.32 percent in 1994-1995.

246 Miller, N.S., Belkin, B.M. & Gold, M.S. (1991). Alcohol and drug dependence among the elderly: Epidemiology, diagnosis and treatment. *Comprehensive Psychiatry*, 32, 153–165.

This describes alcohol and drug dependence among the elderly as common and underdiagnosed. The practice of self-administration of prescribed medications, particularly sedatives, hypnotics, benzodiazepines and nonprescription, over-the-counter medications is prevalent. The clinician's index of suspicion must be high enough to make the proper diagnosis of alcohol- and drug-induced syndromes (e.g., dementia, depression, anxiety).

247 Miller, T.W., Kraus, R.F., Kaak, O., Sprang, R. & Burton, D. (2002). Telemedicine: A child psychiatry case report. *Telemedicine Journal & E-Health*, 8(1), 139-141.

This report examined an innovative model of telehealth care delivery through a rural school system in an underserved regional setting. The goals of this model are offered, as are a number of applications within the broad spectrum of services utilizing telehealth. Changing patterns in clinically based health care delivery in a managed care environment are discussed.

248 Miller-Heyl, J., MacPhee, D. & Fritz, J.J. (1998). DARE to be you: A family-support, early prevention program. *Journal of Primary Prevention*, 18, 257-285.

Over a five-year period, successive cohorts of families were randomly assigned to an experimental (n = 496) or control (n = 301) group. The DARE to Be You program was provided to children, families, preschool teachers, and community professionals who work with youth. Program replicability was tested at four sites, which varied in population density (urban, town, rural) and ethnic composition (Ute, Mountain Ute, Hispanic, Anglo). Evaluation data reveal significant, persistent increases in parental self-appraisals and democratic child-rearing practices, with a corresponding decrease in harsh discipline. Parent satisfaction with social support increased; target children's developmental levels were enhanced and oppositional behavior declined.

249 Minkoff, K. & Pollack, D. (Eds.) (1997). *Managed mental health care in the public sector: A survival manual.* Book Series Title: *Chronic mental illness*, Vol. 4.

This book attempts to answer many troubling questions that have recently emerged regarding managed care in public mental health. Are profit-driven mental health systems eliminating services for people with severe and persistent mental illness? Since when is community mental health a business, and when did the CMHC (community mental health center) become a "behavioral health care provider corporation?"

250 Moffitt, T.E. (1993). Adolescence—limited and lifecourse-persistent antisocial behavior: A developmental taxonomy. *Psychology Review*, 100, 674-701.

The author presents a dual taxonomy to reconcile two incongruous facts about antisocial behavior: 1) It shows impressive continuity over age, but 2) its prevalence changes dramatically over age, increasing almost 10-fold temporarily during adolescence. This article suggests that delinquency conceals two distinct categories of individuals, each with a unique natural history and etiology: A small group engages in antisocial behavior of one sort or another at every life stage, whereas a larger group is antisocial only during adolescence.

251 Mohatt, D. (1997). Rural issues in public sector managed behavioral health care. In: Minkoff, K. & Pollack, D. (Eds.). *Managed mental health care in the public sector: A survival manual. Chronic mental illness*, Vol. 4.

The design of optimal PSMC (public sector managed care) behavioral health care systems is significantly influenced by the nature of the service area. This chapter discusses implementation of PSMC in rural settings. Topics addressed include: an overview of rural issues, innovative public sector solutions, vertical integration and horizontal integration.

252 Mohatt, D.F. (1997). *Access to Mental Health Services in Frontier Areas*: Letter to the Field, No. 4, Nebraska Department of Health and Human Services.

The traditional American health care system of independent providers being reimbursed by patients and indemnity insurers on a fee-for-service basis is rapidly yielding to myriad new payment and delivery systems, multi-provider networks, and innovative private and public efforts to manage the care of beneficiaries. This shift toward what is most often called managed care has been a clear trend in the marketplace for the past decade, and has currently shown a rapid acceleration of pace.

253 Mohatt, D.F. (2000). Access to mental health services in frontier areas. *Journal of the Washington Academy of Sciences*, 86(3), 35-48.

This paper reviews and evaluates the access to mental health services in frontier areas of the United States. It takes into account that the combination of the shortage of providers and limited array of services, coupled with a thin layer of third-party payers, creates a fragile continuum of care for rural residents, especially those residing in remote frontier areas.

254 Mohatt, D.F. & Kirwan, D. (1995). *Meeting the challenge: Model programs in rural mental health.* Rockville, MD: Office of Rural Health Policy.

This report is an overview of the four model programs in Rural Mental Health. It includes information on program achievement, barriers to implementation, and challenges.

255 Mohr, P., Franco, S., Blanchfield,B., et al. (1999). Vulnerability of rural hospitals to Medicare outpatient reform. *Health Care Financial Review*, 21(1), 1-18. Available at: http://cms.hhs.gov/review/99Fall/mohr.pdf. Accessed May 7, 2003.

Because the Balanced Budget Act (BBA) of 1997 requires implementation of a Medicare prospective payment system (PPS) for hospital outpatient services, the authors evaluated the potential impact of outpatient PPS on rural hospitals. Areas examined include: 1) How dependent are rural hospitals on outpatient revenue? 2) Are they more likely than urban hospitals to be vulnerable to payment reform? 3) What types of rural hospitals will be most vulnerable to reform? Using Medicare cost report data, the authors found that small size and government ownership are more common among rural than urban hospitals and are the most important determinants of vulnerability to payment reform.

256 Monti, P.M., Rohsenow, D.J., Michalec, E., Martin, R.A. & Abrams, D.B. (1997). Brief coping skills treatment for cocaine abuse: Substance use outcomes at three months. *Addiction*, 92, 1717-1728.

Coping skills training, a promising treatment approach for alcoholics, was adapted for use with cocaine abusers and effects on outcome were investigated. A cocaine-specific coping skills training (CST) package was compared to an attention placebo control when both were added to a comprehensive treatment program. The sites were two private substance abuse treatment facilities, one residential and rural, and one an urban partial hospital. The CST intervention involved functional analysis of high-risk situations and coping skills training based on the functional analysis. Clients who received CST had significantly fewer cocaine-use days and the length of their longest binge was significantly shorter during the three-month follow-up period compared to clients in the control condition. CST did not affect relapse rates or use of other substances.

257 Moon, J.R. (2001). Establishing a fee-for-service practice in rural settings. In: VandeCreek, L. & Jackson, T.L. (Eds.). *Innovations in clinical practice: A source book*, Vol. 19.

The author describes how to establish a fee-forservice mental health practice in a rural setting, and argues that there are significant needs for a variety of mental health services in rural settings. The following topics are discussed: 1) critical success factors: confidentiality, convenience and affordability; 2) practical considerations in rural settings; 3) marketing the practice in rural settings and 4) business strategies in rural settings.

258 Morris, J.A. (Ed) (1997). *Practicing psychology in rural settings: Hospital privileges and collaborative care.*

This volume is designed to aid the rural psychologist in educating rural hospital administrators, hospital board members, medical staff, and rural citizens about the valuable contribution psychologists can make to patient care. The book covers the history of psychology's advancement in hospital settings.

Contributors also describe successful collaborative models with physicians and community mental health service providers and highlight the challenges and rewards of working in rural areas.

259 Morrissey, J.P., Johnsen, M.C. & Calloway, M.O. (1997). Evaluating performance and change in mental health systems serving children and youth: An interorganizational network approach. *Journal of Mental Health Administration*, 24(1), 4-22.

This presents an approach to system level assessment by viewing children's mental health systems as an interorganizational network. Data are presented on two county-based child mental health systems for children with severe emotional disturbances that participated in the Robert

Wood Johnson Foundation Mental Health Services Program for Youth. Findings indicate that the rural system was outperforming the urban system, but the urban system caught up over the study interval. There was high agreement between the network and stakeholder ratings of system performance at both time periods.

260 Motes, P.S., Melton, G., et al. (1999). Ecologically oriented school-based mental health services: Implications for service system reform. *Psychology in the Schools*, 36(5), 391-401.

In the past several years, there has been a significant growth in the number and type of school-based and school-linked initiatives across the nation. Through work with several State agencies, local school districts, and local community mental health centers, an integrated school-based mental health services model was established in more than 20 pilot schools in largely rural, under-served communities in South Carolina. The ecologically oriented program model that resulted from this initiative is presented. Evaluative findings and implications for service system reform for a Statewide school-based system of mental health care are discussed.

261 Mueller, K., Patil, K. & Ullrich, F. (1997). Lengthening Spells of Uninsurance and their Consequences. *The Journal of Rural Health*, 13(1).

The lengths of time adults are without health insurance have increased since 1988, as shown by data from 1,235 household interviews completed during 1992 in Nebraska. Rural residents without insurance have experienced longer such spells than their urban counterparts. Thus, while rates of uninsurance are nearly the same between urban and rural residents, important differences exist. The relationship between insurance status and physician utilization is consistent during the five years (1989 to 1993) covered in this study. This study points out some differences between rural and urban populations regarding insurance status, even when the overall rates of uninsurance are equal.

262 Mueser, K.T., Essock, S.M., Drake, R.E., Wolfe, R.S. & Frisman, L. (2001). Rural and urban differences in patients with a dual diagnosis. *Schizophrenia Research*, 48, 93-107.

This study evaluated the differences between two cohorts of patients with severe mental illness (schizophrenia-spectrum or bipolar disorder) and co-occurring substance-use disorders, living in either predominantly rural areas or urban areas. Patients in the Connecticut study group had higher rates of cocaine-use disorder, more involvement in the criminal justice system, more homelessness, and were more likely to be from minority backgrounds. The Connecticut group also had a higher proportion of patients with schizophrenia and more severe symptoms, as well as lower rates of marriage, educational attainment, and work than the New Hampshire study group. Alcohol-use disorder was higher in the New Hampshire group.

263 Mulder, P.L., Shellenberger, S., Kenkel, M., Constantine, M. G., Jumper-Thurman, P., et al. (2000). *The behavioral health care needs of rural women.* Washington, DC: American Psychological Association, Committee on Rural Health. Available online:
http://www.apa.org/rural/ruralwomen.pdf

This report presents a review of the literature related to the behavioral health care needs of rural women. The goal of the paper is to help psychologists and other health professionals be able to more effectively plan and deliver services to this population. The authors noted that additional goals for this report included identifying further questions, and providing recommendations for future research, action, and advocacy related to addressing the needs of this underserved population.

264 Mulder, P.L., Linkey, H. & Hager, A. (2003). Needs assessment, identification and mobilization of community resources and conflict management. In: Stamm, B.H. (Ed.). *Rural behavioral health care: An interdisciplinary guide.* Washington, D.C., American Psychological Association.

In this chapter, several procedures commonly used to assess and prioritize actual needs, identify community resources, and mobilize community members to take action are presented with attention to applicability in rural and frontier communities in need of behavioral health care services and to cultural sensitivity issues. The areas of concern addressed include: the direction of approach—assessment of needs or the identification of resources; the interaction of the rural environment with the procedures must be understood; and interventions must be tailored to individual communities, on the basis of a clear understanding of the specific community's needs, cultural norms and values, dynamic structure, history, and available resources.

265 Murray, J.D. & Keller, P.A. (1991). Psychology and rural America. *American Psychologist,* 46(3): 220-231.

Economic developments affecting agriculture, farm families, and rural communities have increased awareness of problems facing rural areas. Psychologists can respond to the unique challenges created by rural mental health needs through research on stress, psychopathology, and community well-being. Training programs should be encouraged to recognize rural concerns. Psychologists are needed to practice in rural areas and to help develop effective rural service models. They can also support the development of State and Federal policies that address rural needs.

266 Myers, M.S. (1998). Empowerment and community building through a gardening project. *Psychiatric Rehabilitation Journal*, 22(2), 181-183.

Gardening activities undertaken by persons with psychiatric disabilities can provide opportunities for empowerment and increased competence, while building bridges to naturally occurring supports and resources within the broader community. Psychosocial components utilized in the process include focus upon abilities rather than upon disabilities, consumer-staff partnerships, and community integration outcomes. This "healing therapy" was demonstrated by a community support program (CSP) project undertaken by a supported-housing supervisor with 18 consumers in 10 garden sites located within rural Chester County, Pennsylvania.

267 National Advisory Committee on Rural Health (1993). *Sixth annual report on rural health.* Rockville, MD: Office of Rural Health Policy, Health Resources and Services Administration, HHS.

This report describes the lack of parity between urban and rural residents in accessing appropriate mental health and substance abuse services. Several of these disparities can be traced to the grossly insufficient supply of qualified professionals in rural areas. Recommendations to address these problems are offered.

268 National Alliance for the Mentally Ill (July 1999). *Families on the brink: The impact of ignoring children with serious mental illness.* Washington, DC: National Alliance for the Mentally Ill.

"Families on the Brink: The Impact of Ignoring Children with Serious Mental Illness" is the first National survey to examine family views of the availability of treatments and services, as well as difficulties encountered in caring for children with severe mental illnesses.

269 National Center on Addiction and Substance Abuse (CASA) at Columbia University (2000). *No place to hide: substance abuse in mid-size cities and rural America.* New York: Author unknown.

This report provides information on the prevalence of substance abuse and addiction by population centers based on a wide variety of data. CASA conducted an analysis of previously unreleased data from the 1999 Monitoring the Future study conducted by the University of Michigan Institute for Social Research and of four other national data sets. This report reveals that for adults, use and abuse of illegal drugs, alcohol and tobacco is as prevalent in small metropolitan and rural areas as in urban America. For teens, use rates are higher in rural areas and smaller cities, and these areas have less availability of services.

270 National Coalition for the Homeless (1997). *Rural homelessness (NCH Fact Sheet No. 13)*. Also available: http://nch.ari.net/rural.html (1998, November 10).

A one-page fact sheet Published by the National Coalition for the Homeless that provides definitions and demographics regarding the rural homeless population. The fact sheet also includes policy issues relevant to this population.

271 National Economic Council/Domestic Policy Council (2000). *Prescription drug coverage & rural Medicare beneficiaries: A critical unmet need.* Available online: clinton4.nara.gov/WH/New/html/20000613.html

This report, prepared in response to a request from Senator Max Baucus (D-MT), shows that rural beneficiaries tend to have a greater need for prescription drug coverage but have fewer coverage options. Their incomes are lower, access to pharmacies is more limited, and out-of-pocket spending higher. The report highlights that the private prescription drug coverage options available to rural beneficiaries are not only severely limited, but extremely expensive.

272 National Institute of Mental Health (2000). Rural mental health research at the National Institute of Mental Health. Available online: http://www.nimh.nih.gov/publicat/ruralresfact.cfm.

This report describes issues facing rural Americans regarding mental health care, such as limited access to and availability of mental health specialists, such as psychiatrists, psychologists, psychiatric nurses and social workers, poverty, geographic isolation and cultural differences. It also describes resources, (i.e., grants and contracts), available to improve mental health care for rural Americans.

273 National Rural Health Association, (1999). *Mental health in rural America: An issue paper prepared by the National Rural Health Association.* Available online:
http//www.nrharural.org/dc/issuepapers/ipaper14.html

This issue paper describes a number of aspects of rural mental health issues, including the scope of such issues, infrastructure, organizational issues, discrimination and consumer issues. It provides recommendations related to each area.

274 Neese, J.B. & Abraham, I.L. (1997). Cluster analysis of psychogeriatric characteristics and service use among rural elders. *Issues in Mental Health Nursing*, 18(1), 1- 18.

This analysis developed profiles of rural elderly, a significant risk population, by subjecting data on the psychogeriatric nursing status and health services utilization of 125 Ss (aged 60-93 years) to cluster-analytic methods. The cluster analysis yielded a three-cluster model: Cluster 1 (n = 39) predominantly comprised unmarried women in moderate health, but with a high degree of health service utilization; Cluster 2 (n = 53) had rural elders with moderate physical impairments, self-perceptions of poor health, and moderate health service utilization and Cluster 3 (n = 33) comprised elders with severe cognitive and physical impairments and high health service utilization.

275 Neese, J.B., Abraham, I.L. & Buckwalter, K.C. (1999). Utilization of mental health services among rural elderly. *Archives of Psychiatric Nursing*, (13)1, 30-40.

These authors developed predictive models of psychiatric hospitalization, use of mental health services, and use of crisis intervention by 152 rural elders (mean age 78 years) participating in an outreach case-management program. Being married and having supplemental insurance in addition to Medicare predicted 23 percent of the variance for utilization of psychiatric hospitalization. Only one variable, Medicaid, predicted 14 percent of the variance for use of mental health services. Type of caregiver, marital status, household composition, and Medicaid insurance accounted for 23 percent of the variance in utilization of crisis intervention by rural elders. Overall, the two variables that most likely predicted use of psychiatric mental health services were marital status and type of insurance.

276 New Freedom Commission on Mental Health. *Subcommittee of Rural Issues: Background Paper*. DHHS Pub. No. SMA-04-3890. Rockville, MD: 2004. Available online at:
http://www.mentalhealthcommission.gov/papers/ Rural.pdf.

This report provides a synopsis of problems facing rural Americans regarding mental health care. It covers problems associated with availability, accessibility, and acceptability. Policy options are offered.

277 Newman, I.M. & Fitzsimmons, M.L. (1994). Newspapers as an evaluation tool of a rural drug education program. *Health Values*, 18(4), 41-50.

Previous studies have shown that rural newspapers set and reflect community agendas. In this study measurement of column inches and content analysis of local newspapers were used for formative and outcome evaluation of a rural community drug education program for adolescents. Newspaper coverage from the first 15 months of the project was analyzed and compared with the 15 months prior to program implementation. Coverage of community activities, attitudes, police activities, and school activities varied significantly among the seven target communities both during and before the project. Results provided insights for program refinements and the assessment of outcomes.

278 Nordal, K.C., Copans, S.A. & Stamm, B.H. (2003). Children and adolescents in rural and frontier areas. In: Stamm, B.H. (Ed). *Rural behavioral health care: An interdisciplinary guide*. Washington, D.C.: American Psychological Association.

In this chapter, the authors discuss issues relating to children and adolescents in rural areas. They begin by considering youth mortality, health risks, and mental health issues. The second section addresses access to care and utilization of services. After the discussion, the authors consider some workforce issues specific to those who care for youth, and proceed to an overview of clinical issues. Recommendations for policy and clinical care are provided in the final section.

279 Oetting, E.R., Edwards, R.W., Kelly, K. & Beauvais, F. (1997). Risk and protective factors for drug use among rural American youth. In: Roberson, E.B., Sloboda, Z., Boyd, G.M., Beatty, L, and Kozel, N.J., eds. *Rural Substance Abuse: State of Knowledge and Issues*. National Institute on Drug Abuse; U.S. Department of Health and Human Services; National Institutes of Health: NIH Publication No. 97-4177. Rockville, MD.

The authors describe commonalities between urban and rural areas when considering personal and social risk factors for drug use among adolescents. The chapter illustrates the links between these risk factors by reviewing self-report data from seventh- and eighth-grade and 11th- and 12th-grade rural students across nine States.

280 Office of Behavioral and Social Sciences Research (2001). *Qualitative methods in health research: Opportunities and considerations in application and review* (NIH Publication No. 02-5046). Bethesda, MD: National Institutes of Health. Available online at: http://obssr.od.nih.gov/Publications/Qualitative.pdf.

This document, a product of the NIH Culture and Qualitative Research Interest Group, is based on discussions and written comments from an expert working group. The purpose of the document was to assist investigators using qualitative methods in submitting competitive applications for support from NIH. The document is not intended to be comprehensive, but rather, to assist applicants in thinking about qualitative research issues to be addressed when applying for NIH funding. While the perspective is on qualitative research, many of the general issues discussed apply to both qualitative and quantitative methodologies.

281 Office of Management and Budget (1990). OMB Circular A-11. Preparation and Submission of Budget Estimates.

This report details the budget process and identifies the central financial agencies.

282 Office of Management and Budget (2003). OMB Bulletin No. 03-04. http://www.whitehouse.gov/omb/bulletins/b03-04.html.

This bulletin establishes revised definitions for the Nation's Metropolitan Statistical Areas and recognizes 49 new Metropolitan Statistical Areas. The bulletin also designates Metropolitan Divisions in those Metropolitan Statistical Areas that have a single core with a population of at least 2.5 million. In addition, the bulletin establishes definitions for two new sets of statistical areas: Micropolitan Statistical Areas and Combined Statistical Areas. New England City and Town Areas also are defined.

283 Office on National Drug Control Policy, Executive Office of The President (ONDCP) (1997). *Pulse Check, Summer 1997: Special Report— Methamphetamine Trends in Five Western States and Hawaii*, 1997. (Order # NCJ-164261). Available online at:
http://www.whitehousedrugpolicy.gov/publications/drugfact/pulsechk/summer97/pcappa.html

This report describes methamphetamine in terms of its history, physical and psychological impact, and data from a number of States regarding prevalence, methods of ingestion, and treatments.

284 Office of Rural Mental Health Research (2003). A rural mental health research agenda: Building on success by planning for the future. Boulder, CO, June 9-10, 2003. Available online at: http://www.nimh.nih.gov/scientificmeetings/ ruralmentalhealthjune03.pdf.

This paper describes the results from a June 2003 workshop put on by the Office of Rural Mental Health Research (ORMHR). The workshop included researchers, policy analysts, and consumers who share a commitment to research for improving the delivery of mental health services to diverse populations in rural and frontier areas. Meeting participants identified critical research areas and their potential benefits.

Participants noted that rural communities offer self-contained environments that provide unique opportunities to study interventions (both treatment and prevention) and other issues in "real world" settings. This meeting focused on several major areas of inquiry and resulted in specific ideas for future research.

285 O'Hara, M.W., Gorman, L.L. & Wright, E.J. (1996). Descriptions and evaluation of the Iowa Depression Awareness, Recognition, and Treatment Program. *American Journal of Psychiatry*, 153(5), 645-649.

The authors evaluated the Depression Awareness, Recognition, and Treatment Programs for professionals who provide services to rural residents in the Midwest. Following the programs, Ss evidenced significant increases in levels of knowledge of depression and a high degree of satisfaction with most elements of the program. The six-month follow-up evaluations indicated a continued positive evaluation of the program.

286 Park, J., Kosterman, R., Hawkins, J.D., Haggerty, K.P., Duncan, T.E., Duncan, S.C. & Spoth, R. (2000). Effects of the "Preparing for the Drug Free Years" curriculum on growth in alcohol use and risk for alcohol use in early adolescence. *Prevention Science*, 1, 125-138.

This study examined the effects of Preparing for the Drug-Free Years (PDFY) on the trajectories of these factors, as well as on the trajectory of alcohol use from early to mid adolescence. The sample consisted of 424 rural families of sixth graders from schools randomly assigned to an intervention or a control condition. PDFY significantly reduced the growth of alcohol use and improved parent norms regarding adolescent alcohol use over time. Implications for prevention and evaluation are discussed.

287 Patterson, G.R., Reid, J.B. & Dishion, T.J. (1992). *Antisocial Boys*. Eugene, OR: Castalia Publishing. This book describes the models of antisocial behavior and delinquency by thoroughly examining the relationship among peer rejection, antisocial parents, social disadvantage, low self-esteem, academic failure, conduct problems, as well as other important factors.

288 Patterson, G.R. (1993). Orderly change in a stable world: The antisocial trait as a chimera. *Journal of Consulting & Clinical Psychology*, 61, 911-919.

Children's traits, such as antisocial behavior, are embedded in a matrix that is changing over time. Although the trait score is stable, there are changes in the form of antisocial acts. Latent growth models were used to demonstrate both changes in form and systematic changes in mean level for a subgroup of boys. There are also qualitative changes brought about by the presence of the antisocial trait itself (e.g., academic failure, peer rejection and depressed mood). Factor analyses carried out at grades four, six and eight showed that, over time, both the changes in form and the addition of new problems are quantifiable and thus represent orderly change.

289 Perkins, D.V., Hudson, B.L., Gray, D.M. & Stewart, M. (1998). Decisions and justifications by community mental health providers about hypothetical ethical dilemmas. *Psychiatric Services*, 49(10), 1317-1322.

Ninety-five staff members (aged 19-66 years) from five community mental health centers read 14 vignettes describing ambiguous ethical dilemmas involving professional role boundaries or client confidentiality. Ss were asked to make and justify a more conservative or a less conservative decision in response to each dilemma. Years of experience as a mental health provider and previous ethics training correlated positively with staff having experienced more situations similar to those in the vignettes; however, these variables were not related to the decision made or the type of ethical justification for it. When the analysis controlled for experience and previous ethics training, Ss made fewer conservative decisions in boundary dilemmas than in confidentiality dilemmas. Compared with nonrural providers, rural providers had experienced more boundary dilemmas and made fewer conservative decisions. Boundary problems occur frequently in community-based services, especially in rural settings.

290 Petterson, S.M. (2003). Metropolitan-nonmetropolitan differences in amount and type of mental health treatment. *Archives of Psychiatric Nursing*, 17(1), 12- 19.

The author examined the extent to which, conditional on receiving treatment, the type of care differs across metropolitan and nonmetropolitan areas. Using data from the Medical Expenditure Panel Survey, the findings indicate that nonmetro residents who obtained mental health care have fewer mental health visits in a calendar year than their metro counterparts after adjusting for individual-level characteristics. Although observed rates of hospitalization and contact with physicians were higher in nonmetro areas than metro areas, this difference is attributable primarily to compositional differences between metro and nonmetro residents.

291 Petti, T.A., Cornely, P.J. & McIntyre, A.A. (1993). A consultative study as a catalyst for improving mental health services for rural children and adolescents. *Hospital & Community Psychiatry*, 44(3), 262-265.

This describes a consultative study in which a team from an academic training center examined the system of mental health and related human services for children and adolescents in a semi-rural county in western Pennsylvania. Improvement in the system of care during the follow-up period included creation and maintenance of a children's unit and a partial hospital program for adolescents at the county's community mental health center.

292 Pickrel, S.G. & Henggeler, S.W. (1996). Multisystemic therapy for adolescent substance abuse and dependence. *Child & Adolescent Psychiatric Clinics of North America*, 5, 201-211.

This article contains the principles of generating multisystemic interventions, with illustrative case examples. MST for substance abusing or dependent adolescent populations is supported by the empiric descriptive and causal modeling literature for substance-abusing youth and by preliminary outcome data regarding the short-term effects of MST on self-reported adolescent substance use, criminal offending, and parent-figure alcohol use among substance-abusing or - dependent youth and their families.

293 Pilgrim, C., Abbey, A., Hendrickson, P. & Lorenz, S. (1998). Implementation and impact of a family-based substance abuse prevention program in rural communities. *Journal of Primary Prevention*, 18, 341-361.

A family-based alcohol, tobacco, and other drug abuse prevention program was evaluated. The program targeted families with students entering middle or junior high school. The goals of the program were to increase resiliency and protective factors including family cohesion, communication skills, school attachment, peer attachment, and appropriate attitudes about alcohol and tobacco use by adolescents. The program was offered to all eligible families in eight rural school districts. Families who chose to participate began the program with lower scores on several protective factors as compared to nonparticipating families. Analyses found several positive effects of program participation at the one year follow-up. The results were strongest for boys.

294 Plaut, T., Landis, S. & Trevor, J. (1993). Focus groups and community mobilization: A case study from rural North Carolina. In: Morgan, D.L.

(Ed). *Successful focus groups: Advancing the State of the art. Sage focus editions*, Vol. 156.

This case study presents work with community-based focus groups demonstrating that effective community-based interventions must do more than meet the needs of the community; they must come from the community, and focus groups are a powerful means of facilitating this process.

295 Plomin, R., Chipuer, H.M. & Neiderhiser, J.M. (1994). Behavioral genetic evidence for the importance of nonshared environment. In: Heatherington, E.M., Reiss, D, and Plomin, R., eds. *Separate Social Worlds of Siblings: The Impact of Nonshared Environment on Development.* Hillsdale, NJ: Erlbaum, pp. 1-31.

This book examines the contributions of genetics, shared environment, and nonshared environment to development. The chapters were written by some of the foremost scholars working in the area of nonshared environment and present their perspectives, concerns, strategies, and research findings with regard to the impact of nonshared environment on individual differences in the development of siblings.

296 President's *New Freedom Commission on Mental Health.* (2004). *Achieving the Promise: Transforming Mental Health Care in America. A final report.* DHHS Pub. No. SMA-03-3832. Rockville, MD.

The New Freedom Initiative is part of President George Bush's administration's commitment to screen all American adults for possible mental illnesses, and every single child for emotional disturbances. The goal is to identify those with suspected disabilities who could then be provided with state-of-the-art treatment, predominantly in the form of psychoactive drugs, and supports. The commission was directed to identify policies that could be implemented by Federal, State and local government agencies to promote psychiatric screening, enhance utilization of treatment interventions, and streamline delivery of medical services. Available: http://www.mentalhealthcommission.gov/.

297 President's *New Freedom Commission on Mental Health. Subcommittee of Rural Issues: Background Paper.* DHHS Pub. No. SMA-04-3890. Rockville, MD: 2004.

The President's New Freedom Commission on Mental Health appointed 15 subcommittees to assist in its review of the Nation's mental health service delivery system. The full Commission appointed a Chair for each subcommittee. The experts prepared initial discussion papers that outlined key issues in rural America and presented preliminary policy options.

298 Puskar, K.R. & Martsolf, D. (1993). Stress in rural families. In: Fawcett, C.S. *Family psychiatric nursing.* University of Pittsburgh, School of Medicine, Graduate Program, Pittsburgh, PA.

These authors discuss the stress and mental health problems of adolescents and their families who live in a rural community, and present a model of care for rural mental health using a psychiatric nurse team (collaborating with the school nurse and guidance counselors in a rural high school), and suggest some guidelines for psychiatric nursing assessment and prevention/intervention.

299 Radley, A., Cramer, D. & Kennedy, M. (1997). Specialist counselors in primary care: The experience and preferences of general practitioners. *Counseling Psychology Quarterly,* 10(2), 165-173.

Three-hundred ninety-four general practitioners who could and who could not refer to an in-house counselor were compared in terms of the characteristics of their practices as well as their views about counseling provision, both within the practice and by agencies outside the practice. Results show that Ss having access to a counselor belonged to practices which were larger and had fund-holding status. No significant difference was found between rural and urban practices in their employment of an in-house counselor, although those Ss working in rural areas were less likely to see this service as having a high priority. Ss without in-house counselors estimated a referral rate for counseling in excess of twice that of the actual rate reported by Ss with practice counselors.

300 Ralph, R.O. & Lambert, D. (1999). Best practices in rural Medicaid Managed Behavioral Health: Consumer Issues. In *Working Papers Series.* Portland, ME: Muskie Institute, University of Southern Maine.

This report recommends best practices for "developing, delivering, and monitoring" Medicaid mental health managed care in rural communities. Recommendations were informed by consumers, healthcare executives, and State officials responsible for developing mental health managed care.

301 Rapp, R.C., Kelliher, C.S., Fisher, J.H. & Hall, J.F. (1996) Strengths-based case management: A role in addressing denial in substance abuse treatment. In H.A. Siegal & R.C. Rapp (Eds.), *Case management and substance abuse treatment: Practice and experience* (pp. 21–36). New York: Springer Publishing Co.

A strengths-based approach to case management is presented as an intervention to assist persons with substance abuse problems to access needed resources. The chapter describes how the same strengths-based practice activities that support resource acquisition are also effective in addressing the denial that can interfere with substance abuse treatment. Both benefits, resource acquisition and a constructive approach to denial, have shown promise for enhancing client participation in treatment and subsequent outcome from that treatment.

302 Rathbone-McCuan, E. (2001). Mental health care provision for rural elders. *Journal of Applied Gerontology*, 20(2), 170-183.

The author suggests that rural mental health service resources and intervention approaches to meet the needs of rural elders are in a State of flux. Even within this fluctuation, some relatively stable and beneficial resources are available to rural elders and their families. This article identifies those resources within the context of the growing influence of managed behavioral health care. Systems of managed care are directing the types of mental health services available and their patterns of coordination with other health and social service resources used by rural elders.

303 Rathbone-McCuan, E. (1993). Rural geriatric mental health care: A continuing service dilemma. In: Bull, C.N. (Ed). *Aging in rural America.* Sage focus editions, 162, 146-160.

The author identifies the major issues contributing to the lack of adequate mental health services for the rural elderly and suggests steps to address the critical shortage of these resources

304 Rawson, R.A., Obert, J.L., McCann, M.J. & Ling, W. (1991). *The Matrix Model for Outpatient Treatment for Alcohol Abuse and Dependency.* Beverly Hills, CA: Matrix.

This manual describes a standardized relapse prevention treatment format that provides a comprehensive framework to learn recovery skills and facilitates participation in recovery activities. This may be a means through which to identify key elements for successful treatment.

305 Regier, D.A., Farmer, M.E., Rae, D.S., Locke, B.Z., Keith, S.J., Judd, L.L., & Goodwin, F.K. (1990). Comorbidity of mental disorders with alcohol and other drug abuse: Results from the Epidemiologic Catchment Area Study. *Journal of the American Medical Association, 264,* 2511-2518.

The prevalence of comorbid alcohol, other drug, and mental disorders in the United States' total community and institutional population was determined from 20,291 persons interviewed in the National Institute of Mental Health Epidemiologic Catchment Area Program. Estimated U.S. population lifetime prevalence rates were 22.5 percent for any non-substance abuse mental disorder, 13.5 percent for alcohol dependence-abuse, and 6.1 percent for other drug dependence-abuse. Among those with a mental disorder, the odds ratio of having some addictive disorder was 2.7, with a lifetime prevalence of about 29 percent (including an overlapping 22 percent with an alcohol and 15 percent with another drug disorder). For those with either an alcohol or other drug disorder, the odds of having the other addictive disorder were seven times greater than in the rest of the population. Among those with an alcohol disorder, 37 percent had a comorbid mental disorder. The highest mental-addictive disorder comorbidity rate was found for those with drug (other than alcohol) disorders, among whom more than half (53 percent) were found to have a mental disorder with an odds ratio of 4.5. Individuals treated in specialty mental health and addictive disorder clinical settings have significantly higher odds of having comorbid disorders. Among the institutional settings, comorbidity of addictive and severe mental disorders was highest in the prison population, most notably with antisocial personality, schizophrenia, and bipolar disorders.

306 Regier, D.A., Narrow, W.E., Rae, D.S., Manderscheid, R.W., Locke, B.Z., & Goodwin, F.K. (1993). The de Facto U.S. Mental and Addictive Disorders Service System: Epidemiologic Catchment Area prospective one-year prevalence rates of disorders and services. *Archives of General Psychiatry, 50*, 85-94.

After initial interviews with 20,291 adults in the National Institute of Mental Health Epidemiologic Catchment Area Program, the authors estimated prospective one-year prevalence and service use rates of mental and addictive disorders in the U.S. population. An annual prevalence rate of 28.1 percent was found for these disorders, composed of a one-month point prevalence of 15.7 percent (at wave 1) and a one-year incidence of new or recurrent disorders identified in 12.3 percent of the population at wave 2. During the one-year follow-up period, 6.6 percent of the total sample developed one or more new disorders after being assessed as having no previous lifetime diagnosis at wave 1. An additional 5.7 percent of the population, with a history of some previous disorder at wave 1, had an acute relapse or suffered from a new disorder in one year. Other descriptive data is provided.

307 Richters, J.E. & Martinez, P.E. (1993). Violent communities, family choices, and children's chances: An algorithm for improving the odds. *Developmental Psychopathology*, 5, 609-627.

The authors investigated the early predictors of adaptational success and failure among 72 children attending their first year of elementary school in a violent neighborhood. Community violence exposure levels were not predictive of adaptational failure or success. Instead, adaptational status was systematically related to characteristics of Ss' homes; Ss' chances of adaptational failure rose dramatically as a function of living in unstable and/or unsafe homes.

308 Ricketts T, Slifkin R, Silberman P. (1998). *The Changing Market, Managed Care and the Future Viability of Safety Net Providers—Special Issues for Rural Providers*. Background Paper for the Institute of Medicine. Chapel Hill: Cecil G. Sheps Center for Health Services Research, University of North Carolina at Chapel Hill.

This paper examines the impact of the growth of Medicaid managed care and other major changes in the health care system on the future viability of safety net providers, with a special emphasis on those providers funded by HRSA. A committee reviewed the literature and analyzed relevant information and data as it pertains to this area; held a public hearing and conducted site visits to assess how safety net providers are being affected both positively and negatively by the new environment and managed care; and, produced and disseminated a report with recommendations.

309 Roberts, L.W., Battaglia, J., Epstein, R.S. (1999). Frontier ethics: Mental health care needs and ethical dilemmas in rural communities. *Psychiatric Services*, 50(4), 497-503.

Important but little-recognized ethical dilemmas affect rural mental health care delivery. Six attributes of isolated settings with limited resources appear to intensify these ethical dilemmas: overlapping relationships, conflicting roles, and altered therapeutic boundaries between caregivers, patients and families; challenges in preserving patient confidentiality; heightened cultural dimensions of mental health care; "generalist" care and multidisciplinary team issues; limited resources for consultation about clinical ethics and greater stresses experienced by rural caregivers. The authors describe these features of rural mental health care and provide vignettes illustrating dilemmas encountered in the predominantly rural and frontier States of Alaska and New Mexico. They also outline constructive approaches to rural ethical dilemmas in mental health care.

310 Robins, L.N. & Reiger, D.A. (Eds). (1991). *Psychiatric disorders in America: The Epidemiologic Catchment Area Study.* New York: The Free Press.

The National Institute of Mental Health multisite Epidemiologic Catchment Area (ECA) program is distinguished by its sample size of at least 3,500 subjects per site (about 20,000 total); the focus on Diagnostic Interview Schedule--defined DSM-III mental disorders; the one-year re-interview-based longitudinal design to obtain incidence and service use data; the linkage of epidemiologic and health service use data and the replication of design and method in multiple sites.

311 Rogers, C.C. (1999). Growth of the oldest old population and future implications for rural areas. *Rural Development Perspectives*, 14, 3, 22-26.

This article discusses the changing geographic distribution of the older population and describes the results of this shift, including disparities between community resources and needs (e.g., medical services, social services, housing and long-term care). Small rural counties are especially challenged in providing services for the elderly. Additionally, there are special problems of transportation, availability of facilities and resources and delivery of services associated with the geographic dispersion and isolation of the population.

312 Rohland, B.M. (2001). Telepsychiatry in the heartland: If we build it, will they come? *Community Mental Health Journal*, 37(5), 449-459.

The author notes that the quality of care provided by telemedicine and its acceptability to persons who live in rural areas is largely undetermined. In this study, service satisfaction and functional status in 24 persons (aged 34-81 years) using telemedicine was compared to those receiving face-to-face services at two rural sites over a two-year study period. Similar ratings of satisfaction and clinical status were observed in 12 patients who received services under both modalities.

313 Rohland, B.M. & Langbehn, D.R. (1998). Use of mental health services in rural areas. *Psychiatric Services*, 49(1), 107-108.

This determined if residents of rural counties in Iowa had less access to the same types of services as their urban counterparts. Results show that Medicaid beneficiaries living in a rural county did not report less overall mental health service usage than those in urban areas, but they were less likely to use group therapy. Persons who did not have schizophrenia and had been hospitalized during 1993 were more likely to report a greater lifetime cumulative number of days hospitalized if they lived in urban areas.

314 Rohland, B.M. & Rohrer, J.E. (1998). County funding of mental health services in a rural State. *Psychiatric Services*, 49(5), 691-693.

This examined the relationships between funding for mental illness in Iowa counties and county wealth, political activism, need for public services, rural culture, and policy makers' attitudes. Counties with fewer people, lower proportions of persons with college education, higher proportions of rural and elderly residents, higher rates of poverty, and a higher proportion of income from farms spent less money on mental health services. Regression analysis indicated that the size of the county population and the proportion of persons receiving Medicaid funds explained 96 percent of the variation between county budgets.

315 Rohland, B.M., Rohrer, J.E. & Etsey, Y.K. (1998). The impact of case management on utilization of community support services in a rural State. *Administration & Policy in Mental Health*, 26(2), 125-135.

This tested the hypothesis that persons with serious mental illness (SMI) would report more utilization of community support services if they had a case manager. Two hundred sixty-nine individuals (ages 20-81 years) with SMI were asked to complete a survey reporting their use of ten community support services and case management. Having a case manager was not associated with increased utilization of any support service or case management by Ss with SMI in this rural State.

316 Rohland, B.M., Rohrer, J.E., Tzou, H. (1998). Broker model of case management for persons with serious mental illness in rural areas. *Administration & Policy in Mental Health*, 25(5), 549-553.

Ninety-one case managers from 61 counties in Iowa State were surveyed in order to assess the application of a broker model of case management for persons with serious mental illness who live in a rural State. Results show that three weaknesses—inconsistent and inappropriate training, restrictions from role as direct service provider, and limited service availability— diminished the practicality of the broker model. While the resources expended on case managers may be less than it is in other models, the cost-effectiveness of this approach in regard to assuring comprehensive service provision to persons with serious mental illness is less evident. It is suggested that alternative models for case management that are less dependent on referral to existing community resources (e.g., assertive community treatment) may be more effective in rural areas and should be the subject of future studies.

317 Rohland, B.M., Rohrer, J.E., Tzou, H. (1998). Perceived shortages of community support services. *Administration & Policy in Mental Health*, 25, 321-326.

This examined whether the perception of service availability and adequacy would be correlated with county funding and the presence of a community mental health center in the county. Sixty-two case managers from urban and rural counties completed a survey regarding community support services in their counties. The results show that the perception of service availability was not correlated with county per capita expenditures on mental illness. The presence of a community mental health center within the county, however, was correlated to the perception of availability for the service components of crisis response, mental health treatment, housing, identification and outreach, and family support.

318 Rokke, P.D. & Klenow, D.J. (1998). Prevalence of depressive symptoms among rural elderly: Examining the need for mental health services. *Psychotherapy: Theory, Research, Practice, Training*, 35(4), 545-558.

This reexamined the prevalence of depressive symptoms among 1,724 rural, noninstitutionalized older adults and documented the need for mental health services as they relate to depression and potential barriers to receiving needed services. Results indicate that the prevalence of depression was relatively low.

Controlling for potential alcohol abuse, cognitive impairment and medical problems, the study found that five percent of older adults reported current depressive symptomatology. When using a cutoff score that is likely to correspond to a diagnosis of major depression, the study found a prevalence rate of 1.6 percent. Of those reporting significant levels of depression, only 27.6 percent were currently being treated for an emotional problem.

319 Rosenheck, R. & Fontana, A. (1995). Do Vietnam-era veterans who suffer from post-traumatic stress disorder avoid VA mental health services? *Military Medicine, 160,* 136-142.

It has been suggested that Vietnam veterans who suffer from PTSD avoid Department of Veterans Affairs (VA) health services because their experiences in the military engendered a profound distrust of the Federal government and its institutions. Data from a national survey of 1,676 veterans who served during the Vietnam era show that veterans with PTSD were 9.6 times more likely than other veterans to have used VA mental health services; but only 3.3 times more likely to have used non-VA services. After controlling for other factors, veterans suffering from PTSD were 1.8 times more likely than other veterans to have used VA services, but were no more likely to have used non-VA services. Contrary to conventional belief, veterans with PTSD show a preference for VA compared to non-VA mental health services.

320 Rosman, M. & Van Hook, M.P. (1998). Changes in rural communities in the past twenty-five years: Policy implications for rural mental health. Available online: http://www.narmh.org/pages/refone.html.

This article identifies key changes in the structures of rural American society during the past 25 years and discusses accompanying shifts in mental health care to rural Americans. It also discusses the implications for policy of these changes and ways in which policy changes have affected rural mental health services. The following discussion reflects the reality that mental health is intricately linked with health generally and with family and community well-being.

321 Rost, K., Fortney, J., Fischer, E., Smith, J. (2002). Use, quality and outcomes of care for mental health: The rural perspective. *Medical Care Research and Review*, 59(3), 231-265.

This reviews literature published during the period 1989-1997 concerning the determinants of use, quality, and outcomes of mental health services usage in rural areas. Examined are: (1) how key constructs are operationalized; (2) the influence of constructs on the care process; (3) reported differences between usage by nonmetropolitan and metropolitan individuals or within nonmetropolitan individuals; (4) salient issues raised by rural advocates and (5) key research questions.

322 Rost, K.M., Owen, R.R., Smith, J. & Smith, Jr., G.R. (1998). Rural-urban differences in service use and course of illness in bipolar disorder. *Journal of Rural Health*, 14(1), 36-43.

Authors tested the hypothesis that depressed rural individuals would receive less outpatient treatment and report higher rates of hospital admittance and suicide attempts than their urban counterparts. Although there were no rural-urban differences in the rate, type, or quality of outpatient depression treatment, rural Ss made significantly fewer specialty care visits for depression. Depressed rural Ss had 3.05 times the odds of being admitted to the hospital for physical problems and 3.06 times the odds of being admitted for mental health problems during the year. Elevated rates of hospital admittance disappeared in models controlling for number of specialty care depression visits in the previous month. Rural Ss reported significantly more suicide attempts during the study period.

323 Rowe, W.E. (1997). Changing ATOD norms and behaviors: A Native American community commitment to wellness. *Evaluation & Program Planning*, 20, 323- 333.

In September 1991, a five-year GAP-funded community substance abuse prevention program was launched in this Native American community. A small (550 member) rural community, it had a history of serious alcohol and drug problems. The Chi-e-thee ("workers") grass-roots program sought to address substance abuse through a strategy using community collaboration between tribal agencies, community empowerment and education, cultural enhancement and development of support networks and services for people engaged in healing and recovery. This program was successful in sponsoring over 215 cultural and educational events, and has resulted in 96 community members making a commitment to sobriety, a community-wide change in norms about wellness and substance abuse, the creation of new networks of communication and collaboration and new tribal policies and enforcement practices to curtail drug and alcohol abuse. The number of clean and sober individuals was determined to have increased from 25 percent of the adult population in 1992 to 40 percent of the adult population in 1996.

324 Rowland, D. & Lyons, B. (1989). Triple Jeopardy: Rural, Poor and Uninsured. *Health Services Research*, 23, (6): 975-1004.

This article reports that current knowledge on health care for the rural poor and uninsured demonstrates little descriptive and empirical evidence on this population.

Policy strategies are called for to get a better understanding of the gaps in insurance coverage and the special problems of rural residents, especially those with low incomes.

325 Rueter, M.A., Conger, R.D. & Ramisetty-Mikler, S. (1999). Assessing the benefits of a parenting skills training program: A theoretical approach to predicting direct and moderating effects. *Family Relations: Interdisciplinary Journal of Applied Family Studies*, 48, 67-77.

Using a theoretical model to ground this investigation, the authors tested specific hypotheses about factors that moderate the benefits of attending the Preparing for the Drug-Free Years (PDFY). These hypotheses were experimentally tested on a sample of families that each included a sixth or seventh grade child. The results for 144 fathers supported the study hypotheses, while 150 mothers who benefited most from program participation showed the weakest pre-program communication skills and reported the greatest marital difficulties.

326 Ryland, S.A. & Lucas, L. (1996). A rural collaborative model of treatment and recovery services for pregnant and parenting women with dual disorders. *Journal of Psychoactive Drugs*, 28(4), 389-395.

This discusses the organization of services for the treatment of rural women with dual disorders in Fresno County, California. The overall goal of the Fresno County Health Service Agency Mental Health Department is to assist clients in developing coping skills that will promote and sustain productive and fulfilling lives. This is done by providing comprehensive treatment for both mental illness and substance abuse, parenting skills, prenatal and postnatal medical support, and case management and focusing on women-specific issues.

327 Sammons, M.T. (2003). Nonphysician prescribers in rural settings: Unique roles and opportunities for enhanced mental health care. In: Stamm, B.H. (Ed). *Rural behavioral health care: An interdisciplinary guide*. Washington, D.C.: American Psychological Association.

Two areas of expanded practice are the acquisition of independent prescribing authority and collaborative drug therapy management. These trends are analyzed in light of long-extant shortcomings in the provision of rural mental health services. The positive implications of expanded nonphysician scopes of practice for rural residents in need of mental health services are discussed, and recommendations are made for instituting changes in training programs and scope of practice to the benefit of rural populations.

328 Sampson, R.J. & Groves, W.B. (1989). Community structure and crime: Testing social-disorganization theory. *American Journal of Sociology*, 94, 774-802.

The authors analyzed data from 1982 national crime surveys of England and Wales that replicated and significantly extended C. Shaw and H. McKay's (1942) systemic model of community social disorganization. Community-level measurement (of sparse friendship networks, unsupervised teenage peer groups, and low organizational participation) provides a step toward directly testing macrosocial control theory.

329 Sandrick, K. (1990). Expanded delivery system needed for post-traumatic stress. *Hospitals*, 64(11), 44-45.

For many Vietnam combat veterans, the war never ended. They fight it over and over again in their minds. Their condition is called post-traumatic stress disorder. The Department of Veterans Affairs has made significant strides in treating these vets, but the VA is able to meet only a small part of the veterans' demand for treatment. A need exists at the community level, particularly in rural areas, where many veterans do not have access to the specialized treatment they need without traveling great distances and navigating red tape.

330 Santos, A.B., Deci, P.A., Lachance, K.R., Dias, J.K, et al. (1993). Providing assertive community treatment for severely mentally ill patients in a rural area. *Hospital and Community Psychiatry*, 44, 34-39.

This evaluated the effect of an assertive community treatment program on rates of hospital utilization and cost of care. Twenty-three patients (ages 18-61 years) with chronic psychotic disorders were studied. The intervention was associated with a 79 percent decrease in hospital days per year, a 64 percent decrease in the number of admissions per year, a 75 percent decrease in the average length of stay per admission and a 52 percent reduction in estimated direct cost of care.

331 Sawyer, D. & Beeson, P. (1998). Rural Mental Health: Vision 2000 and Beyond. Available online: http://www.narmh.org/pages/future.html.

This report is the result of an intensive effort by the National Association for Rural Mental Health (NARMH) to define a strategic direction for rural mental health in the year 2000 and beyond. The work began in May of 1997 with a focus group that explored policies, issues, strategies, solutions and recommendations regarding the provision of mental health services in rural areas.

332 Sawyer, D.A. & Moreines, S.F. (1995). A model for rural children's mental health services. *Administration & Policy in Mental Health*, 22(6), 597-605.

The authors present the Rural Partnership model for service delivery in rural areas, which has strengthened the mental health network for children and youth in New York. The Rural Partnership model is designed to improve mental health service provision and access by focusing on local planning, service coordination, reallocation and redirection of existing financial resources, service providers and communication. It includes overlapping and cumulative services composed of a system of coordination and development, treatment, support and educational components. It involves shared partnerships among service providers and service recipients and is transferable to other rural settings.

333 Scattolon, Y. (2003). "I just went on ... there was no feeling better, there was no feeling worse": Rural women's experiences of living with and managing "depression." In: Stoppard, J.M. & McMullen, L.M. (Eds.).

Situating sadness: Women and depression in social context. New York, NY, US: New York University Press.

How do women living in rural communities understand, experience, and cope with being depressed on their own, without professional help? To answer this question, the author talked to 15 women living in rural communities who described themselves as depressed or under a great deal of stress. None of the women had sought professional help to cope with their distress. Although they did not utilize professional mental health services, their reasons for not doing so provide valuable information for mental health professionals.

334 Schank, J.A. & Skovholt, T.M. (1997). Dual-relationship dilemmas of rural and small-community psychologists. *Professional Psychology-Research & Practice*, 28(1), 44-49.

Sixteen licensed psychologists who lived and practiced in rural areas and small communities participated in interviews about ethical dilemmas they faced in daily practice. Dilemmas involving professional boundaries were identified as significant concerns for all of the psychologists. Major themes were the reality of overlapping business relationships, the effects of overlapping relationships on members of the psychologist's own family and the dilemmas of working with more than one family member as clients or with others who have friendships with individual clients. The psychologists knew the content of ethical codes but often struggled in choosing how to apply those codes in the best interest of clients.

335 Schauer, P.M. & Weaver, P. (1993). Rural elder transportation. In Krout, J.A. (Ed.), *Providing Community-Based Services to the Rural Elderly.* Thousand Oaks, CA: Sage.

This chapter describes changes in rural America (e.g., land use) that have presented challenges for transporting elderly persons to various locations (e.g., small rural communities becoming polycentric, losing the central business district to strip malls and shops with parking).

336 Schur, L. & Franco, S. (1999). Access to health care. In: Ricketts, T. (Ed.). *Rural health in the United States.* New York: Oxford University Press.

This chapter describes the rural economy of the United States and its relation to considerable health care access problems in terms of health insurance coverage and provider supply. Rural residents are less likely to have employer-sponsored health insurance and are more likely to be uninsured than urban residents. In addition, the rural poor are less likely to be covered by Medicaid than the urban poor. Although it does not appear that rural residents are unable to obtain needed care, rural residents are more likely to report delaying needed care because of financial barriers than are urban residents.

337 Sears, S.F. & Evans, G.D. et al. (2003). Rural social services systems as behavioral health delivery systems. In: Stamm, B.H. *Rural behavioral health care: An interdisciplinary guide.* Washington, DC, American Psychological Association.

The purpose of this chapter is to review four systems spanning education, health, and religious systems that could accommodate the provision of behavioral services to rural areas in the U.S. and to examine the assets and barriers to reach such collaboration. Collaboration among school-based health and social services can be along a continuum of informal, coordinated, partnerships, collaborative, and integrated. The delivery systems presented in this chapter have been explored as conduits for rural behavioral health care to some degree, and are presented as possibilities that possess inherent strengths and weaknesses.

338 Sheldon-Keller, A.E.R., Koch, J.R., Watts, A.C. & Leaf, P.J. (1996). The provision of services for rural youth with serious emotional and behavioral problems: Virginia's comprehensive services act. *Community Mental Health Journal,* 32(5), 481-495.

This details the Commonwealth of Virginia's experience of implementing the Comprehensive Services Act in rural areas for youth with serious emotional and behavioral problems. The State-level effort provides an interagency plan for providing and funding a minimum level of community services for youth with serious emotional and behavioral problems. Five general goals include encouraging a private and public partnership in the delivery of services. The role of the local government in the implementation is outlined. Issues in funding and support are also discussed. An evaluation report from five demonstration model projects, one being a rural community, is included.

339 Shelton, D.A. & Frank, R., (1995). Rural mental health coverage under health care reform. *Community Mental Health Journal,* 31(6), 539-552.

This discusses the impact of health care (HC) reform efforts on the mentally ill in rural areas. Although the utilization rates for inpatient and residential beds have increased over the years, the number is still less than in urban areas. Managed competition can improve care in rural areas, while taking into consideration the local culture. Mental health in reform must include coverage for catastrophic illness, rural mentally ill persons, supportive and case management services. Important issues facing rural mental health under HC reform are inclusion of mental health benefits, avoiding biased selection under insurance plans and rural service availability.

340 Shelton, D.A., Merwin, E. & Fox, J. (1995). Implications of health care reform for rural mental health services. *Administration & Policy in Mental Health*, 23(1), 59-69.

Efforts toward health care reform for people with mental illness in rural America must take into consideration the unique characteristics of these areas. Universal coverage, for example, would remove the financial barriers to accessing care for this population, but its focus on cost control in managed health care would not assure an expansion of services or providers in rural areas. Special incentives (e.g., loan forgiveness for selected provider groups and subsidies for troubled rural hospitals) are necessary to address the needs of rural populations.

341 Sher, K.J., Walitzer, K.S., Wood, P.K. & Brent, E.E. (1991). Characteristics of children of alcoholics: Putative risk factors, substance use and abuse and psychopathology. *Journal of Abnormal Psychology*, 100, 427-488.

A sample of 253 children of alcoholics (COAs) and 237 children of nonalcoholic (non-COAs) were compared on alcohol and drug use, psychopathology, cognitive ability, and personality. COAs reported more alcohol and drug problems, stronger alcohol expectancies, higher levels of behavioral undercontrol and neuroticism, and more psychiatric distress in relation to non-COAs. They also evidenced lower academic achievement and less verbal ability than nonCOAs. Although gender differences were found, there were few Gender x Family History interactions; the effects of family history of alcoholism were similar for men and women. When gender effects were found, they showed greater family history effects for women.

342 Shuff, I.M. (1997). Rural practice. In: Winiarski, M.G. (Ed). *HIV mental health for the 21st century.*

This chapter presents a discussion of the literature regarding the treatment and spread of HIV/AIDS in rural communities. The literature is divided into four general areas: general policy and public health, service provider preparation, rural practice, and homophobia. The author then discusses recommendations for future practice and points he considers to be critical in developing a system for HIV/AIDS services delivery in nonurban areas.

343 Simons, R.L., Whitbeck, L.B., Beaman, W.J. & Conger, R.D. (1994b). The impact of mother's parenting, involvement by nonresidential fathers, and parental conflict on the adjustment of adolescent children. *Journal of Marriage and Family*, 56, 356-374.

This examined the influence of mothers' parenting practices, involvement of nonresidential fathers, and parental conflict on the adjustment of adolescents living in mother-headed households. Results show that adolescents experienced a high level of contact with their fathers. The quality of both mothers' and fathers' parenting influenced adolescents' externalizing and internalizing problems. Parental conflict was related to internalizing problems for male Ss but not for female Ss.

344 Simons, R.L., Wu, C., Conger, R.D. & Lorenz, F.O. (1994a). Two routes to delinquency: Differences between early and late starters in the impact of parenting and deviant peers. *Criminology*, 32, 247-276.

This tests hypotheses concerning differences in the determinants of involvement with the criminal justice system for adolescents who show early vs. late onset of delinquency. It also tests various contentions about the nature of the associations between parenting practices, deviant peers, and involvement in criminal activities. Four waves of data collected on 177 adolescent boys living in small towns in the Midwest were used to test the hypotheses. Data were collected annually from families when the target child was in grades seven, eight, nine, and ten.

345 Smith, H.A. (1999). Rural telepsychiatry is economically unsupportable: Comment. *Psychiatric Services*, 50(2), 266-267.

The author comments on the article by A. Werner and L. Anderson, suggesting that the authors took a short-sighted approach, which predictably would indicate that telepsychiatry is economically unsupportable. Smith argues that region-wide advances in continuity of care, treatment and discharge planning are far-reaching benefits of telepsychiatry, along with increased consumer and family involvement and greater opportunities for staff education and training.

346 Smith, M., Mitchell, S., Buckwalter, K.C. & Garand, L. (1994). Geropsychiatric nursing consultation: A valuable resource in rural long-term care. *Archives of Psychiatric Nursing*, 8(4), 272-279.

This provides an overview of the challenges confronting rural long-term care (LTC) facilities and describes a model of service delivery in which geropsychiatric nurses indirectly exert a positive influence on the day-to-day mental health nursing care provided in geographically remote facilities. Results indicate that the dual approach of providing necessary information via training and promoting application of that knowledge through consultee-centered consultation may be effective in changing day-to-day interventions in rural LTC facilities.

347 Snustad, D.G., Thompson-Heisterman, A.A., Neese, J.B. & Abraham, I.L. (1993). Mental health outreach to rural elderly: Service delivery to a forgotten risk group. *Clinical Gerontologist*, 14(1), 95-111.

This explores the special challenges confronting a multi-disciplinary team attempting mental health outreach to rural elders. Outreach services offer an approach to increasing the equity and accessibility of mental health services to this at-risk vulnerable population. The services that are provided and the principles that guide these services are discussed and illustrated by case studies. Services include (1) multidisciplinary assessment and intervention, (2) integrating community services, (3) assuring access, (4) counseling, (5) caregiver support, (6) family counseling, (7) psychiatric diagnosis and treatment, (8) crisis intervention and (9) advocacy.

348 Sobel, S.N., Anisman, S. & Hamdy, H.I. (1998). Factors affecting emergency service utilization at a rural community mental health center. *Community Mental Health Journal*, 34(2), 157-163.

Five years of data on adult and child emergency service contacts at a rural community mental health center were analyzed retrospectively to clarify which of an array of potential factors actually affect the utilization of emergency services. Significant associations with number of emergency contacts were found for season, day of week, holidays, school vacations and weather conditions. This study helps to elucidate those factors affecting psychiatric emergency service utilization at a rural community mental health center.

349 Spoth, R., Redmond, C., Haggerty, K. & Ward, T. (1995). A controlled parenting skills outcome study examining individual difference and attendance effects. *Journal of Marriage & the Family*, 57, 449-464.

The study tested a theory-based, family-focused prevention program entitled Preparing for the Drug Free Years with 209 families, all of whom had a sixth or seventh grader. The findings showed significant intervention effects on both measures for mothers and fathers. Results also indicated that both mothers' and fathers' level of intervention attendance and expressed readiness for parenting change were significant predictors of the targeted parenting outcome, as was parent self-efficacy among mothers. The targeted parenting outcome, in turn, significantly affected the general child management outcome for both mothers and fathers.

Finally, findings showed a significant interaction of intervention attendance and intervention-targeted parenting behaviors at pretest for fathers.

350 Spoth, R., Redmond, C., Hockaday, C. & Yoo, S. (1996). Protective factors and young adolescent tendency to abstain from alcohol use: A model using two waves of intervention study data. *American Journal of Community Psychology*, 24, 749-770.

This model used two waves of data from a family-focused preventive intervention project, called Preparing for the Drug Free Years, to test a model of the influence of protective factors (e.g., positive parent-child interactions and effective parenting) on young adolescents' tendency toward alcohol abstinence. Although the hypothesized cross-time paths relating prosocial peer affiliation and affectional relationship with parents were not supported, the modeling results did provide support for the cross-time effects of affectional relationship with parents and prosocial peer affiliation on young adolescent mastery-esteem.

351 Spoth, R., Yoo, S., Kahn, J.H. & Redmond, C. (1996). A model of the effects of protective parent and peer factors on young adolescent alcohol refusal skills. *Journal of Primary Prevention*, 16, 373-394.

This describes the specification and testing of a model of protective parent and peer factors on young adolescent alcohol refusal skills. Covariance structure modeling of data from 209 families participating in a controlled study of a family-oriented skills training, Preparing for the Drug FreeYears (Hawkins, J.D., et al, 1991), was used to test two versions of the model, one version addressed attachment and skills training attendance specific to mothers and one specific to fathers. The revised model shows a strong fit with the data and accounted for a substantial portion of the variance in the alcohol refusal outcome. Hypothesized protective factor effects and skills training effects were significant.

352 Spoth, R., Redmond, C. & Shin, C. (1998). Direct and indirect latent-variable parenting outcomes of two universal family-focused preventive interventions: Extending a public health-oriented research base. *Journal of Consulting & Clinical Psychology*, 66, 385- 399.

This article illustrates a program evaluation approach for the study of family intervention outcomes in general populations. Thirty-three rural schools were randomly assigned to one of three conditions: the Preparing for the Drug Free Years Program (PDFY), the Iowa Strengthening Families Program (ISFP) or the minimal-contact control group. Analyses were conducted to ensure initial and attrition-related group equivalencies and to assess school effects. Structural equation models of the hypothesized sequence of direct and indirect effects for both PDFY and ISFP were then fit to the data. All hypothesized effects were significant for both interventions. The discussion addresses the potential public health benefits of evaluation research on universal preventive interventions.

353 Spoth, R., Reyes, M.L., Redmond, C. & Shin, C. (1999). Assessing a public health approach to delay onset and progression of adolescent substance use: Latent transition and log-linear analyses of longitudinal family preventive intervention outcomes. *Journal of Consulting & Clinical Psychology*, 67, 619-630.

This study examined the effects of the Iowa Strengthening Families Program (ISFP) and the Preparing for the Drug Free Years program (PDFY) on young adolescent transitions from nonuse of substances to initiation and progression of substance use. Effects on delayed substance use initiation were shown for both the ISFP and the PDFY at a two-year follow-up. Also at this follow-up, the PDFY showed effects on delayed progression of use among those previously reporting initiation.

354 Spoth, R., Goldberg, C., Neppl, T., Trudeau, L. & Ramisetty-Mikler, S. (2001). Rural-urban differences in the distribution of parent-reported risk factors for substance abuse among young adolescents. *Journal of Substance Abuse*, 13, 609-623.

This compared the effects of rural and urban residence on cumulative risk for substance usage among young adolescents. Nine-hundred thirty-two parents (mean ages 37-40 years) having a young adolescent (ages 11-13 years) completed surveys concerning parenting practices, attitudes toward substance use, other adolescent substance use risk factors, parental social relationships, use of community social services and demographic characteristics. Results show higher levels of cumulative risk among rural youth.

355 Spoth, R.L., Redmond, C. & Shin, C. (2001). Randomized trial of brief family interventions for general populations: Adolescent substance use outcomes 4 years following baseline. *Journal of Consulting & Clinical Psychology*, 69, 627-642.

This study examined the long-term substance use outcomes of two brief interventions designed for general population families of young adolescents. Significant intervention-control differences in initiation and current use were found for both interventions. It is concluded that brief family skills-training interventions designed for general populations have the potential to reduce adolescent substance use and thus have important public health implications.

356 Spoth, R., Redmond, C., Shin, C. & Azevedo, K. (2004). Brief Family Intervention Effects on Adolescent Substance Initiation: School-Level Growth Curve Analyses 6 Years Following Baseline. *Journal of Consulting & Clinical Psychology*, 72, 535-542.

This study examined the effects of two brief family-focused interventions on the trajectories of substance initiation over a period of six years following a baseline assessment. Alcohol and tobacco composite use indices—as well as lifetime use of alcohol, cigarettes and marijuana—and lifetime drunkenness, were examined. Significant intervention– control differences were observed, indicating favorable delays in initiation in the intervention groups.

357 Stack, S. (1982). Suicide: A decade of review of the sociological literature. *Deviant Behavior: An Interdisciplinary Journal*, 4, 41-66.

This reviews major works on suicide and classifies them into four analytic categories according to their theoretical emphasis: cultural, economic, modernization and social integration perspectives. The research under these paradigms is assessed in terms of four themes: 1) Attention is drawn to research evidence that questions traditional theories, 2) The review notes several new theories including D.P. Phillips's imitation thesis and the present author's own model of migration's effects on suicide, 3) The paper observes and reviews explanations of new trends in suicide rates, such as the rapid increase in youth suicide and the decline in suicide among the elderly and 4) The review calls attention to explanations of suicide, such as that linking suicide to low marital solidarity, that have withstood the test of the more rigorous empirical testing of recent times.

358 Stamm, B. Hudnall (Ed) (2003). *Rural behavioral health care: An interdisciplinary guide*. Washington, DC, U.S.: American Psychological Association.

This edited volume presents a comprehensive analysis of the public and Federal policy, clinical trends, and empirical literature relevant to the provision of health care services in rural and frontier areas. Leading experts from different professional disciplines examine the economic and social problems of rural and frontier areas, collaborative methods for service delivery, and the specific needs of special populations. Contributors also explain the unique cultural characteristics of rural areas compared with urban areas and offer a detailed look at the differences between frontier and rural areas.

359 Stanton, M.D. & Shadish, W.R. (1997). Outcome, attrition, and family-couples treatment for drug abuse: A meta-analysis and review of the controlled, comparative studies. *Psychological Bulletin*, 122, 170- 191.

This review synthesizes drug abuse outcome studies that included a family-couples therapy treatment condition. The meta-analytic evidence, across 1,571 cases involving an estimated 3,500 patients and family members, favors family therapy over a) individual counseling or therapy, b) peer group therapy and c) family psychoeducation. Family therapy is as effective for adults as for adolescents and appears to be a cost-effective adjunct to methadone maintenance.

360 Starr, S., Campbell, L.R. & Herrick, C.A. (2002). Factors affecting use of the mental health system by rural children. *Issues in Mental Health Nursing*, 23(3), 291-304.

This study examined rural parents' (80 percent over the age of 30 years) expectations about outcomes related to mental health treatment, the provider-client-parent relationships, social and cultural factors, and accessibility to mental health services. The parents' knowledge of the prevalence of mental health disorders in children and adolescents was also examined. Results show that stigma toward the use of the mental health system was evident. More than half the parents were concerned that mental health professionals would not care for their child. Although negative relationship outcome expectations were revealed, positive treatment outcome expectations also emerged. Structural outcome expectations were not shown to be a major deterrent in receiving care.

361 Stell, J. & Rodgers, J. (2004). *The Medicare Prescription Drug Benefit: Potential Impact on Beneficiaries.* AARP Public Policy Institute: Washington, DC. Available online: http://www.aarp.org/ppi.

Under the Medicare Prescription Drug, Improvement, and Modernization Act of 2003, Medicare will offer prescription drug coverage to beneficiaries who choose to enroll in the Part D benefit, beginning in 2006. This report examines the potential impact of this new benefit plan in the AARP Public Policy Institute Issue Paper by Jack Rodgers and John Stell of Health Policy Economics at PricewaterhouseCoopers.

362 Stein, L.I. & Santos, A.B. (1998). *Assertive community treatment of persons with severe mental illness.*

This book describes the ACT approach as a vehicle for providing treatment, rehabilitation, supportive services, and practical help. It first gives a historical perspective on the management of persons with severe mental illness and places the ACT model within that context. It then explains the model's conceptual framework and development, details its day-to-day workings, and describes how its multidisciplinary team (from secretary to psychiatrist) work with one another, make group decisions, and share their expertise through cross-training.

363 Stevens, M.M., Mott, L.A. & Youells, F. (1996). Rural adolescent drinking behavior: Three year follow-up in the New Hampshire Substance Abuse Prevention Study. *Adolescence*, 31, 159-166.

Among 4,406 children from rural school districts and who were in elementary or junior high school or the 10th grade, a thee-year follow-up study showed that neither a comprehensive school curriculum nor a community intervention was successful in preventing adolescent drinking. Predictor variables for drinking are discussed and the importance of tolerance and encouragement of drinking by adult role models are noted.

364 Stohr, M.K., Hemmens, C., Shapiro, B., Chambers, B. & Kelley, L. (2002). Comparing inmate perceptions of two residential substance abuse treatment programs. *International Journal of Offender Therapy & Comparative Criminology*, 46, 699-714.

Residential Substance Abuse and Treatment (RSAT) programs were developed to address the drug and alcohol treatment needs of inmates in prisons. Typically, such programs range in length from six to 12 months, have an Alcoholics Anonymous and/or Narcotics Anonymous component, and occur in a therapeutic community environment. Some programs also include a cognitive self-change component. In this research, the authors describe, compare, and contrast the perceptions of inmate clients (ages 19-50 years) of two RSAT programs in a rural mountain State.

365 Stout, M. (1998). Impact of Medicaid managed mental health care on delivery of services in a rural State: An AMI perspective. *Psychiatric Services*, 49(7), 961-963.

In March 1995 Iowa implemented a Statewide mental health carve-out program under a Medicaid Section 1915b waiver. A goal was to provide equal access across counties for Medicaid recipients by introducing a Statewide network of service providers. Problems have included the contractor's authorizing only services considered medically necessary for persons with serious mental illness, who also need community supports; contractor staff's lack of knowledge about regional resources and the limited availability of community-based services in most rural areas; clients' difficulty in gaining access to the new system; denial of inpatient hospitalization; untimely provider payments and lack of education for providers, consumers and families.

366 Stromwall, L.K. Mental health needs of TANF recipients. *Journal of Sociology & Social Welfare*, 28(3), 129-137.

This paper reports the findings of a study of 489 female Temporary Aid to Needy Families (TANF) recipients and non-recipients (aged 18-40 years) receiving behavioral health services in the rural Southwest. TANF recipients were more likely to be seriously mentally ill than non-recipients, suggesting that a subgroup of TANF recipients may face significant barriers to employment given the new TANF regulations.

367 Stroul, B.A. & Friedman, R.M. (1986). *A system of care for seriously emotionally disturbed children and youth*. Washington, DC: CASSP Technical Assistance Center, Georgetown University Child Development Center.

This monograph provides States and communities a conceptual model for a system of care for children and youth with emotional disorders. The 1994 update includes an introduction summarizing progress in children's mental health and provides additional emphasis on family involvement, cultural competence, dual diagnosis and juvenile justice.

368 Susman, J.L., Crabtree, B.F. & Essink, G. (1995). Depression in rural family practice. Easy to recognize, difficult to diagnose. *Archives of Family Medicine*, 4, 427-431.

This study explored rural family physicians' decision-making processes when they encounter depression. Themes included the following: depression is easy to recognize but difficult to diagnose; depression is readily treatable but requires negotiation to manage; and depression is important, but time and resources are limited. Depression is commonly recognized by rural family physicians; however, they hesitate to diagnose this condition because of diagnostic uncertainty, perceived stigma, the desire to preserve the physician-patient relationship, time and financial pressures and a lack of supporting resources.

369 Swaim, R.C. (1991). Childhood risk factors and adolescent drug and alcohol abuse. Educational *Psychology Review*, 3(4), 363-398.

This reviews literature on childhood risk factors for adolescent drug and alcohol abuse. Childhood personality manifesting the difficult child syndrome and psychopathological features of hyperactivity and antisocial traits are predictive of later substance abuse, especially when these traits persist into adolescence. Key interpersonal risk factors include family mismanagement, parental substance use, low academic performance and commitment and association with substance-using peers.

370 Szeftel, R. (1999). Rural telepsychiatry is economically unsupportable: Comment. *Psychiatric Services*, 50(2), 267.

The author comments on the article by A. Werner and L. Anderson, disagreeing with their pessimism expressed on telepsychiatry. Szeftel lists several things that differentiate his telemedicine financially viable program from others.

371 Taylor P, Blewett L, Brasure M, et al. Small town health care safety nets: report on a pilot study. *J Rural Health* 2003 Spring;19(2):125-34.

Very little is known about the health care safety net in small towns, especially in towns where there is no publicly subsidized safety-net health care. This pilot study of the primary care safety net in seven such communities was conducted to start building knowledge about the rural safety net. State and National government policy makers should consider subsidy programs for private primary care practices that attempt to meet the needs of the inadequately insured in the many rural communities where no publicly subsidized primary safety-net care is available. Subsidies should be directed to physicians in primary care shortage areas who provide safety-net care; this will improve safety-net access and, at the same time, improve physician retention by bolstering physician incomes. Options include enhanced Medicare physician bonuses and grants or tax credits to support income-related sliding fee scales.

372 The Hay Group. (1998). *Health care plan design and trends*. Arlington, VA: The Hay Group.

Reported on changes in the health plans of medium and large employers provides more recent evidence for these trends. Between 1988 and 1997, the proportion of such plans with day limits on inpatient psychiatric care increased from 38 percent to 57 percent, whereas the proportion of plans with outpatient visit limits rose from 26 percent to 48 percent. On the basis of this and other information, the Hay Group estimated that the value of behavioral health care benefits within the surveyed plans decreased from 6.1 percent to 3.1 percent from 1988 to 1997 as a proportion of the value of the total health benefit.

373 Thombs, D.L. (2000). A retrospective study of DARE: Substantive effects not detected in undergraduates. *Journal of Alcohol & Drug Education*, 46, 27-40.

This retrospective study examined the long-term effects of DARE by assessing substance use among 630 undergraduates (58.6 percent females, ages 18-24 years) attending a large public university in Ohio. Results from a multiple discriminant analysis found that after accounting for the effects of age, there were no substantial group differences in substance use. Participation in the DARE program during elementary school, middle school, or high school did not appear to deter subsequent use in the undergraduate years.

374 Thornberry, T.P. (1987). Toward an interactional theory of delinquency. *Criminology*, 25, 863-891.

The author addresses the notion of an age-varying effect of delinquent peers, suggesting that the influence of delinquent peer associations should increase during mid-adolescence and then decline gradually. The reasoning, derived in part from social learning theory, is that peer networks become increasingly central to an individual's identity during adolescence and then less so as they begin to develop commitments to conventional activities and institutions, such as education, career, family, and so forth.

375 Thornberry, T.P., Lizotte, A.J., Krohn, M.D.,Farnworth, M. & Jang, S.J. (1991). Testing interactional theory: An examination of reciprocal causal relationships among family, school and delinquency. *Journal of Criminal Law and Criminology*, 82, 3-35.

Using data from the Rochester Youth Development Study, the authors test an interactional model of attachment to parents and commitment to school. They found that weakened bonds to family and school do cause delinquency and, additionally, delinquent behavior further attenuates the strength of the bonds to family and school. They note that there is no single, direct pathway to delinquency. They also suggest that family interventions should start relatively early in life.

376 Torrey, W.C., Drake, R.E., Dixon, L., Burns, B.J., Flynn, L., Rush, A.J., Clark, R.E. & Klatzker, D. (2001). Implementing evidence-based practices for persons with severe mental illness. *Psychiatric Services*, 52(1), 45- 50.

As part of an effort to promote the implementation of evidence-based practice, the authors summarize perspectives on how best to change and sustain effective practice from the research literature and from the experiences of administrators, clinicians, family advocates, and services researchers. They describe an implementation plan for evidence-based practices based on the use of toolkits to promote the consistent delivery of such practices. The toolkits include integrated written material, Web-based resources, training experiences, and consultation opportunities.

377 Troester, A.I., Paolo, A.M., Glatt, S.L., Hubble, J.P., et al. (1995). "Interactive video conferencing" in the provision of neuropsychological services to rural areas. *Journal of Community Psychology*, 23(1), 85-88.

Describes the use of interactive videoconferencing in providing neuropsychological services to residents of rural areas. The advent of interactive videoconferencing via digital telephone lines has greatly reduced the cost associated with earlier rural health care efforts requiring satellite communication. Interactive videoconferencing enhances availability and accessibility of neuropsychological services to rural residents. Furthermore, initial informal evaluation of the program indicates that it meets with patient acceptance and satisfaction.

378 U.S. Census Bureau (2003). http://www.ers.usda.gov/Briefing/Rurality/NewDefinitio ns/. Describes the rural/urban continuum codes.

379 United States Committee for Refugees (1997). *A cry for help: Refugee mental health in the United States. Refugee Reports*, 19, 9.

This report describes the rising awareness among mental health providers and resettlement workers that refugees and survivors of torture need greater, earlier access to culturally appropriate mental health services to help them deal with both the trauma from which they fled and the challenge of adjusting to life in the United States. It goes on to describe some factors associated with these needs and programs to address them.

380 United States Congress, Office of Technology Assessment (1995). *Impact of health reform on rural areas: Lessons from the States*. Washington, DC: Author.

This paper examines the impact of health care reform in the context of two different categories of reforms: 1) the effects of insurance market reforms and 2) effects of reforms aimed at the health care delivery system.

381 United States Department of Agriculature Economic Research Service (ERS). Rural-urban commuting area (RUCA) codes. http://www.ers.usda.gov/briefing/Rurality/RuralUrbanC ommutingAreas/. Describes the rural-urban commuting area (RUCA) codes.

382 U.S. Department of Health and Human Services, Substance Abuse and Mental Health Services Administration, Office of Applied Studies (1999). *National household survey on drug abuse*, 1997 [Computer file; ICPSR version]. Ann Arbor, MI: Inter-university Consortium for Political and Social Research (Distributor).

This report contains 1999 national and State estimates of rates of use, numbers of users, and other measures related to illicit drugs, alcohol, cigarettes and other forms of tobacco. These estimates are from the National Household Survey on Drug Abuse (NHSDA), an ongoing survey of the civilian noninstitutionalized population of the United States, 12 years old or older.

383 U. S. Department of Health and Human Services Rural Task Force (2002). *One department serving rural America* (Report to the Secretary). Washington, DC: U.S. Department of Health and Human Services. http://ruralhealth.hrsa.gov/PublicReport.htm#summary

On July 25, 2001, Secretary of Health and Human Services Tommy G. Thompson charged all HHS agencies and staff offices to examine ways to improve and enhance health care and human services for rural Americans. As the former governor of a predominantly rural State, Secretary Thompson recognizes the unique characteristics and needs of rural America and the important role HHS plays in ensuring healthy rural communities.

384 United States Public Health Service Office of the Surgeon General (2001). *Mental health: Culture, race, and ethnicity.* Rockville, MD: Department of Health and Human Services.

This report is a supplement to the Surgeon General's Report on Mental Health, *Mental Health: A Report of the Surgeon General* (U.S. Department of Health and Human Services [DHHS], 1999). It was undertaken to probe more deeply into mental health disparities affecting racial and ethnic minorities.

385 Van Hook, M.P. & Ford, M.E. (1998). The linkage model for delivering mental health services in rural communities. *Health & Social Work*, 23(1), 53-60.

This article presents the results of a study involving 28 mental health staff placed in these arrangements in rural health centers. Staff identified roles, benefits, and barriers to linkages. Benefits included increased access and coordination and promotion of a more holistic sense of health care. Barriers were lack of space, differences among health disciplines and administrative logistic problems. Social workers need good clinical and communication skills to work effectively in these programs.

386 Vaughan-Sarrazin, M.S., Hall, J.A. & Rick, G.S. (2000). Impact of case management on use of health services by rural clients in substance abuse treatment. *Journal of Drug Issues*, 30, 435-464.

This evaluated the effects of case management, the proximity of case manager to treatment facility, and telephone use on use of medical and mental health services by residential substance abuse treatment clients.

Results show that case managers located at the treatment facility increased Ss' use of substance abuse treatment and medical services. Use of mental health services did not vary by group.

387 Vega, W.A., Kolody, B., Aguilar-Gaxiola, S. & Catalano, R. (1999). Gaps in service utilization by Mexican Americans with mental health problems. *American Journal of Psychiatry*, 156(6), 928-934.

These authors examined the degree of underutilization of mental health services (MHSs) among urban and rural Mexican American adults. Among Ss with Mental Disorders-III-Revised (DSM-IIIR)-defined disorders, only one-fourth had used an MHS or a combination of MHSs in the past 12 months. Overall use of MHS providers by persons with diagnosed mental disorders was 8.8 percent, use of providers in the general medical sector was 18.4 percent, use of other professionals was 12.7 percent, and use of informal providers was only 3.1 percent. Factors associated with utilization of MHSs included female sex, higher educational attainment, unemployment, and comorbidity. Immigrants are unlikely to use MHSs, even when they have a recent disorder, but may use general practitioners, which raises questions about the appropriateness, accessibility and cost-effectiveness of MHSs for this population.

388 Vega, W.A., Kolody, B., Aguilar-Gaxiola, S., Alderete, E., Catalano, R. & Caraveo-Anduaga, J. (1998). Lifetime prevalence of DSM-III-R psychiatric disorders among urban and rural Mexican Americans in California. *Archives of General Psychiatry*, 55, 771- 778.

This presents the results of the Mexican American Prevalence and Services Survey (MAPSS), which was designed to cover Diagnostic and Statistical Manual of Mental Disorders-III-Revised (DSM-III-R) disorders in a community sample of Mexican Americans living in urban and nonurban residential settings. MAPSS results reveal two key findings. First, rates of lifetime disorders were highest in urban areas but, after controlling for demographic factors, only substance abuse or dependence disorders were clearly more frequent in urban centers, and immigrants had only one half the total DSM-III--R disorders as the U.S.-born. The total lifetime DSM-III--R prevalence rate of any disorder in the MAPSS survey is lower than reported for Hispanics or White non-Hispanics in the National Catchment Survey.

389 Vicary, J.R., Swisher, J.D., Doebler, M.K., Yuan, J., Bridger, J.C., Gurgevich, E.A. & Deike, R.C. (1996). Rural community substance abuse prevention and intervention. *Family & Community Health*, 19, 59-72.

This assessed alcohol, tobacco and other drug (ATOD) awareness, and knowledge, prevention service use and behaviors among 18-35 year old females in a disadvantaged rural community before (1991) and after (1994) exposure to the Community Health's Demonstration Project. Results indicate increased awareness and knowledge of problems associated with ATOD use during pregnancy and postpartum, new services adopted by local agencies and organizations, more cooperative efforts to provide prevention programs for all ages throughout the community, a range of new or expanded programs to enhance development and a reduction in ATOD use during and after pregnancy by women in this rural area.

390 Voss, S.L. (1996). The church as an agent in rural mental health. *Journal of Psychology & Theology*, 24(2), 114-123.

Many rural communities lack adequate mental health services. Additionally, there are specific problems associated with delivery of services to rural citizens. This article suggests that the church can be an active agent in the delivery of services to rural populations. Ideas presented include (1) identification and referral, (2) counseling networks utilizing local churches, (3) Christian counseling centers, (4) education and enrichment activities, (5) support groups, (6) lay counseling, (7) volunteer workers with the chronically mentally ill and (8) clergy collaboration with local mental health practitioners.

391 Vuchinich, S., Bank, L. & Patterson, G.R. (1992). Parenting, peers, and the stability of antisocial behavior in preadolescent boys. *Developmental Psychology*, 28, 510-521.

This study examined the linkages between parental discipline practices, peer relationships, and antisocial behavior in a two-year longitudinal study (N = 206) of preadolescent boys (ages nine and ten years at first assessment). The results showed that preadolescent antisocial behavior had substantial concurrent negative effects on the quality of parental discipline and peer relationships. Evidence for a reciprocal relationship between parental discipline and child antisocial behavior was found. The study specifies how parental discipline practices are involved in maintaining the stability of antisocial behavior in preadolescents. Low popularity with peers did not directly influence the child's antisocial behavior.

392 Wagenfeld, Morton O. A snapshot of rural and frontier America. Stamm, B. Hudnall (Ed). (2003). *Rural behavioral health care: An*

interdisciplinary guide. (pp. 33-40). Washington, DC, US: American Psychological Association. xiv, 250pp. (Chapter: 2003-04375-002).

This chapter addresses difficulties in defining rural, in separating fact from myth, and in understanding the heterogeneity of the demography and economic base of rural and frontier America. Particular attention is paid to the most sparsely populated subset of rural areas, what is called frontier. The frontier areas are largely concentrated in the western U.S. with population densities of seven or fewer people per square mile. These areas, along with other rural areas, tend to have unstable economics, which may have an impact on the mental health of its residents.

393 Wagenfeld, M.O. & Buffum, W.E. (1983). Problems in, and prospects for, rural mental health services in the United States. *International Journal of Mental Health*, 12(1-2), 89-107.

Evidence suggests that psychopathology is more prevalent in rural than urban areas because of the high incidence of poverty, the lack of services, the abundance of dependent and high-risk populations, the stresses caused by recent immigration, and the reluctance of rural people to seek mental health services. Issues related to the delivery of mental health services are examined in relation to organization and management; recruitment, retention, and staffing; relationships with the community and the impact of changing demographic patterns and of the "new Federalism."

394 Wagenfeld, M.O., Goldsmith, H.F., Stiles, D. & Manderscheid, R.W. (1993). Inpatient mental health services in rural areas: An interregional comparison. *Journal of Rural Community Psychology*, 12(2), 3-19.

A classification of counties developed by the Economic Research Service using 1980 Census data was applied to the 1983 National Institute of Mental Health inventories of mental health organizations and general hospital mental health services. Inpatient mental health services are most likely to be found in the "specialized government," "manufacturing-dependent," and "ungrouped" types of nonmetropolitan counties. The types least likely to have services are the "persistent poverty" and "farming-dependent," which are the least urban and also contain high concentrations of black and elderly persons shown to have a high need for mental health services.

395 Wagenfeld, M.O., Murray, J.D., Mohatt, D.F. & DeBruyn, J.C. (Eds.) (1994). *Mental health and rural America: 1980 – 1993* (NIH Publication No. 94-3500). Washington, DC: US Government Printing Office.

This is the second publication of this chapter and covers the same areas.

396 Wagenfeld, M.O., Murray, J.D., Mohatt, D.F. & DeBruyn, J.C. (1997). Mental health service delivery in rural areas: Organizational and clinical issues. In: Roberson, E.B., Sloboda, Z., Boyd, G.M., Beatty, L, and Kozel, N.J., eds. *Rural Substance Abuse: State of Knowledge and Issues*. National Institute on Drug Abuse; U.S. Department of Health and Human Services; National Institutes of Health: NIH Publication No. 97- 4177. Rockville, MD.

The authors describe models of service delivery to rural areas developed in the decade prior to their writing from a clinical and organizational perspective. They debunk myths of rural life and describe challenges, such as under-funding, understaffing, cultural barriers and inappropriate application of urban models to rural areas.

397 Wagenfeld, M.O. (2000). Organization and delivery of mental health services to adolescents and children with persistent and serious mental illness in frontier areas. *Journal of the Washington Academy of Sciences*, 86(3), 81-88.

This articles deals with different aspects of delivery of mental health services to persons in sparsely-populated frontier areas - a historically-underserved group living in a special and unique part of the United States. Specifically, it is concerned with the organization and delivery of services to children and adolescents with serious mental illness (SMI). It is based on published and unpublished literature, and interviews with planners and providers.

398 Waitzfelder, B.E., Engel Jr., C.C. & Gilbert Jr., F.I. (1998). Substance abuse in Hawaii: Perspectives of key local human service organizations. Substance Abuse, 19, 7-22.

Available evidence suggests that substance abuse in Hawaii is a substantial problem. The three major objectives of this study were to determine qualitatively Hawaii's human service organizations' perspective regarding (1) the magnitude of the Statewide substance abuse problem, (2) the unmet needs of the State's substance abuse treatment system and (3) the features of the problem unique to Hawaii's many ethnic and other subgroups. The study targeted those human service organizations most burdened by the substance abuse problem. Respondents perceived the magnitude of the Hawaii substance abuse problem to be at least comparable to that of the mainland United States. Although most respondents viewed the problem using a medical model, the problem was generally thought to be exacerbated by a community context in which substance abuse is accepted, excused, or denied. Cultural alienation, exacerbated by the State's prevailing multiculturalism, was thought to contribute to the substance abuse problem among all ethnic groups, but especially among Native Hawaiians.

399 Walker, J. (2002). Rural women with HIV and AIDS: Perceptions of service accessibility, psychosocial and mental health counseling needs. *Journal of Mental Health Counseling*, 24(4), 299-316.

This study examined rural women with HIV and AIDS and the staff members who work with them, using a qualitative design. Interviews and observations (documents were collected) were conducted with four women and eight staff members. Results of the study revealed a) barriers to these women regarding the accessibility of services, including mental health counseling; b) a need to empower these women to be proactive in their health care; c) a stronger social support system and sense of hope in women identified as doing well; d) a better quality of life may be obtained with protease inhibitors and e) empowerment may accrue through support groups.

400 Wakefield, M. (2004). IOM Report: *Quality Through Collaboration*; ORHP Technical Assistance Meeting of Rural Health Research Centers; Center for Rural Health. November 2, 2004.

This rural health quality report calls for both the Federal government and rural communities to pursue new approaches to maintain quality in rural health care, citing strategies in five key areas including: 1) Address personal and population health needs at the community level,) Establish quality improvement support structure, 3) Strengthen the rural health care workforce, 4) Provide adequate and targeted financial resources and 5) Utilize information and communications technology.

401 Warner, B.D. & Leukefeld, C.G. (2001). Rural-urban differences in substance use and treatment utilization among prisoners. *American Journal of Drug & Alcohol Abuse*, 27, 265-280.

This study examines differences between urban and rural drug use patterns and treatment utilization among chronic drug abusers to determine whether, and in what ways, rurality may affect substance abuse and treatment seeking. Findings show significant differences in drug use and treatment utilization of urban and rural offenders. Chronic drug abusers from rural and very rural areas have significantly higher rates of lifetime drug use, as well as higher rates of drug use in the 30 days prior to their current incarceration than chronic drug abusers from urban areas.

Nonetheless, being from a very rural area decreased the likelihood of having ever been in treatment after controlling for the number of years using and race.

402 Weigel, D.J. & Baker, B.G. (2002). Unique issues in rural couple and family counseling. *Family Journal: Counseling & Therapy for Couples & Families*, 10(1), 61-69.

During the past several decades, a variety of authors has suggested that rural mental health practice differs significantly from that of urban practice. Several studies have examined rural mental health service delivery issues. Frequently, couple and family counseling issues have not been addressed in these studies. The purpose of this article is to review the available literature regarding rural couple and family counseling, in conjunction with the findings of research in closely related fields. This review is conducted in an effort to identify unique practice issues facing rural couple and family counselors.

403 Weisheit, R.A., Wells, E.L. & Falcome, D.N. (1994). Community policing in small town and rural America. *Crime & Delinquency*, (40)4, 5449-567.

This article describes the role of law enforcement in rural areas, including mental health.

404 Weist, M.D. (1997). Expanded school mental health services: A national movement in progress. *Advances in Clinical Child Psychology*, 19, 319-352.

This provides an overview of the limitations and advantages of expanded school mental health services. Traditional school mental health services are generally limited to students in special education, placing overwhelming demands on school psychologists and social workers. The author presents several models of expanded school mental health programs, which could help alleviate this problem, and reviews the challenges confronting school systems and individual school clinicians.

405 Weist, M.D., Myers, C.P., Danforth, J., McNeil, D.W., Ollendick, T.H. & Hawkins, R. (2000). Expanded school mental health services: Assessing needs related to school level and geography. *Community Mental Health Journal*, 36(3), 259-273.

The authors surveyed 62 school administrators on factors relevant to developing school-based mental health programs grouped in five categories: 1) Stressful conditions, 2) Internalizing behavioral problems, 3) Externalizing behavioral problems, 4) Substance abuse and 5) Barriers to mental health care, and provided open-ended comments on needs of youth and mental health programs for them. They rated behavioral and substance abuse problems as progressively more serious as students advanced in school level. Urban youth were reported to encounter higher stress and present more severe internalizing problems than suburban or rural youth. Suburban and rural schools provided more health and mental health services than urban schools. Across geographic locales, physical health services far outnumbered mental health services.

406 Welsh, J., Domitrovich, C.E., Bierman, K. & Lang, J. (2003). Promoting Safe schools and healthy students in rural Pennsylvania. *Psychology in the Schools*, 40(5), 457-472.

The Safe Schools/Healthy Students (SS/HS) Initiative involves reducing risk and building competencies for students and their families through integration of law enforcement and mental health into school-based prevention efforts. The programs include early childhood, elementary, and secondary school components; and district-wide components that span these developmental levels. Despite challenges associated with the integration of different professional perspectives into the school environment, the initiative has been quite successful. Program evaluation is varied, and reflects the different programs and student populations served.

407 Werner, A. & Anderson, L.E. (1999). Rural telepsychiatry is economically unsupportable: Reply. *Psychiatric Services*, 50(2), 267-268.

This responds to professional criticism regarding their article on telepsychiatry in rural environments. They argue that Chen et al and Smith mistakenly seem to think that they are against telepsychiatry. They ignore what is said and misinterpret the purpose of their analysis. And they fail to address the issues of costs that were originally raised. Werner and Anderson welcomes R. Szeftel's comments and said that she suggests the kind of detail and support that is necessary for a viable telepsychiatry service.

408 Whitbeck, L.B., Hoyt, D.R., Chen, X. & Stubben, J.D. (2002). Predictors of gang involvement among American Indian Adolescents. *Journal of Gang Research*, 10, 11-26.

This study is an investigation of factors associated with gang involvement among 212 fifth through eighth-grade American Indian adolescents whose families lived on or near three American Indian Reservations in the Upper Midwest. Gang involvement was highly associated with delinquency and substance abuse. Predictors of gang involvement other than delinquency and substance abuse included age of adolescent, living in single-mother household, mother's history of antisocial behaviors, number life transitions and losses in the past year, traditional activities and perceived discrimination.

409 Wilker, H.I. & Lowell, B. (1996). Bereavement services development in a rural setting. *Hospice Journal - Physical, Psychosocial & Pastoral Care of the Dying*, 11(4), 25-40.

This identifies ways to offer bereavement follow-up to hospice and non-hospice families, including ways to mix together survivors of different types of death in a support group atmosphere. The focus is on how the Bereavement Services of St. Rita's Medical Center and Hospice Program in Ohio expanded in response to the needs of communities in the three counties they serve. Bereavement needs were determined from several sources, including surveys completed by 75 pastors, 42 doctors and five mental health agencies.

410 Williams, R.W. & Bowman, M.L. (2002). Current issues on neuropsychological assessment with rural populations. In: Ferraro, F.R. (Ed). *Minority and cross-cultural aspects of neuropsychological assessment. Studies on neuropsychology, development, and cognition.* Bristol, PA, US: Swets & Zeitlinger Publishers.

Examines the literature related to urban versus rural place of residence upon cognitive functioning. The authors address the question of whether people in rural settings perform different on intellectual and neuropsychological tests. Studies of children and adults are discussed. The authors review the research concerning the mental health problems and needs of rural people and the availability of services in rural settings. The implications of the research for conducting neuropsychological assessments in rural settings are outlined.

411 Windle, C. (1994). Social values and services research: The case of rural services. *Administration & Policy in Mental Health*, 22(2), 181-188.

The author suggests a framework for planning research evaluations of mental health service system changes, emphasizing the inclusion of measures of the availability of satisfying and remunerative work for both mental health patients and service providers. Working conditions for mental health workers are influenced by general societal conditions, the U.S. health care system, health care reform and the special conditions of mental health. The mental health service system, in turn, is affected by perceptions of mental illness, perceptions of treatment and the recognized importance of work. One of the many problems to be addressed is how to accommodate the special problems of rural areas. Possible approaches include service outreach procedures, telecommunication to bring expertise to rural practitioners and development of alternative care providers.

412 Worley, N.K & Sloop, T. (1996). Psychiatric nursing in a rural outreach program. *Perspectives in Psychiatric Care*, 32(2), 10-14.

This describes a program in which psychiatric nurses provide mental health services to clients in rural areas in South Carolina. Candidates for the program are ages 18-65 years, have a primary diagnosis of a psychotic disorder, and have a history of long-term and/or multiple hospital admissions or ongoing use of psychiatric services. Goals of the program include improving compliance with prescribed aftercare treatment programs, decreasing the number of psychiatric hospitalizations, and providing supportive and rehabilitative services to enhance the client's capacity for independent living. Information is provided to both clients and their families on medication and symptom monitoring, as well as relevant community resources available.

413 Wysong, E., Aniskiewicz, R. & Wright, D. (1994). Truth and DARE: Tracking drug education to graduation and as symbolic politics. *Social Problems*, 41, 448-472.

These authors used a multidimensional impact and process evaluation framework to explore the Drug Abuse Resistance Education (DARE) program in terms of long-term effects, political potency, and implementation issues. Questionnaire data from 288 high school seniors exposed to DARE as seventh-graders were compared with that of 331 nonexposed seniors. No significant differences in drug use behaviors or attitudes were found between the two groups. After tracking DARE for five years, data indicate no long-term effects for the program in preventing or reducing adolescent drug use.

414 Yawn, B.P. & Yawn, R.A. (1993). Adolescent pregnancies in rural America: A review of the literature and strategies for primary prevention. *Family and Community Health*, 16(1), 36-45.

This review discusses primary and secondary preventions of adolescent pregnancies in rural America. Many factors may reinforce or interdict the activities of adolescent sexual intercourse and pregnancy. These factors include biology and maturation; social influences; racial, cultural, and economic factors; media exposure; the role of parents; peer environments and dating behavior; personality and self-esteem; perception of risk and benefit and societal trends. A review of the literature identifies the following prevention programs: abstinence, school, community-based and male-only programs. The importance is noted for adopting programs only after their application to the rural situation is assessed.

415 Yuen, E.J., Gerdes, J.L. & Gonzales, J.J. (1996). Patterns of rural mental health care: An exploratory study. *General Hospital Psychiatry*, 18(1), 14-21.

This study analyzed the ambulatory, partial, emergency room, and inpatient medical claims of patients who had a mental health visit within fiscal year 1991 from the same HMO. Ss who had weaker mental health consultative linkages, higher rurality and less availability of mental health specialty care used more mental health services by primary care providers, received more ambulatory care from joint mental health/primary care providers and had more mental health hospital utilization.

416 Zarate, Jr., C.A., Weinstock, P., Cukor, C., Morabito, L., Leahy, Burns, C., and Baer, L. (1997). Applicability of telemedicine for assessing patients with schizophrenia: Acceptance and reliability. *Journal of Clinical Psychiatry*, 58(1), 22-25.

This study was conducted to assess the reliability and acceptance of videoconferencing equipment in the assessment of patients with schizophrenia. It assessed reliability of the Brief Psychiatric Rating Scale (BPRS), Scale for the Assessment of Positive Symptoms (SAPS) and Scale for the Assessment of Negative Symptoms (SANS) under three conditions: (1) in person, (2) by videoconferencing at low (128 kilobits per second [kbs]) bandwidth, (3) by videoconferencing at high (384 kbs) bandwidth. Total score on the SANS was less reliably assessed at the low bandwidth, as were several specific negative symptoms of schizophrenia that depend heavily on nonverbal cues. Video interviews were well accepted by patients in both groups, although patients in the high bandwidth group were more likely to prefer the video interview to a live interview. Global severity of schizophrenia and overall severity of positive symptoms were reliably assessed by videoconferencing technology. Higher bandwidth resulted in more reliable assessment of negative symptoms and was preferred over low bandwidth, although patients' and raters' acceptance of video was good in both conditions.

In: Mental Health and Rural America
Editor: Pamela Rhodes

ISBN: 978-1-63321-122-3
© 2014 Nova Science Publishers, Inc.

Chapter 2

PREVALENCE OF MENTAL ILLNESS IN THE UNITED STATES: DATA SOURCES AND ESTIMATES[*]

Erin Bagalman and Angela Napili

SUMMARY

Determining how many people have a mental illness can be difficult, and prevalence estimates vary. While numerous surveys include questions related to mental illness, few provide prevalence estimates of *diagnosable mental illness* (e.g., major depressive disorder as opposed to feeling depressed, or generalized anxiety disorder as opposed to feeling anxious), and fewer still provide *national* prevalence estimates of diagnosable mental illness. This report briefly describes the methodology and results of three large surveys (funded in whole or in part by the U.S. Department of Health and Human Services) that provide *national prevalence estimates of diagnosable mental illness*: the National Comorbidity Survey Replication (NCS-R), the National Comorbidity Survey Replication Adolescent Supplement (NCS-A), and the National Survey on Drug Use and Health (NSDUH). The NCS-R and the NCS-A have the advantage of identifying specific mental illnesses, but they are a decade old. The NSDUH does not identify specific mental illnesses, but it has the advantage of being conducted annually.

---

[*] This is an edited, reformatted and augmented version of Congressional Research Service Publication, No. R43047, dated February 28, 2014.

Between February 2001 and April 2003, NCS-R staff interviewed more than 9,000 adults aged 18 or older. Analyses of NCS-R data have yielded different prevalence estimates. One analysis of NCS-R data estimated that 26.2% of adults had a mental illness within a 12-month period (hereinafter called 12-month prevalence). Another analysis of NCS-R data estimated the 12- month prevalence of mental illness to be 32.4% among adults. A third analysis of NCS-R data estimated the 12-month prevalence of mental illness *excluding substance use disorders* to be 24.8% among adults. The 12-month prevalence of *serious* mental illness was estimated to be 5.8% among adults, based on NCS-R data.

Between February 2001 and January 2004, NCS-A staff interviewed more than 10,000 adolescents aged 13 to 17. Using NCS-A data, researchers estimated the 12-month prevalence of mental illness to be 40.3% among adolescents. Some have suggested that the current approach to diagnosing mental illness identifies people who should not be considered mentally ill. The 12- month prevalence of *serious* mental illness was estimated to be 8.0% among adolescents, based on NCS-A data.

The NSDUH is an annual survey of approximately 70,000 adults and adolescents aged 12 years or older in the United States. According to the 2012 NSDUH, the estimated 12-month prevalence of mental illness *excluding substance use disorders* was 18.6% among adults aged 18 or older. The estimated 12-month prevalence of *serious* mental illness (excluding substance use disorders) was 4.1% among adults. Although the NSDUH collects information related to mental illness (e.g., symptoms of depression) from adolescents aged 12 to 17, it does not produce estimates of mental illness for that population.

The prevalence estimates discussed in this report may raise questions for Congress. Should federal mental health policy focus on adults or adolescents with *any* mental illness (including some whose mental illnesses may be mild and even transient) or on those with *serious* mental illness? Should substance use disorders be addressed through the same policies as other mental illnesses? Members of Congress may approach mental health policy differently depending in part on how they answer such questions.

INTRODUCTION

Congress has demonstrated an interest in mental health and mental illness,[1] and knowing how many people have a mental illness may be helpful in addressing related policy issues. Determining how many people have a mental illness can be difficult, and prevalence[2] estimates vary. While numerous surveys include questions related to mental illness, few provide prevalence estimates of *diagnosable mental illness*, and fewer still provide *national* prevalence estimates of diagnosable mental illness.[3]

This report briefly describes the methodology and selected findings of three large federally funded surveys that provide *national prevalence estimates of diagnosable mental illness*: the National Comorbidity Survey Replication (NCS-R), the National Comorbidity Survey Replication Adolescent Supplement (NCS-A), and the National Survey on Drug Use and Health (NSDUH). This report presents prevalence estimates of *any* mental illness and *serious* mental illness[4] based on each survey and ends with a brief discussion of how these prevalence estimates might inform policy discussions.

One data source may be preferred over another in specific situations. For example, the NCS-R and the NCS-A are a decade old, so the NSDUH (which is conducted annually) may be preferred for more recent prevalence estimates. On the other hand, the NCS-R and the NCS-A provide prevalence estimates for specific disorders,[5] which the NSDUH does not provide.[6]

ESTIMATING PREVALENCE OF MENTAL ILLNESS

In clinical practice, mental health professionals diagnose mental illnesses based on criteria in the American Psychiatric Association's *Diagnostic and Statistical Manual of Mental Disorders* (DSM)[7] and exercise clinical judgment in doing so.[8] Large surveys, however, may not allow for lengthy interviews and use of clinical judgment. Considerations in generating national prevalence estimates of diagnosable mental illness[9] through large surveys include (1) what survey instrument (i.e., set of questions) is used, (2) who administers it, and (3) how generalizable the findings are. Each of these considerations is discussed briefly below.

When designing surveys, researchers must weigh the value of detailed information against the time required to collect that information. Longer survey instruments may be better able to identify mental illness accurately by asking all or most of the questions necessary to assess DSM diagnostic criteria. Shorter survey instruments, while more practical to include in a survey, may not identify mental illness as accurately as longer instruments. **Table 1** provides examples of survey instruments assessing mental illness.

Table 1. Examples of Survey Instruments Assessing Mental Illness

Instrument	What It Assesses	Who Administers It	How Long It Takes	Examples of Surveys Using It
Structured Clinical Interview for DSM Disorders (SCID)a	Diagnoses	Trained mental health professionals	Approximately 30–60 minutes	NSDUH (for a subsample of respondents)
World Mental Health Survey Initiative version of the Composite International Diagnostic Interview (WMH-CIDI)b	Diagnoses, functioning, treatment, risk factors, socio-demographic characteristics, and more	Trained lay interviewers	Approximately 2 hours, but modular so that some sections can be excluded	NCS-R; NCS-A uses a modified Composite International Diagnostic Interview (CIDI)
World Health Organization Disability Assessment Schedule (WHODAS)c	Difficulties (due to health conditions) in the areas of cognition, mobility, self-care, getting along, life activities, and participation	Either self-administered or administered by an interviewer (no training required)	Different versions are available; the longest (36 items) takes approximately 15–20 minutes	NSDUH uses a modified version
Kessler-6 Psychological Distress Scale (K6)d	Frequency and severity of feeling nervous, hopeless, restless/fidgety, sad/depressed, and worthless	Either self-administered or administered by an interviewer (no training required)	No more than 2 minutes	NSDUH uses a modified version

Note: A *survey instrument* is a tool for systematically collecting information from survey respondents; each instrument listed in this table is a set of questions that may be asked as part of a larger questionnaire.

a DSM = Diagnostic and Statistical Manual of Mental Disorders. Information about the SCID in this table is drawn from U.S. Department of Health and Human Services (HHS), Centers for Disease Control and Prevention (CDC), "Mental Illness Surveillance in the United States," *Morbidity and Mortality Weekly Report*, vol. 60, Supplement (September 2, 2011).

[b] Information about the WMH-CIDI in this table is drawn from Ronald C. Kessler and T. Bedirhan Üstün, "The World Mental Health (WMH) Survey Initiative Version of the World Health Organization (WHO) Composite International Diagnostic Interview (CIDI)," *International Journal of Methods in Psychiatric Research*, vol. 13, no. 2 (2004), pp. 93-121.

[c] Information about the WHODAS in this table is drawn from World Health Organization, Classifications, *Classification of Functioning, Disability and Health (ICF)*, http://www.who.int/classifications/icf/whodasii/en/.

[d] Ronald C. Kessler et al., "Screening for Serious Mental Illness in the General Population with the K6 Screening Scale: Results from the WHO World Mental Health (WMH) Survey Initiative," *International Journal of Methods in Psychiatric Research*, vol. 19 (Supplement 1) (2010), pp. 4-22.

Survey instruments may be administered in different ways, which may affect both the accuracy of their assessment of mental illness and the feasibility of their inclusion in large surveys. Some, such as the Structured Clinical Interview for DSM Disorders (described in **Table 1**), require trained mental health professionals. Others require trained interviewers who need not be mental health professionals. Still others may be self-administered or administered by interviewers without extensive training.

The prevalence estimates described in this report are weighted to reflect the general U.S. population as closely as possible.[10] This is accomplished by assigning a weight to each survey respondent based on information that is available for both the survey respondents and the general U.S. population (e.g., age and gender, among others). Weighting can correct for known differences between the survey respondents and the general U.S. population (e.g., if people in a certain age range are overrepresented in the survey). Weighting cannot, however, correct for subpopulations that are excluded from the survey altogether (e.g., the homeless). Prevalence estimates are not generalizable to excluded subpopulations.[11]

NATIONAL COMORBIDITY SURVEY REPLICATION

The National Comorbidity Survey Replication (NCS-R) replicated the original National Comorbidity Survey (conducted between 1990 and 1992), which was the first survey to use fully structured research diagnostic interviews to assess a wide range of DSM disorders among a national sample of adults in the United States.[12] The NCS-R was funded primarily by the National Institute of Mental Health within the National Institutes of Health (NIH) of the Department of Health and Human Services (HHS), with supplemental support from the National Institute on Drug Abuse (also within NIH), the Substance Abuse and Mental Health Services Administration (of HHS), the Robert Wood Johnson Foundation, and the John W. Alden Trust.[13] Between February 2001 and April 2003, NCS-R staff conducted in-person interviews with more than 9,000 adults aged 18 or older, drawing the sample from households in the contiguous United States. The sample did not include the homeless, individuals in institutions, or non-English speakers; these exclusions limit the generalizability of findings based on the NCS-R.[14]

Prevalence of Any Mental Illness Among Adults

The NCS-R determined the presence of any mental illness based on the World Health Organization's World Mental Health Survey Initiative version of the Composite International Diagnostic Interview (WMH-CIDI), which assessed 19 specific DSM diagnoses.[15] Analyses of NCS-R data have yielded different prevalence estimates. One analysis of NCS-R data estimated that 26.2% of adults had a mental illness within a 12-month period (hereinafter called 12-month prevalence).[16] Another analysis of NCS-R data estimated the 12-month prevalence of mental illness to be 32.4% among adults; the difference may be attributable to the use of more recent information about the U.S. population in weighting the NCS-R data.[17] Both of these estimates include substance use disorders as mental illness; an analysis of NCS-R data estimated the 12- month prevalence of mental illness *excluding substance use disorders* to be 24.8% among adults.[18]

Prevalence of Serious Mental Illness Among Adults

Additional analyses of NSC-R data were conducted to determine the 12-month prevalence of mental illness at three levels of severity: serious,[19] moderate,[20] or mild.[21] Among the 26.2% of adults identified with a mental disorder in the analysis, serious disorders (22.3% *among adults with a disorder*) were less common than moderate disorders (37.3%) or mild disorders (40.4%). The estimated 12-month prevalence of serious mental illness among *all* adults was 5.8%.[22]

NATIONAL COMORBIDITY SURVEY REPLICATION ADOLESCENT SUPPLEMENT

The National Comorbidity Survey Replication Adolescent Supplement (NCS-A) was the first survey to use fully structured research diagnostic interviews to assess a wide range of DSM disorders among a national sample of adolescents in the United States. Like the NCS-R, the NCSA was funded primarily by the National Institute of Mental Health, with supplemental support from the National Institute on Drug Abuse, the Substance Abuse and Mental Health Services Administration, the Robert Wood Johnson Foundation, and the John W. Alden Trust.[23] Between February 2001 and January 2004, NCS-A staff interviewed more than 10,000 adolescents aged 13 to 17, drawing the sample from both schools and households in the coterminous United States. Adolescent participants were interviewed in person, and one parent of each participating adolescent was asked to complete a self-administered questionnaire about the adolescent's developmental history and mental health. The sample did not include the homeless, individuals in institutions, or non-English speakers; these exclusions limit the generalizability of findings based on the NCS-A.[24]

Prevalence of Any Mental Illness Among Adolescents

The NCS-A determined the presence of any mental illness based on a modified Composite International Diagnostic Interview (CIDI), which assessed 15 specific DSM diagnoses. Using NCS-A data, researchers estimated the 12-month prevalence of mental illness to be 40.3% among adolescents.[25] Some have suggested that the current version of the DSM identifies people who should not be considered mentally ill.[26]

Prevalence of Serious Mental Illness Among Adolescents

Additional analyses of NCS-A data were conducted to determine the presence of serious mental illness (called serious emotional disturbance in NCS-A), which was defined as at least one diagnosis accompanied by an estimated score of 50 or less on the Children's Global Assessment Scale (CGAS), indicating either severe functional impairment in one area of living or moderate functional impairment in most areas of living. The CGAS score was not measured directly as part of the NCS-A. Instead the NCS-A used a sophisticated approach that involved (1) selection of a subsample of 347 adolescent-parent pairs from the main study; (2) follow-up telephone interviews conducted by mental health professionals who assigned CGAS scores; (3) development of a statistical model linking CGAS scores to responses to questions in the main study; and (4) application of the statistical model to the full sample to impute CGAS scores based on responses to questions in the main study.[27]

Using the imputed CGAS scores, researchers assessed serious mental illness among 6,483 adolescent NCS-A participants with complete data (including parent questionnaires). This analysis yielded a 12-month prevalence of any mental illness (42.6%) that was slightly higher than the previous estimate and found most cases to be mild (58.2% *among adolescents with a disorder*) or moderate (22.9%), rather than serious (18.8%). The estimated 12-month prevalence of serious mental illness among *all* adolescents was 8.0%. Some people have suggested that most adolescents with mental disorders do not need treatment because their disorders are mild and will resolve on their own; however, some research has shown that mild disorders during adolescence may predict serious disorders during adulthood.[28]

NATIONAL SURVEY ON DRUG USE AND HEALTH

The National Survey on Drug Use and Health (NSDUH) focuses primarily on the use of illegal drugs, alcohol, and tobacco and also includes several modules that focus on mental health issues.[29] The NSDUH is funded by the Substance Abuse and Mental Health Services Administration. Each year, the NSDUH surveys approximately 70,000 non-institutionalized civilians aged 12 years or older in the United States, divided roughly between 45,000 adults (aged 18 or older) and 25,000 adolescents (aged 12 to 17).[30] The NSDUH is conducted in both English and Spanish. Participants are interviewed in their homes using a combination of personal interviewing and audio computer-assisted self-interviewing, which offers more privacy in order to encourage honest reporting of sensitive topics such as illicit drug use. The sample does not include the homeless, individuals in institutions, those who speak a language other than English or Spanish, or military personnel on active duty; these exclusions limit the generalizability of findings based on the NSDUH.[31]

NSDUH-based prevalence estimates of any mental illness and serious mental illness among adults aged 18 or older are described below. Although the NSDUH collects information related to mental illness (e.g., symptoms of depression) from adolescents aged 12 to 17, it does not produce *prevalence estimates of mental illness* for that population.

Prevalence of Any Mental Illness Among Adults

The NSDUH determines the presence of any mental illness based on a combination of relatively short modules of questions (including modified versions of the K6 and WHODAS described in **Table 1**) in the main survey and information from an additional follow-up interview conducted with a subsample of adults from the main survey.[32] Unlike the NCS-R and the NCS-A, the core component of NSDUH does not include questions designed to identify specific DSM diagnoses. Instead, the NSDUH uses an approach similar to the one used by NCS-A to impute the CGAS, involving (1) selection of a subsample of adults from the main study; (2) follow-up telephone interviews conducted by mental health professionals who conduct the Structured Clinical Interview for DSM Disorders (SCID); (3) development of a statistical model linking the SCIDbased diagnosis of mental illness to responses to questions in the main study; and (4) application of the statistical model to the full sample to impute the presence of mental illness based on responses to questions in the main study.[33] According to the 2012 NSDUH, the estimated 12- month prevalence of mental illness *excluding substance use disorders* is 18.6% of adults (aged 18 or older).[34]

Prevalence of Serious Mental Illness Among Adults

The NSDUH identifies adults (aged 18 or older) as having a serious mental illness if (1) they have a mental illness (excluding substance use disorders and developmental disorders) and (2) the illness substantially interferes with or limits at least one major life activity. The same approach used to impute any mental illness is applied to impute serious mental illness. According to the 2012 NSDUH, the estimated 12-month prevalence of serious mental illness *excluding substance use disorders* is 4.1% among adults (aged 18 or older).[35]

CONCLUSION

Knowing how many people are likely to be affected by policies related to mental illness may help policy makers identify specific problems as well as their scope; however, the national prevalence estimates discussed in this report may raise as many questions as they answer. For example, given the difference in prevalence estimates between *any* mental illness and *serious* mental illness among adolescents, might policy makers choose to focus on a large group of adolescents that includes many whose mental illnesses may be mild and even transient, or might they choose to focus more narrowly on adolescents with serious mental illness? As clinical practice is moving toward more integrated care,[36] should substance use disorders be included in the definition of mental illness (as in the NCS-R and the NCS-A) and addressed through the same policies, or should they be identified separately (as in the NSDUH) and addressed through different policies? How might policy makers address mental illness among populations that are excluded from the prevalence estimates (e.g., the homeless)? Policy makers may come to different conclusions about the best policy approach depending in part on how they answer such questions.

End Notes

[1] See, for example, U.S. Congress, Senate Committee on Health, Education, Labor, & Pensions, *Assessing the State of America's Mental Health System*, 113th Cong., 1st sess., January 24, 2013, http://www.help.senate.gov/hearings/ hearing/?id=b2048a10-5056-a032-529c-340d7ae5f237; and U.S. Congress, House Committee on Energy and Commerce, Subcommittee on Oversight and Investigations, *After Newtown: A National Conversation on Violence and Severe Mental Illness*, 113th Cong., 1st sess., March 5, 2013, http://energycommerce.house.gov/event/after-newtownnational-conversation-violence

[2] Prevalence is the share of a population affected by a given condition during a specified period of time. The term "12- month prevalence" refers to the share of study participants with symptoms that could be identified as mental illness in the 12 months before the interview. Another way to express prevalence is "lifetime prevalence," which is based on the share of study participants that had *ever* had a mental illness as of the time of the interview. This report focuses on 12- month prevalence because it more closely reflects the number of people with mental illness at a given time, which might translate into need for services at a given time.

[3] See U.S. Department of Health and Human Services (HHS), Centers for Disease Control and Prevention (CDC), "Mental Illness Surveillance in the United States," *Morbidity and Mortality Weekly Report*, vol. 60, Supplement (September 2, 2011), http://www.cdc.gov /mmwr/preview/mmwrhtml/su6003a1.htm; and HHS, Substance Abuse and Mental Health Services Administration (SAMHSA), Center for Behavioral Health Statistics and Quality (CBHSQ), *Comparison of NSDUH Mental Health Data and Methods with Other Data Sources*, March 2012, http://www.samhsa.gov/data /NSDUH/2k12Findings/CBHSQ DataReviewC2MentalHealth2012.pdf.

[4] Severity of mental illness is generally defined by the number of symptoms (i.e., whether the individual has just enough symptoms to meet diagnostic criteria or has excess symptoms) and/or the degree of functional impairment (e.g., whether an individual with mental illness is unable to work as a consequence of the illness). Each survey discussed in this report uses its own definition of serious mental illness.

[5] Estimates of specific disorders are not presented in this report; they are available in the cited documents.

[6] The NSDUH provides more detailed information about substance use disorders, but not other mental illness.

[7] American Psychiatric Association, *Diagnostic and Statistical Manual of Mental Disorders, Fourth Edition, Text Revision (DSM-IV-TR),* (Washington, DC: American Psychiatric Association, 2000). Some of the interviews designed for research are based on the fourth edition prior to the text revision (DSM-IV), published in 1994. A fifth edition (DSM-5) is scheduled for release in 2013.

[8] A diagnosis of mental illness may be based on what an individual reports about himself or herself; what other people report about the individual (if, for example, a family member is available); and what the mental health professional observes about the individual. People may not be forthcoming with information about certain behaviors (e.g., drug use) or symptoms (e.g., hallucinations); this is a challenge in both clinical settings and research settings.

[9] This report uses the term "diagnosable" as distinct from "diagnosed" in acknowledgement of the potential for surveys to identify people suffering from mental illnesses that have not been diagnosed by a mental health professional. Also important is the distinction between symptoms of mental illness (e.g., feelings of depression or anxiety) and a combination of symptoms meeting DSM criteria for a diagnosis of mental illness (e.g., major depressive disorder or generalized anxiety disorder). While all DSM disorders may be considered mental illnesses, surveys generally do not assess all of them. In this report, some of the prevalence estimates include substance use disorders and others do not.

[10] The weighting was done by the researchers whose published results CRS cites in this report, not by CRS.

[11] Excluded subpopulations may have higher or lower risk of mental illness than the general population. Thus if these subpopulations had been included in the surveys, the overall prevalence estimates would have been slightly higher or lower accordingly. Policy approaches that might be appropriate for excluded subpopulations such as the homeless or non-English speakers may be different than policy approaches for the general population.

[12] Harvard Medical School, Department of Health Care Policy, *National Comorbidity Survey,* http://www.hcp.med.harvard.edu/ncs/.

[13] Ronald C. Kessler et al., "Prevalence, Severity, and Comorbidity of Twelve-month DSM-IV Disorders in the National Comorbidity Survey Replication (NCS-R)," *Archives of General Psychiatry,* vol. 62, no. 6 (June 2005), pp. 617-627. Hereinafter, Kessler et al., NCS-R Prevalence, (2005).

[14] Kessler et al., NCS-R Prevalence, (2005).

[15] The DSM includes more than 19 diagnoses. While all of them may be considered mental illnesses, some are often excluded from definitions of mental illness (e.g., learning disorders).

[16] Kessler et al., NCS-R Prevalence, (2005).

[17] Harvard Medical School, Department of Health Care Policy, *National Comorbidity Survey,* "NSC-R Twelve-Month Prevalence Estimates" link at http://www.hcp.med.harvard.edu/ncs/. This later analysis was based on updated data as of July 19, 2007, and "reflect[s] the latest diagnostic, demographic and raw variable information."

[18] Benjamin G. Druss et al. "Impairment in Role Functioning in Mental and Chronic Medical Disorders in the United States: Results from the National Comorbidity Survey Replication." *Molecular Psychiatry,* vol. 14, no. 7 (July 2009), pp. 728-737.

[19] Kessler et al., NCS-R Prevalence, (2005). Any of the following qualified a case of mental illness as serious: "a 12- month suicide attempt with serious lethality intent; work disability or substantial limitation due to a mental or substance disorder; positive screen results for non-affective psychosis; bipolar I or II disorder; substance dependence with serious role

impairment (as defined by disorder-specific impairment questions); an impulse control disorder with repeated serious violence; or any disorder that resulted in 30 or more days out of role in the year" (p. 618).

[20] Kessler et al., NCS-R Prevalence, (2005). Among cases of mental illness not defined as serious, any of the following qualified a case as moderate: "suicide gesture, plan, or ideation; substance dependence without serious role impairment; at least moderate work limitation due to a mental or substance disorder; or any disorder with at least moderate role impairment in 2 or more domains of the Sheehan Disability Scale [which] assessed disability in work role performance, household maintenance, social life, and intimate relationships" (p. 618).

[21] Kessler et al., NCS-R Prevalence, (2005). All cases of mental illness that were not defined as serious or moderate were considered mild (p. 618).

[22] Kessler et al., NCS-R Prevalence, (2005).

[23] Ronald C. Kessler et al., "Prevalence, Persistence, and Sociodemographic Correlates of DSM-IV Disorders in the National Comorbidity Survey Replication Adolescent Supplement," *Archives of General Psychiatry*, vol. 69, no. 4 (April 2012). Hereinafter, Kessler et al., NCS-A Prevalence, (2012).

[24] Ronald C. Kessler et al., "Severity of 12-Month DSM-IV Disorders in the National Comorbidity Survey Replication Adolescent Supplement," *Archives of General Psychiatry*, vol. 69, no. 4 (April 2012). Hereinafter, Kessler et al., NCSA Severity, (2012).

[25] Kessler et al., NCS-A Prevalence, (2012).

[26] Kessler et al., NCS-A Severity, (2012).

[27] Kessler et al., NCS-A Prevalence, (2012); Kessler et al., NCS-A Severity, (2012); and Ronald C. Kessler et al., "The National Comorbidity Survey Adolescent Supplement (NCSA): III. Concordance of DSM-IV/CIDI Diagnoses with Clinical Reassessments," *Journal of the American Academy of Child and Adolescent Psychiatry*, vol. 48, no. 4 (April 2009), pp. 386-399.

[28] Kessler et al., NCS-A Severity, (2012).

[29] U.S. Department of Health and Human Services (HHS), Substance Abuse and Mental Health Services Administration (SAMHSA), Center for Behavioral Health Statistics and Quality (CBHSQ), *Results from the 2012 National Survey on Drug Use and Health: Mental Health Findings*, (SMA) 13-4805, Rockville, MD, December 2013, http://www.samhsa.gov/data/NSDUH/2k12MH_FindingsandDetTables/Index.aspx. Hereinafter, *2012 NSDUH: Mental Health Findings*.

[30] In 2012, 68,309 respondents completed a NSDUH interview, including 45,817 adults and 22,492 adolescents. (*2012 NSDUH: Mental Health Findings,*Table B.4 Weighted Percentages and Sample Sizes for 2011 and 2012 NSDUHs, by Final Interview Code).

[31] *2012 NSDUH: Mental Health Findings*. The NSDUH has been ongoing since 1971; prior to 2002, it was called the National Household Survey on Drug Abuse.

[32] *2012 NSDUH: Mental Health Findings*.

[33] This approach, called the Mental Health Surveillance Study, began with the 2008 NSDUH.

[34] *2012 NSDUH: Mental Health Findings*.

[35] *2012 NSDUH: Mental Health Findings*.

[36] Like clinical practice, financing is moving toward including substance use disorders with the rest of mental illness. The Mental Health Parity Act of 1996 (MHPA, P.L. 104-204) did not apply to coverage of substance use disorders. The more recent Paul Wellstone and Pete Domenici Mental Health Parity and Addiction Equity Act of 2008 (MHPAEA, P.L. 110-343) applies to both substance use disorders and the rest of mental illness. See CRS Report

R41768, *Mental Health Parity and Mandated Coverage of Mental Health and Substance Use Disorder Services After the ACA.*

INDEX

#

20th century, 11, 154
21st century, 6, 100, 155, 229

A

Abraham, 32, 34, 39, 144, 147, 209, 231
abuse, 17, 20, 35, 41, 42, 43, 44, 45, 53, 54, 56, 57, 59, 60, 61, 63, 64, 67, 68, 73, 76, 137, 147, 152, 155, 156, 160, 163, 166, 173, 185, 208, 216, 217, 224, 229, 242, 245, 247, 248
academic performance, 238
accessibility, 9, 25, 26, 29, 55, 102, 130, 140, 145, 164, 165, 178, 209, 231, 235, 240, 242, 246
accountability, 83, 111, 118, 140, 156
accounting, 239
acculturation, 59, 147
activism, 221
AD, 145
ADA, 151
adaptation(s), 145, 156, 182, 196
ADHD, 146
adjustment, 67, 73, 131, 151, 152, 181, 197, 230
administrators, 28, 64, 80, 86, 194, 204, 239, 247
adolescent adjustment, 151
adolescent boys, 67, 151, 230
adolescent development, 152
adolescent drinking, 75, 152, 236
adulthood, 63, 69, 173, 261
advancement, 143, 156, 163, 172, 204
advocacy, 100, 104, 108, 109, 158, 189, 206, 231
affective disorder, 183
African Americans, 10, 58, 125, 127, 131, 133, 140, 193
African-American, 47, 67, 140
age, 4, 10, 21, 49, 51, 59, 92, 106, 129, 135, 147, 162, 164, 174, 179, 183, 186, 193, 202, 209, 235, 239, 248, 258
aggregation, 164
aggression, 130
agriculture, 9, 206
AIDS, 174, 183, 229, 246
Alaska, 12, 42, 64, 91, 96, 97, 107, 170, 194, 219
Alaska Natives, 107, 194
alcohol abuse, 60, 75, 142, 155, 222, 224, 237
alcohol consumption, 51, 59
alcohol dependence, 183, 184, 218
alcohol problems, 58, 141, 182
alcohol use, 45, 47, 48, 51, 52, 56, 58, 59, 61, 63, 66-68, 72, 74, 143, 144, 147, 152, 155, 157, 159, 160, 170, 172, 174, 212, 214, 232
alcoholics, 56, 73, 204, 229

alcoholism, 61, 66, 149, 229
algorithm, 73, 219
alienation, 61, 246
American Psychiatric Association, 255, 264
amphetamines, 44
anger, 64, 136
antisocial acts, 212
antisocial behavior, 42, 44, 60, 71, 76, 202, 212, 243, 249
antisocial personality, 183, 218
antisocial personality disorder, 183
anxiety, 135, 183, 201, 264
anxiety disorder, 183
APA, 104, 105, 110
appointments, 29, 139, 140
appraisals, 51, 202
arrests, 54, 149
articulation, 96
assault, 37, 61, 122, 190
assertiveness, 49, 51, 172
assessment, 48, 53, 66, 70, 77, 81, 89, 95, 101, 108, 119, 135, 142, 146, 166, 168, 170, 175, 185, 204, 206, 210, 216, 231, 234, 243, 249, 251, 258
assets, 77, 78, 228
asylum, 33, 135, 136
atmosphere, 249
attachment, 50, 51, 129, 172, 214, 232, 239
attitudes, 31, 50, 51, 56, 58, 80, 129, 152, 154, 155, 172, 178, 181, 210, 214, 221, 233, 250
authority(s), 15, 99, 111, 134, 190, 225
autonomy, 83
avoidance, 82, 130
awareness, 28, 32, 52, 175, 206, 240, 243

B

bandwidth, 135, 251
barriers, 20, 22, 23, 25, 26, 28, 29, 77, 78, 107, 111, 136, 141, 145, 154, 158, 166, 167, 171, 174, 178, 180, 182, 184, 191, 192, 193, 197, 199, 203, 222, 228, 229, 237, 241, 245, 246
barriers to entry, 180

base, vii, 1, 74, 84, 98, 232, 244
basic needs, 15
battered women, 156
behavioral disorders, 27
behavioral genetics, 131
behavioral problems, 22, 43, 55, 161, 228, 247
behaviors, 21, 43-44, 49-50, 73, 151-152, 171, 186, 199, 224, 232, 243, 249-250, 264
beneficiaries, 18, 24, 37, 38, 133, 147, 187, 198, 203, 208, 220, 235
benefits, 2, 14, 18, 29, 32, 73, 83, 107, 113, 120, 184, 197, 217, 224, 229, 230, 233, 238, 241
binge drinking, 60
bipolar disorder, 40, 64, 148, 205, 218, 223
bivariate analysis, 131
Blacks, 131
board members, 204
bonding, 46, 49, 171
bonds, 49, 239
bonuses, 238
Britain, 33, 138
BTC, 165
building blocks, 116

C

campaigns, 32, 48, 104, 120
cannabis, 174
capacity building, 129
care model, 82, 83
caregivers, 17, 144, 145, 165, 177, 181, 219
caregiving, 176
case examples, 214
case study(s), 130, 214, 215, 231
catalyst, 214
Caucasians, 189
causal relationship, 75, 116, 175, 239
CDC, 256, 263
Census, 5, 6, 7, 8, 9, 18, 240, 244
certification, 106, 147
Chad, 5

challenges, 1, 2, 17, 34, 35, 77, 79, 87, 96, 100-102, 139, 143, 153, 161, 167, 194, 203, 204, 206, 219, 227, 230, 231, 245, 247, 248
changing environment, 96
Chicago, 71, 191, 192
Child Behavior Checklist, 46
child rearing, 49
childcare, 21
childhood, 42, 43, 49, 98, 237, 248
childhood disorders, 98
childrearing, 151, 199
child-rearing practices, 43, 51, 202
chimera, 72, 212
Christianity, 146
city(s), 6, 7, 35, 36, 59, 64, 72, 159, 176, 178, 207, 208, 211
citizens, vii, 1, 9, 204
clarity, 158
classification, 6, 7, 8, 10, 46, 116, 244
classroom, 48
clients, 34, 53, 54, 55, 56, 57, 63, 64, 68, 75, 80, 98, 109, 134, 136, 140, 141, 148, 150, 156, 158, 163, 176, 187, 190, 196, 197, 204, 225, 227, 236, 241, 250
climate, 12
clinical judgment, 255
close relationships, 16
cluster analysis, 209
cluster model, 209
clusters, 7, 8, 54
cocaine, 44, 56, 58, 62, 64, 71, 203, 204, 205
cocaine abuse, 56, 71, 203, 204
coercion, 152
cognition, 249, 256
cognitive ability, 229
cognitive function, 249
cognitive impairment, 222
cognitive-behavioral therapy, 56, 153
collaboration, 4, 20, 32, 60, 96, 97, 110, 129, 132, 141, 155, 161, 186, 224, 228, 243
College Station, 35, 87, 167
college students, 50

colleges, 103
color, 10, 134, 161, 175
communication, 49, 50, 52, 60, 78, 82, 102, 121, 158, 186, 191, 214, 224, 225, 226, 240, 241
communication skills, 214, 225, 241
community service, 21, 35, 133, 155, 163, 166, 228, 231
community support, 166, 176, 178, 179, 207, 221, 222, 236
community-based services, 15, 65, 132, 163, 213, 236
comorbidity, 37, 66, 70, 142, 164, 183, 184, 218, 242
competition, 191, 228
complement, 48, 157
complexity, 175
compliance, 113, 114, 139, 250
complications, 53
composition, 79, 140, 180, 186, 187, 202
computer, 55, 130, 261
conceptual model, 200, 237
conditioning, 130
conduct disorder, 71, 192
conference, 105
confidentiality, 53, 65, 82, 83, 111, 178, 204, 213, 219
configuration, 135
conflict, 46, 50, 51, 73, 89, 206, 230
Congress, ix, 9, 10, 11, 12, 18, 38, 72, 114, 167, 198, 240, 254, 263
Congressional Budget Office, 113
congruence, 33
consciousness, 175
consensus, 117
Consensus, 94, 98
conspiracy, 159
consumers, 14, 29, 30, 59, 77, 81, 82, 83, 91, 96, 97, 103, 104, 105, 106, 107, 110, 117, 119, 121, 140, 155, 156, 158, 165, 181, 199, 207, 211, 216, 237
consumption, 44, 63
content analysis, 210
control condition, 56, 186, 195, 204, 212
control group, 232

controlled studies, 173
cooperation, 2
coordination, 3, 4, 32, 83, 86, 93, 101, 109, 114, 132, 145, 165, 166, 217, 226, 241
coping strategies, 50, 61, 172
cost, 14, 27, 29, 80, 82, 86, 99, 108, 112, 113, 115, 120, 135, 140, 148, 149, 165, 180, 187, 190, 203, 221, 226, 229, 235, 240, 242
cost benefits, 82
cost saving, 82
counsel, 4
counseling, 51, 52, 146, 176, 201, 216, 231, 235, 243, 246, 247
covering, 14, 190
credentials, 93, 106
crimes, 37, 122, 190
criminal behavior, 131
criminal justice system, 23, 63, 64, 68, 77, 98, 133, 169, 191, 205, 230
criminality, 191, 192
crises, 23, 26
criticism, 248
cross-sectional study, 64
CST, 56, 204
CT, 35, 163
cultural beliefs, 31
cultural differences, 23, 83, 175, 208
cultural influence, 31
cultural norms, 86, 103, 144, 206
cultural values, 13, 145, 147
culture, 20, 31, 32, 53, 57, 58, 65, 77, 86, 103, 153, 155, 178, 190, 221, 228
curricula, 136
curriculum, 33, 49, 51, 52, 53, 72, 110, 131, 137, 172, 212, 236

D

daily living, 151
data collection, 7, 129
data set, 159, 207
database, 167
deaths, 54
decision makers, 86

decision-making process, 237
deficiencies, 133
deficit, 146, 161
degradation, 135
delinquency, 43, 44, 49, 50, 71, 74, 75, 152, 160, 176, 191, 192, 195, 202, 212, 230, 239, 248
delinquent behavior, 60, 239
Delta, 114
dementia, 23, 138, 168, 201
demographic characteristics, 64, 131, 233, 256
demographic data, 150
demographic factors, 151, 242
demography, 244
denial, 56, 73, 216, 217, 236
Department of Agriculture, 17, 116, 159
depression, ix, 20, 21, 31, 35, 37, 61, 88, 142, 151, 162, 164, 173, 191, 201, 212, 222, 223, 226, 237, 254, 261, 264
depressive symptomatology, 222
depressive symptoms, 21, 173, 178, 222
deprivation, 145
depth, 94, 142, 159
detection, 21, 179
detention, 182
developmental disorder, 262
developmental process, 191
Diagnostic and Statistical Manual of Mental Disorders, 184, 185, 242, 255, 256, 264
diagnostic criteria, 63, 185, 255, 263
direct cost, 80, 226
directors, 33, 95, 130, 176, 185
disability, 150, 264, 265
disclosure, 57
discontinuity, 111
discriminant analysis, 239
discrimination, 113, 208, 249
disorder, 20, 21, 22, 33, 35, 39, 44, 59, 61, 64, 81, 117, 132, 142, 146, 150, 163, 164, 166, 183, 192, 205, 218, 242, 250, 259, 261, 264, 265
dispersion, 220
displaced persons, 194
disposition, 164

Index

dissatisfaction, 63
distance education, 96
distance learning, 106, 107
distress, 36, 104, 178, 227, 229
distribution, 27, 74, 94, 180, 220, 233
diversification, 82, 139
diversity, 5, 6, 7, 8, 77, 85, 161, 175, 200
doctors, 21, 194, 249
Domestic Policy Council, 38, 208
drawing, 104, 258, 260
drinking pattern(s), 59
drug abuse, 21, 48, 62, 66, 68, 73-75, 137-139, 142, 158, 173, 214, 217, 235, 240, 246
drug abusers, 62, 246
drug dependence, 71, 191, 201, 218
drug education, 48, 76, 145, 209, 210, 250
drug testing, 57
drug therapy, 225
drug treatment, 54, 195
drugs, 24, 41, 44, 46, 47, 48, 50, 52, 58, 61, 63, 68, 159, 160, 176, 185, 208, 240, 261
DSM, 255, 256, 258, 259, 260, 262, 264
DSM-IV-TR, 264
dysphoria, 152

E

ecology, 153
economic downturn, 200
Economic Research Service (ERS), 6, 10, 17, 116, 123, 159, 161, 240, 244
economics, 13, 194, 244
economies of scale, 145
ecstasy, 45
editors, 3, 144
education, 12, 20, 21, 23, 46, 59, 60, 67, 68, 78, 85, 92, 94-96, 99, 104, 106, 108, 121, 146, 147, 154, 157, 158, 162, 170, 176, 200, 221, 224, 228, 230, 237, 239, 243
educational attainment, 64, 206
educational institutions, 95
educational opportunities, 20
educational programs, 48
educators, 51, 79, 157

elderly population, 14, 144, 145
elders, 22, 23, 34, 36, 136, 144, 189, 209, 217, 231
elected leaders, 106
elementary school, 52, 158, 201, 219, 239
eligibility criteria, 173
emergency, 56, 77, 78, 139, 164, 189, 231, 251
emergency response, 189
emotional disorder, 175, 237
emotional dispositions, 44
emotional health, 173
emotional responses, 43, 44
emotionality, 149
employees, 29, 113
employers, 14, 112, 113, 190, 238
employment, 7, 9, 10, 21, 47, 62, 63, 94, 98, 161, 164, 199, 200, 216, 237
employment growth, 10
employment opportunities, 200
employment status, 21, 164
empowerment, 60, 153, 207, 224, 246
encouragement, 166, 236
enforcement, 27, 60, 224
England, 138, 225
environment(s), vii, 2, 3, 12, 16, 22, 62, 72, 79, 81, 109, 146, 149, 178, 189, 201, 206, 212, 215, 219, 236, 248, 250
environmental influences, 170
epidemic, 56
epidemiologic, 19, 130, 144, 162, 220
epidemiology, 119, 128, 179, 194
equipment, 111, 251
equity, 231
ERS, 8, 9, 10, 11, 17, 159, 161
ethical issues, 17
ethics, 18, 39, 73, 103, 213, 219
ethnic background, 25
ethnic groups, 61, 103, 133, 193, 246
ethnic minority, 31, 32, 41, 57
ethnicity, 31, 41, 79, 241
etiology, 42, 202
Europe, 33, 135, 136
evidence-based practices, 28, 33, 42, 98, 107-109, 121, 123, 133, 155, 186, 239

exercise, 255
expenditures, 14, 120
expertise, 17, 23, 91, 107, 118, 236, 250
exploitation, 17
exposure, 219, 243, 250

F

faith, 77, 86, 110
family conflict, 46, 50, 152
family factors, 58, 192
family history, 45, 229
family income, 29, 131
family interactions, 70, 186
family life, 151, 152
family members, 43, 44, 49, 110, 235
family physician, 83, 237
family support, 222
family therapy, 55, 177, 235
Farm Bill, 27
farmers, 9, 159, 200
farms, 9, 152, 221
fatalism, 56
fear(s), 23, 31, 104
Federal Government, 84
feelings, 46, 190, 264
fidelity, 79
financial, 16, 26, 29, 46, 80, 83, 95, 96, 102, 103, 108, 112, 114, 148, 151, 211, 226, 228, 229, 237, 246
financial incentives, 96, 103
financial performance, 114
financial resources, 16, 29, 112, 226, 246
financial stability, 80, 102, 148
financial support, 114
financial system, 114
first responders, 27
flexibility, 78, 115, 133, 136, 145, 148
focus groups, 215
food, 159
force, 52, 148, 149
Ford, 78, 83, 89, 241
formation, 104, 194
formula, 195
foundations, 16

friendship, 80, 148, 225
functional analysis, 56, 204
funding, 27, 29, 32, 61, 77-78, 83, 94-96, 98-99, 102, 106-108, 110-112, 114-115, 136, 148-149, 175, 188, 211, 221-222, 228, 245
funds, 15, 16, 30, 85, 156, 175, 221

G

gender differences, 160, 229
gender effects, 229
gender role, 190
General Accounting Office, 113
general practitioner, 216, 242
generalizability, 258, 260, 261
generalized anxiety disorder, viii, 253, 264
genetics, 215
Geographic Information System, 165
geography, 7, 57, 77, 89, 247
Georgia, 54, 161
gerontology, 192
glue, 174
God, 47
governance, 111
government policy, 238
governments, 115
governor, 241
GPA, 131
grades, 45, 49, 52, 59, 213, 230
grant programs, 115
grants, 42, 94, 110, 112, 114, 115, 208, 238
grass, 60, 224
grassroots, 48
group therapy, 108, 220
growth, 8, 9, 10, 11, 57, 71, 72, 83, 172, 195, 205, 212, 219
growth models, 212
guidance, 4, 216
guidance counselors, 216
guidelines, 54, 102, 155, 216

H

hallucinations, 264
harmful effects, 48
Hawaii, 54, 57, 60, 61, 64, 72, 76, 91, 92, 166, 211, 245
healing, 60, 207, 224
Health and Human Services, 18, 106, 178, 241
health care professionals, 145, 195
health care system, 22, 29, 114, 192, 198, 202, 203, 219, 249
health condition, 256
health education, 81
health insurance, 2, 14, 29, 113, 200, 205, 227
health practitioners, 81, 243
health problems, 81, 85, 104, 132, 162, 164, 168, 195
health promotion, 77, 192
health risks, 210
health status, 23, 34, 94, 145, 146, 159, 172
helplessness, 61
heritability, 43
heroin, 58, 61
heterogeneity, 244
HHS, 3, 6, 13, 18, 38, 75, 92, 100, 207, 241, 256, 258, 263, 265
high school, 12, 58, 131, 174, 201, 216, 239, 250
high school diploma, 12
higher education, 12, 81, 96, 97, 129, 242
high-risk populations, 244
highways, 5
Hispanics, 10, 242
history, 34, 44, 60, 64, 77, 98, 100, 112, 136, 143, 154-155, 172, 183-184, 194, 202, 204, 206, 211, 218, 224, 229, 248, 250, 260
HIV, 84, 174, 183, 229, 246
HIV/AIDS, 84, 174, 229
homelessness, 12, 18, 64, 149, 205, 208
homes, 181, 219, 261
hopelessness, 61
horizontal integration, 202
hospice, 249
hospitalization, 78, 80, 148, 149, 209, 213, 237
host, 199
House, 18, 263
House of Representatives, 18
household composition, 209
housing, 22, 64, 80, 148, 207, 220, 222
human, 7, 9, 12, 61, 76, 102, 111, 124, 145, 200, 214, 241, 245
human resources, 111
Hunter, 36, 177
Hurricane Andrew, 81
hyperactivity, 146, 237
hypothesis, 153, 164, 196, 221, 223

I

ideal(s), 79, 171
identification, 89, 109, 119, 142, 148, 173, 206, 222, 243
identity, 239
ideology, 190
illicit drug use, 57, 261
illicit substances, 137
image, 9
imitation, 234
immigrants, 12, 17, 31, 59, 160, 194, 242
immigration, 23, 160, 194, 244
impairments, 17, 209
improvements, 63, 186
impulsive, 44
in vivo, 187
incarceration, 62, 201, 246
incidence, 2, 10, 13, 19, 42, 63, 108, 147, 218, 220, 244
income, 9, 20, 21, 29, 59, 111, 131, 147, 151, 221, 238
increased access, 22, 83, 111, 241
independence, 56, 83, 196, 200
independent living, 250
Indian reservation, 60
Indians, 194
indirect effect, 199, 233
individual character, 191

individual characteristics, 191
individual differences, 215
industry(s), 194
informal sector, 146
information sharing, 96
infrastructure, 16, 77, 102, 112, 114, 115, 129, 145, 208
ingestion, 211
ingredients, 79, 88, 198
initiation, 45, 50, 52, 180, 233, 234
inmates, 41, 57, 62, 191, 236
insane, 31
institutions, 77, 103, 104, 171, 222, 239, 258, 260, 261
integration, 35, 49, 55, 58, 78, 82, 83, 87, 96, 107, 111, 139, 149, 167, 194, 207, 248
integrity, 69, 171
interaction effect, 141
internalizing, 152, 230, 248
intoxication, 63
Iowa, 27, 45, 54, 81, 132, 144, 170, 212, 220, 221, 232, 233, 236
isolation, 21, 23, 53, 111, 145, 150, 153, 178, 208, 220

J

junior high school, 52, 214, 236
justification, 213
juvenile delinquency, 131
juvenile justice, 137, 237

L

labeling, 31
landscape(s), 2, 5, 6, 9
language barrier, 95
languages, 6
Latinos, 130, 131, 193
law enforcement, 27, 189, 247, 248
laws, 97, 105, 113, 155, 181
lead, 7, 13, 63, 82, 151
leadership, 3, 4, 47, 107, 136

Leahy, 122, 123, 135, 251
learning, 99, 106, 154, 182, 264
legislation, 24, 114, 155
legislative proposals, 106
leisure, 80, 148, 149
life course, 43
life satisfaction, 23, 181
lifetime, 20, 44, 59, 62, 113, 183, 184, 218, 221, 234, 242, 246, 263
light, 31, 225
linear model, 117
linear modeling, 117
local community, 2, 82, 205
local government, 215, 228
locus, 109
longitudinal study, 67, 152, 162, 179, 243
Louisiana, 54, 114
love, 15
LTC, 230

M

magnitude, 46, 50, 60, 61, 157, 171, 245
major depression, 39, 184, 222
major depressive disorder, viii, 253, 264
major issues, 158, 217
major life activity, 262
majority, 5, 24, 27, 81, 110, 151, 184, 187
man, 69
MANOVA, 141
manpower, 170
manufacturing, 10, 161, 244
mapping, 56
marijuana, 44, 45, 47, 49, 50, 52, 58, 59, 62, 154, 172, 176, 234
marital conflict, 151, 152
marital status, 46, 209
marketing, 28, 82, 120, 121, 136, 204
marketplace, 2, 14, 203
marriage, 64, 206
Maryland, 54
masculinity, 190
MAST, 61, 142
materials, 53
matrix, 212

matter, 7
measurement, 7, 209, 225
media, 48, 139, 250
mediation, 66, 149
Medicaid, 14, 18, 24, 29, 37, 39, 84, 85, 91, 112, 121, 138, 161, 167, 187, 209, 216, 219, 220, 221, 227, 236
medical, 21, 26, 27, 32, 54, 55, 61, 81, 83, 84, 86, 99, 110, 113, 115, 134, 141, 154, 160, 161, 165, 194, 204, 215, 220, 222, 225, 241, 242, 245, 251
medical care, 134
Medicare, 14, 24, 27, 29, 34, 38, 40, 83, 84, 85, 99, 112, 115, 121, 138, 147, 161, 167, 198, 203, 208, 209, 235, 238
medication, 79, 80, 108, 176, 193, 198, 250
medicine, 185
membership, 149, 179
memory, 149, 150
mental disorder, 17, 28, 32, 44, 73, 81, 87, 91, 134, 140, 151, 166, 168, 179, 182, 186, 195, 197, 217, 220, 242, 259, 261
mental health professionals, 2, 21, 22, 25-28, 32, 76, 79, 82, 91-93, 103, 105, 110, 111, 119, 131, 134, 136, 158, 172, 180, 194, 196, 200, 227, 235, 255, 256, 258, 260, 262
mentally ill, viii, 19, 20, 23, 29, 89, 119, 130, 140, 144, 148, 149, 153, 165, 170, 178, 181, 196, 199, 226, 228, 237, 243, 254, 260
mentally ill persons, 149, 165, 228
meridian, 5
meta-analysis, 55, 74, 117, 192, 235
methadone, 235
Methamphetamine, 56, 68, 72, 158, 166, 211
methodology, vii, viii, 25, 98, 116, 253, 255
metropolitan areas, 5, 6, 85, 189
Mexico, 54, 59, 91, 129, 147, 160, 219
Michigan Alcoholism Screening Test, 61
microcosms, 144
migration, 12, 234
military, 222, 261
minimum wage, 9

minorities, 65, 130, 193, 241
minority groups, 119
minors, 51
mission, 95, 97, 115, 133, 158
Mississippi River, 5
Missouri, 114
misunderstanding, 101
misuse, 44, 63, 160
MMA, 24
moderates, 141
modernization, 234
modules, 106, 261
momentum, 4
Montana, 54, 57, 91, 166
Moon, 204
morbidity, 119
mortality, 210
motivation, 62, 82, 188
motor skills, 191
multiculturalism, 61, 246
multidimensional, 250
multivariate analysis, 117, 131

N

National Comorbidity Survey Replication, vii, viii, 253, 255, 258, 259, 264, 265
National Comorbidity Survey Replication Adolescent Supplement, vii, viii, 253, 255, 259, 265
National Economic Council, 38, 208
National Health Service, 28, 84, 93, 94, 95, 103
National Institute of Mental Health, 4, 37, 38, 61, 75, 115, 120, 142, 185, 208, 218, 220, 244, 258, 259
National Institutes of Health, 66, 67, 68, 70, 72, 76, 123, 138, 147, 152, 155, 157, 159, 182, 210, 245, 258
national policy, 2
National Survey, vii, viii, 253, 255, 261, 265
National Survey on Drug Use and Health, vii, viii, 253, 255, 261, 265
Native Americans, 10, 60

NCS, vii, viii, 184, 253, 254, 255, 256, 258, 259, 260, 262, 263, 264, 265
NCS-A, vii, viii, 253, 254, 255, 256, 259, 260, 262, 263, 265
NCS-R, vii, viii, 253, 254, 255, 256, 258, 259, 262, 263, 264, 265
negative effects, 243
negative relation, 199, 235
neglect, 181
negotiation, 237
networking, 48, 114
neuropsychological tests, 249
neuropsychology, 28, 249
neutral, 82
New England, 54, 196, 211
New Freedom Initiative, 215
non-institutionalized, 59, 261
nonverbal cues, 251
North America, 34, 68, 72, 129, 145, 153, 160, 214
Northern Ireland, 168
NSDUH, vii, viii, 253, 254, 255, 256, 261, 262, 263, 265
nurses, 23, 97, 99, 144, 146, 208, 230, 250
nursing, 23, 94, 143, 156, 165, 182, 185, 196, 209, 216, 230, 250
nursing care, 230
nursing home, 23, 94, 165

O

obsessive-compulsive disorder (OCD), 122, 135, 193
obstacles, 25, 38, 111, 140, 144, 170, 199, 200
occupational health, 183
offenders, 182, 192, 246
Office of Management and Budget (OMB), 6, 7, 8, 18, 116, 117, 211
officials, 98, 216
Oklahoma, 35, 159
old age, 44
ONDCP, 57, 72, 211
open spaces, 146
operant conditioning, 130
operating costs, 111
operations, 114, 115
opiates, 62
opportunities, vii, 1, 15, 25, 49, 95, 96, 103, 114, 121, 192, 207, 212, 225, 230, 239
oral tradition, 31
outpatient, 22, 25, 28, 55, 78, 115, 133, 141, 142, 164, 167, 176, 189, 199, 203, 223, 238
outreach, 23, 29, 31, 41, 61, 79, 82, 93, 97, 104, 122, 136, 140, 144, 158, 184, 187, 188, 209, 222, 231, 250
outreach programs, 31
overlap, 116
ownership, 203

P

Pacific, 10, 69
Pacific Islanders, 10
pain, 38, 143, 194
parallel, 4, 82, 102
parental influence, 192
parenting, 50, 55, 73, 74, 81, 151, 152, 186, 199, 224, 225, 230, 231, 232, 233
parents, 15, 30, 43, 48, 49, 50, 51, 55, 64, 67, 129, 132, 137, 139, 146, 151, 152, 157, 162, 168, 186, 192, 199, 212, 232, 233, 235, 239, 250
parity, 112, 113, 180, 207
participants, 51, 55, 80, 102, 107, 109, 129, 159, 169, 174, 193, 211, 260, 263
pathways, 64, 149, 189
patient care, 204
PCP, 174
peer group, 131, 225, 235
peer influence, 45, 50, 154
peer rejection, 212, 213
peer relationship, 243
peer support, 16
per capita expenditure, 222
performance measurement, 37, 118, 188
personal values, 196
personality, 191, 229, 237, 250
personality traits, 191

pessimism, 238
pharmaceutical, 198
pharmacokinetics, 63
phobia, 183
physical health, 80, 81, 82, 180, 248
physicians, 21, 27, 37, 77, 81, 84-88, 110, 134, 143, 146, 150, 156, 160, 161, 191, 204, 213, 237, 238
physiology, 63
pilot study, 37, 40, 88, 166, 187, 191, 238
placebo, 204
pleasure, 1
police, 50, 172, 210
policy initiative, 100
policy issues, 37, 157, 185, 208, 254
policy levels, 175
policy makers, 8, 32, 64, 101, 102, 109, 130, 194, 221, 262
policy options, 92, 216
policymakers, 7, 32, 80
politics, 76, 250
population density, 6-7, 100, 116, 150, 177, 201
population growth, 7, 11
positive relationship, 199
posttraumatic stress, 35, 39, 163, 164, 192
post-traumatic stress disorder, 222, 225
potential benefits, 211
poverty, 10, 20, 24, 29, 43, 146, 160, 161, 208, 221, 244
preadolescents, 243
precipitation, 5
pregnancy, 52, 243, 250
preparation, 53, 96, 147, 229
preschool, 201
prescription drugs, 14, 24, 147
President, 4, 8, 18, 19, 41, 65, 72, 89, 92, 93, 95, 101, 114, 211, 215
prevalence rate, 20, 45, 218, 222, 242
primacy, 193
principles, 65, 109, 110, 196, 214, 231
prisoners, 57, 76, 246
prisons, 62, 133, 236
privatization, 112, 121
probability, 43, 47, 119, 146, 150, 176

probation officers, 63
probe, 241
problem behavior(s), 42, 43, 45, 46, 49, 64
problem-solving, 49, 150, 154
problem-solving skills, 49
professional literature, 105
professionals, 16, 21, 27, 28, 31, 48, 49, 77, 80, 81, 84, 85, 91, 95, 103, 105, 110, 129, 187, 195, 200, 201, 206, 207, 212, 242, 258
profit, 121, 202
programming, 52, 62
project, 4, 41, 52, 63, 83, 96, 119, 133, 136, 165, 169-171, 180, 197, 201, 207, 210, 232
protease inhibitors, 246
protection, 65, 66, 137, 199
protective factors, 45, 47, 50, 53, 69, 72, 139, 154, 173, 176, 210, 214, 232
protective role, 58
prototype, 34, 156
psychiatric diagnosis, 22, 151, 194, 231
psychiatric disorders, 20, 37, 59, 61, 70, 75, 81, 120, 132, 142, 183, 184, 242
psychiatric hospitals, 111
psychiatric illness, 178
psychiatric morbidity, 131
psychiatric patients, 23
psychiatrist, 80, 108, 153, 170, 198, 236
psychiatry, 65, 88, 95, 99, 122, 132, 135, 188, 201
psychoactive drug, 215
psychologist, 204, 227
psychology, 87, 88, 103, 106, 143, 146, 155, 172, 181, 184, 189, 190, 204
psychopathology, 73, 206, 229, 244
psychosis, 264
psychotherapy, 29, 34, 156, 193
psychotropic drugs, 167
PTSD, 24, 222
public assistance, 57
public education, 29, 104
public health, 27, 35, 74, 87, 121, 132, 153, 167, 229, 232, 233, 234
Public Health Service Act, 86

public policy, 156
public sector, 202
public service, 221
punishment, 130

Q

qualitative research, 116, 211
quality improvement, 102, 115, 246
quality of life, 64, 80, 149, 163, 246
questionnaire, 45, 130, 190, 256, 260

R

race, 10, 41, 58, 79, 131, 140, 162, 241, 247
racial differences, 58
racism, 175
radio, 30
random assignment, 148
rating scale, 135
reactions, 141, 194
reality, 4, 9, 47, 91, 99, 105, 137, 153, 179, 223, 227
reasoning, 239
rebelliousness, 174
reciprocity, 105, 106, 185
recommendations, 32, 92, 93, 98, 106, 138, 146, 155, 173, 174, 178, 179, 189, 190, 192, 199, 206, 208, 219, 225, 226, 229
recovery, 57, 60, 133, 158, 217, 224, 225
recreation, 47
recruiting, 177
reform(s), 32, 53, 86, 88, 89, 111, 122, 132, 138, 140, 148, 175, 181, 192, 203, 205, 228, 229, 240, 249
refugee status, 33, 135, 136
refugees, 25, 33, 38, 135, 136, 194, 240
regional policy, 130
regulations, 53, 78, 139, 178, 237
regulatory bodies, 181
rehabilitation, 28, 79, 133, 187, 235
rejection, 192
relevance, 133
reliability, 108, 123, 135, 251

relief, 63, 169
religion, 47
replication, 169, 220
requirements, 106, 113, 181, 185
researchers, viii, 42, 49, 109, 117, 118, 211, 239, 254, 255, 260, 264
Reservations, 248
resettlement, 240
Residential, 236
resilience, 44
resistance, 48, 50, 68, 77, 158, 159
resource allocation, 86
resource management, 81
response, 13, 25, 28, 29, 46, 77, 81, 98, 118, 130, 170, 208, 213, 222, 249
restrictions, 78, 140, 221
restructuring, 121
retirement, 92
revenue, 203
rewards, 49, 130, 143, 204
risk factors, 45-46, 48, 61, 73-75, 137, 142, 159, 173, 179, 185, 210, 229, 233, 237, 256
risk-taking, 46
role playing, 157
roots, 60, 224
routes, 74, 230
rules, 152
rural counties, 10, 11, 16, 26, 90, 114, 166, 197, 220, 222
rural people, 175, 244, 249
rural population, 5, 7, 9, 10, 11, 12, 20, 30, 42, 45, 105, 141, 193, 225, 229, 243, 249
rural poverty, 10
rural schools, 80, 232, 248
rural women, 21, 36, 38, 61, 66, 141, 142, 145, 173, 183, 206, 225, 246

S

sadness, 227
safety, 25, 27, 40, 83, 84, 88, 97, 173, 196, 219, 238
SANS, 251
SAP, 22

Index

SAPS, 251
savings, 83
scarcity, 17
schizophrenia, 35, 64, 123, 148, 163, 189, 197, 205, 218, 220, 251
scholarship, 84, 95
school achievement, 45, 52
school activities, 210
school work, 201
science, 107
scope, 15, 47, 92, 106, 113, 116, 133, 156, 208, 225, 262
secondary school students, 180
SED, 16, 30
sedatives, 201
self-efficacy, 49, 174, 231
self-employed, 29
self-esteem, 46, 50, 51, 53, 58, 129, 149, 159, 172, 212, 250
self-interest, 82
self-monitoring, 48
self-perceptions, 209
self-report data, 55, 210
self-reports, 174
self-sufficiency, 56
self-view, 61
Senate, 29, 41, 175, 263
sensitivity, 32, 132, 158, 206
service organizations, 47, 61, 76, 245
service provider, 25, 29, 32, 102, 110, 111, 143, 144, 177, 190, 197, 204, 221, 226, 229, 236, 249
SES, 175
settlement class, 116
settlements, 6, 7
sex, 242
sexual abuse, 61, 182
sexual behavior, 21
sexual intercourse, 21, 250
sexual orientation, 57
shape, 170
short supply, 178
shortage, 16, 26, 28, 53, 90, 91, 92, 103, 114, 170, 178, 200, 203, 217, 238
showing, 141

sibling, 199
siblings, 199, 215
signs, 104, 110
sixth grade teachers, 157
skills training, 56, 73, 204, 224, 232
small businesses, 29
small communities, 227
smoking, 46, 49, 143, 174
sobriety, 60, 224
sociability, 149, 174
social activities, 149
social adjustment, 25
social behavior, 46
social consequences, 58
social construct, 189
social context, 42, 43, 58, 64, 67, 152, 154, 227
social control, 49
social development, 49
social environment, 43, 58
social events, 48
social influence(s), 67, 152, 250
social institutions, 31
social integration, 234
social learning, 49, 65, 130, 152, 239
social learning theory, 49, 130, 239
social life, 265
social network, 120
social norms, 171
social phobia, 183
social policy, 170
social problems, 234
social relations, 233
social relationships, 233
social services, 28, 40, 140, 174, 220, 228, 233
social skills, 56, 71, 190
social skills training, 56
social support, 23, 51, 80, 109, 148, 174, 202, 246
social workers, 16, 26, 79, 85, 90, 99, 180, 194, 208, 247
socialization, 192
society, 223
socioeconomic status, 183

sole proprietor, 9
solidarity, 234
solution, 147
South Dakota, 91, 92, 96
special education, 146, 247
specialists, 17, 82, 150, 180, 200, 208
speculation, 145
spending, 24, 147, 208
spirituality, 47, 176
Spring, 238
SS, 248
stability, 76, 80, 163, 243
stabilization, 27
staff members, 213, 246
staffing, 199, 244
stakeholders, 118, 119, 130, 167, 179
state, 54, 163, 215
statistics, 8, 10, 20, 89, 91
stereotypes, 83
stigma, 16, 17, 22, 23, 31, 32, 39, 53, 65, 104, 178, 200, 235, 237
stigmatized, 178
strategic planning, 96
stress, 20, 33, 40, 46, 55, 67, 70, 149, 151, 152, 164, 166, 175, 181, 184, 200, 206, 216, 225, 227, 248
structural changes, 158
structure, 73, 86, 108, 111, 131, 182, 206, 225, 232, 246
student populations, 248
style, 3, 49
subgroups, 61, 245
subsidy(s), 16, 238
Substance Abuse and Mental Health Services Administration (SAMHSA), 4, 17, 33, 36, 42, 45, 48, 92, 93, 94, 95, 97, 104, 107, 138, 258, 263, 265
substance use disorders, vii, viii, ix, 1, 2, 41, 42, 54, 63, 64, 65, 132, 152, 183, 254, 259, 262, 263, 264, 265
substance-abuse treatment, 191
suicide, 13, 20, 174, 179, 223, 234, 264, 265
suicide attempts, 20, 179, 223
suicide rate, 13, 20, 234
supervision, 158, 192

supervisor, 207
support services, 221
surplus, 161
survival, 136, 172, 202
survivors, 25, 156, 240, 249
susceptibility, 46
sustainability, 27, 81, 102
symptoms, ix, 13, 21, 26, 28, 35-36, 61, 64, 80, 104, 110, 132, 135-136, 152, 163, 173, 178, 181, 206, 251, 254, 261, 263-264
syndrome, 237
synthesis, 159

T

target, 28, 102, 104, 120, 175, 187, 202, 210, 230
target population, 102
Task Force, 13, 18, 104, 241
tax credits, 238
taxonomy, 71, 202
teachers, 48, 129, 143, 147, 201
teaching strategies, 95
teams, 49, 77, 79, 80, 86, 118, 132, 138, 186, 187, 198
technical assistance, 96, 97, 114, 118, 129
techniques, 49, 139, 141, 142, 148, 153
technology(s), 32, 93, 101, 102, 106, 108, 111, 133, 149, 155, 162, 169, 246, 251
teens, 208
telephone, 30, 82, 135, 139, 174, 188, 240, 241, 260, 262
territory, 116
test scores, 186
testing, 98, 165, 225, 232, 234
therapeutic community, 62, 236
therapeutic relationship, 134
therapist, 196
therapy, 56, 72, 108, 190, 193, 207, 214, 235
thinning, 6
thoughts, 174, 190
threats, 61, 64, 136, 142
time constraints, 137

time frame, 170
time periods, 205
tobacco, 44, 46, 49, 52, 71, 129, 143, 170, 172, 199, 208, 214, 234, 241, 243, 261
torture, 25, 136, 240
trade, 14, 28, 172
traditionalism, 59
traditions, 30, 31
trainees, 95
training programs, 28, 32, 48, 99, 103, 110, 225
traits, 212, 237
trajectory, 212
transmission, 135
transport, 189
transportation, 13, 14, 22, 23, 28, 29, 40, 61, 111, 220, 227
trauma, 25, 136, 190, 240
traumatic experiences, 61
trial, 71, 74, 170, 187, 195, 233
triggers, 57
turnover, 53, 178

U

U.S. Department of Agriculture (USDA), 9, 17, 161
U.S. Department of Commerce, 5
UK, 136
underwriting, 129
unemployment rate, 10, 20, 160
uniform, 5, 106
uninsured, 29, 37, 84, 137, 224, 227
universities, 103
urban areas, 6, 7, 9, 10, 12, 13, 20, 23, 44, 45, 62, 64, 76, 78, 91, 116, 120, 121, 147, 177, 200, 205, 220, 228, 234, 242, 244, 246
urban population, 19, 20, 46, 205
urban schools, 80, 248
urban youth, 46
urbanization, 7, 116, 159, 169

V

variables, 13, 20, 42, 43, 46, 69, 116, 159, 171, 172, 185, 192, 209, 213, 236
variations, 54, 134, 135, 144, 181, 187
vertical integration, 202
Vietnam, 39, 222, 225
violence, 17, 61, 142, 153, 183, 219, 263, 265
Visa Waiver Program, 86
vision, 3, 83, 96, 101, 133
vitamins, 160
volunteer work, 243
vulnerability, 203

W

wages, 9
waiver, 86, 236
Wales, 225
war, 15, 225
wealth, 221
web, 5, 155
websites, 15
welfare, 137
well-being, 80, 160, 161, 162, 194, 206, 223
wellness, 60, 73, 224
Western Europe, 136
Wisconsin, 54, 176
workers, 7, 9, 10, 14, 27, 53, 60, 79, 93, 94, 178, 180, 224, 240, 241, 249
workforce, 3, 4, 16, 17, 28, 33, 36, 77, 80, 85, 86, 89-97, 99, 100, 101, 103, 115, 139, 148, 161, 180, 210, 246
working families, 9
World Health Organization (WHO), 256, 257, 259
World War I, 170

Y

yield, 119

young adults, 12
young people, 46, 48, 53
young women, 36, 173